British Built Aircraft

Volume 3
South East England

British Built Aircraft

Volume 3
South East England

Ron Smith

TEMPUS

First published 2004

Tempus Publishing Ltd
The Mill, Brimscombe Port
Stroud, Gloucestershire GL5 2QG
www.tempus-publishing.com

© Ron Smith, 2004

The right of Ron Smith to be identified as the Author
of this work has been asserted by him in accordance with the
Copyrights, Designs and Patents Act 1988.

All rights reserved. No part of this book may be reprinted
or reproduced or utilised in any form or by any electronic,
mechanical or other means, now known or hereafter invented,
including photocopying and recording, or in any information
storage or retrieval system, without the permission in writing
from the Publishers.

British Library Cataloguing in Publication Data.
A catalogue record for this book is available from the British Library.

ISBN 0 7524 2993 0

Typesetting and origination by Tempus Publishing.
Printed and bound in Great Britain.

Contents

Introduction	6
Section One:	
The Evolution of the British Aircraft Industry	11
1 Pioneers (1908–1914)	12
2 First World War Mass Production (1914–1918)	14
3 Collapse and Re-birth Between the Wars (1919–1939)	20
4 Second World War Mass Production (1939–1945)	25
5 Post-war (1945–1960)	31
6 Rationalisation – The BAC and the Hawker Siddeley Years (1960–1977)	36
7 Modern Times	41
8 The Genealogy of British Aerospace/BAE SYSTEMS	47
Section Two:	
The Aircraft Manufacturers of South East England	52
Bibliography	209
Index	215

Introduction

This volume is the third in a series, which, when completed, will provide a complete record of aircraft construction in Britain. Each volume of this work focuses on a different regional area, documenting activity over the whole period from 1908 until the present day, keyed to the places where this enterprise was actually performed. The objective of the whole work is to pay tribute to the heritage of the British aircraft industry, and to create and preserve a record of its lost endeavours. The preceding two volumes covered, respectively, aircraft built in Greater London, and in South West and Central Southern England.

As soon as one starts to examine the history of the aircraft industry, it becomes clear that it has developed through a number of distinct phases. These phases can be characterised as the Pioneers (1908–14); First World War Mass Production (1914–18); Collapse and Re-birth Between the Wars (1919–39); Second World War Mass Production (1939–45); Post-war (1945–60); and Modern Times. A discussion of the evolution of the industry covering these six main periods of activity can be found in Section One. The aim of this review of the evolution of the industry is to place the remainder of the work within the overall context, while highlighting developments that are specific to the area of South East England.

Some twenty-five years ago, on the formation of British Aerospace (BAe), the American magazine *Aviation Week and Space Technology* wryly commented that the final phase of development of the SBAC had now taken place. Whereas previously the numerous members of the Society of British Aircraft Constructors (SBAC) had reflected the vigour, diversity and inventive spirit of the British industry, it had, following restructuring in 1960, been reduced to the 'Society of Both Aircraft Companies' (i.e. the British Aircraft Corporation and Hawker Siddeley Aviation Ltd). The formation of BAe was the final act in the process, with the once-great industry reduced to the 'Single British Aerospace Company'.

This light-hearted comment contains an important message. British aircraft industry names, which were once well known to the public, have disappeared from the day-to-day business of manufacturing aeroplanes. Indeed, in many instances, their operating sites have even disappeared from the map. At first sight it seems as if the once vibrant British aircraft industry has contracted virtually to the point of extinction since the Second World War. The entire industry has been reduced to the firms of BAE SYSTEMS, AgustaWestland, Slingsby, and Britten-Norman (surviving, as I write, in its latest manifestation: B-N Group), together with sundry microlight and homebuilt aircraft suppliers.

Many British aircraft manufacturers have disappeared altogether and this has provided the inspiration for this survey of the industry. South East England has seen the demise of such company names as Phillips & Powis/Miles, Fairey, Hawker, de Havilland, Handley Page, Vickers-Armstrongs, Percival, Short Brothers, Martinsyde, Sopwith and Beagle. Simultaneously, aircraft manufacture has ceased at Woodley, Langley, Dunsfold, Hatfield, Leavesden, Radlett, Brooklands/Weybridge, Gravesend, Rochester and the Isle of Sheppey. Having pondered on these closures, the idea grew that an effort should be made to record something of Britain's aircraft construction history and heritage.

The first outcome of this desire to document the past achievements of the British aircraft industry was a successful entry in the 1994 *Pooley's* International Dawn to Dusk Flying Competition by the author, with his colleague Colin Dodds. The entry, under the title *Lost Names in British Aviation*, consisted of the record of a flight made on a single day (between dawn and dusk) in a 1936 de Havilland Hornet Moth, over sites in Britain where aircraft had once been built, by companies that no longer exist. The research carried out in support of that competition entry has been greatly extended to provide the basis for this record of British achievement, innovation, failure and success.

Content

This series of books records British aircraft manufacture in nearly all its manifestations, in the form of a regional survey of the United Kingdom. The scope of the work is deliberately wide, including as many locations as possible where aircraft have been built, whether by their original designers or by contractors. Exclusions are limited to balloons; the majority of gliders and microlight aircraft; and homebuilt aircraft of foreign design, unless substantially modified in the form flown in the United Kingdom.

Being centred on the various manufacturing sites, the book allows a wider scope than a mere litany of product histories, allowing additional discussion of people, places and events. As a result, the major players of the industry are recorded alongside the wealth of early activity, light aircraft and one-off designs that provide a rich background to the main scene. Such is the scope of this record, that the space that can be allocated to any individual firm is necessarily limited. This mainly has the effect of producing a somewhat condensed view of some of the largest and best-known companies. This limitation is, hopefully, compensated for by some of the fascinating but unfamiliar material presented, covering many companies that are likely to be unfamiliar to the reader.

Those interested in the detailed history of the major manufacturers will be able to find many excellent books with which to fill in the detail if they wish. The same cannot be said for companies such as East Anglian Aviation Co. Ltd; Eastbourne Aviation Co. Ltd; Fairfield Aviation Ltd; Glenny & Henderson Ltd; Hordern-Richmond Aircraft Ltd; Kent Aircraft Services Ltd; Wycombe Aircraft Constructors Ltd; and a number of other lesser-known companies from South East England that are included here.

Structure

These introductory remarks are followed by a discussion of the evolution of the aircraft industry, highlighting the activities that characterise each of the main periods identified above, and tailored to the specific region covered by this volume. The contraction through successive mergers that has given rise to the present shape of the industry is presented, together with a family tree of British Aerospace (which contains all of the aircraft heritage of the present BAE SYSTEMS).

The main content of the volume follows in Section Two, which is a survey of aircraft manufacture in South East England (outside Greater London), as defined by the following counties: Berkshire, Buckinghamshire, Essex, Hertfordshire, Kent, Surrey, East Sussex and West Sussex. The presentation is alphabetical by county, and then alphabetical by location. For most locations, individual manufacturers are then presented alphabetically in sequence.

Where activity at a single site has only involved one firm at any time, or where the evolution of a single major firm has dominated a particular site, the presentation is chronological, rather than alphabetical. Hatfield and Dunsfold are examples of such a variation.

When the series is complete it will provide a comprehensive geographic and product history of United Kingdom aircraft construction. I have attempted to cover all sites where aircraft manufacture took place, and to select photographs which provide a balanced mix of example products, locations as they are now and as they were during their heyday, or combinations of these. A number of the photographs are of the sites as seen from the air during the 1994 Dawn to Dusk competition.

Information Sources and Acknowledgements

A number of major reference sources were used to create this survey of the British aircraft industry. Chief among these were magazines such as *Flight*, *The Aeroplane*, and *Aeroplane Monthly*, and the following books and publications, which provide particularly useful material across the whole spectrum of the Industry: Terence Boughton's excellent *History of the British Light Aeroplane*; A.J. Jackson's *British Civil Aircraft since 1919*; the individual company histories published by Putnam; Ken Ellis' *British Homebuilt Aircraft Since 1920*; R. Dallas Brett's *History of British Aviation 1909–14*; Arthur Ord-Hume's encyclopaedic *British Light Aeroplanes – Their Evolution, Development and Perfection 1920–40*; the equally outstanding *British Aircraft Before The Great War* by Michael H. Goodall and Albert E. Tagg; many editions of *Jane's All the World's Aircraft*; a wide range of test pilot autobiographies; and numerous other sources.

In setting out to document the British aircraft industry I wish to give a flavour of the breadth of the endeavour in terms of the diversity of both products and places used for aircraft manufacture. It is not my intention to provide a definitive record of every aircraft built, nor an encyclopaedia of production quantities. In some cases, I have found the latter aspect clouded with uncertainty; unless clearly definitive data are available, I have used Bruce Robertson's *British Military Aircraft Serials 1878–1987* as a guide when indicating production quantities. I have not hesitated to highlight areas where conflicting information may be found in readily available references. It is for others to research and clarify these issues.

Particular thanks are due to my colleague Rob Preece for the loan of his original, unbound, copies of *Flight* covering the period 1911 to 1923, and to Liz and Peter Curtis for access to a complete collection of *Aeroplane Monthly* magazines. Thanks are also due to Chris Ilett for the loan of *Flight* magazines from 1929 and 1930. A further acknowledgement must be made to The Royal Aeronautical Society library; not only are their early copies of *The Aeroplane* bound complete with their advertising pages, but here I also found a copy of R. Borlase Matthews' *Aviation Pocket-Book 1919–20*, whose Gazetteer of the Industry put me on the track of many unfamiliar companies. I am most grateful for the assistance provided by George Jenks (AVRO Heritage Centre) and Barry Abraham (Airfield Research Group).

Acknowledgement is due to those companies still extant (and not today associated with the aircraft industry) who answered my correspondence. Mention must also be made of the information and photographs supplied for this series by Ken Ellis, and by Mr A.H. Fraser-

Hornet Moth G-AELO is seen here at Pocklington prior to the 1994 Dawn to Dusk competition flight by Colin Dodds and the author. (Author)

Mitchell (Handley Page Association); Fred Ballam (Westland); Chris Hodson (Folland Aircraft Ltd); Olivia Johnston (Bombardier Aerospace, Belfast); Robin Heaps (Medway Branch of the Royal Aeronautical Society); and Del Hoyland (Martin-Baker Aircraft Co. Ltd). For this volume in particular, I acknowledge the helpful comments made by Julian Temple on the draft text concerning activity at Brooklands and the access provided by the Brooklands Museum to their photographic archive. Julian also provided a number of images of Miles products for use in this volume. I must further acknowledge the access provided to photographic material by my present employer, BAE SYSTEMS. In making this acknowledgement, I should also stress that all opinions expressed herein are entirely my own. I also acknowledge the permission received from BAE SYSTEMS plc, which enables me to reproduce a number of advertisements from BAE SYSTEMS legacy companies in this volume. Every effort has been made to provide the correct attribution for the illustrations used. If any errors or omissions have been made please inform the publisher; they will be rectified at the earliest opportunity.

Finally, as indicated earlier, the research for this book was triggered by the successful entry in the 1994 *Pooley's* International Dawn to Dusk competition. This could not have been made without the support, encouragement, experience and competence of my colleague Colin Dodds who flew the aircraft and the generosity of David Wells who made his aircraft, G-AELO, available for the competition flight.

Not Yet Found (and Imperfect Knowledge Disclaimer)

In a work of this scope, it is inevitable that mistakes and omissions will be made; for these I apologise, throwing myself upon the mercies of a hopefully sympathetic readership. Any additions and corrections made known to me will be most welcome and will be incorporated in any further edition that the publisher sees fit to print.

While the original intention was to list companies that built complete aircraft, lack of information about the actual products of some companies means that (particularly in the First World War) the content has certainly strayed into the component supply industry. Although this may stretch the scope of the menu beyond the taste of some, it does at least add richness to the feast.

Some firms which sound like aircraft factories may have only built parts (for example, Wycombe Aircraft Constructors Ltd, and Cowper-Coles Aircraft Co.); others, which entered the industry as flying schools, ended up building complete machines (for example, Hewlett & Blondeau and the Henderson School of Flying at Brooklands); finally there are those which may have done almost anything (for example, the Croydon Aviation & Engineering Co. of High Wycombe). Once again, I must trust that any blurring of definitions as to what to include or exclude will be forgiven.

The scope of the content has also been broadened in respect of a number of companies, such as Airtech Ltd at Thame, which carried out conversions and modifications to wartime aircraft to make them suitable for freight or passenger use after the Second World War. In the modern era I have also chosen to include the contributions of a number of companies that specialise in aircraft restoration and replica construction. The scope, quality and complexity of the work undertaken by these firms exceeds, in many cases, the difficulty of the original manufacturing task. Furthermore, I wish to draw specific attention to the contribution of these organisations to the preservation of Britain's aviation heritage.

Mention must also be made of aircraft and companies that are definitely known to have existed, but for which I have been quite unable to establish a location. At the time of writing, these are:

The **Buckle** parasol monoplane. Illegally flown, unregistered, in 1929, the Buckle monoplane was constructed by Mr S.L. Buckle for the princely sum of £17. Sopwith Snipe wings, ailerons, rudder, elevator and tailplane were used. A simple rectangular section fuselage was built, and power was supplied by a 45hp 6 cylinder Anzani radial. The propeller was obtained from a shed at Brooklands and cut down until the Anzani provided a satisfactory rpm. (Source: *Aeroplane Monthly*, April 1979).

The **Newport Aircraft Company** – A question was asked in Parliament in November 1918 in relation to unpaid wages and bonuses at this company.

In addition, the following companies whose addresses are unknown: **Cambrian Aircraft Constructors Ltd** and **Northwold Aircraft Co. Ltd**.

The Evolution of the British Aircraft Industry

This section presents a summary of the overall development of the aircraft industry in Britain, highlighting specifically (in this volume) activities in South East England ouside Greater London. This area was the most active in Britain in terms of pioneer flying, with major centres at Brooklands, Eastchurch and Shoreham. The area is also notable for the activities of a number of important companies. Chief among these are:

- The Sopwith Aviation & Engineering Co. Ltd and its successors Hawker Aircraft Ltd through to British Aerospace at, variously, Brooklands, Langley and Dunsfold.
- The de Havilland Aircraft Co. Ltd and its successors at Hatfield and Leavesden.
- The Fairey Aviation Co. Ltd activity at White Waltham.
- Handley Page Ltd at Radlett and (as Handley Page (Reading)) Woodley.
- Phillips & Powis (Aircraft) Ltd/Miles Aircraft Ltd at Woodley.
- The Short Brothers on the Isle of Sheppey and at Rochester.
- Vickers Ltd and its successors, including Vickers-Armstrongs Ltd and the British Aircraft Corporation, initially in Kent and then at Brooklands/Weybridge and Wisley.

To these major firms one can add Beagle Aircraft Ltd at Shoreham, Percival Aircraft Ltd at Gravesend, Aviation Traders & Engineering Ltd at Southend and Stansted, Campbell Aircraft Ltd at Hungerford and the glider manufacturer Elliotts of Newbury Ltd.

The closure of many airfields as a result of increasing pressure for housing, development for other industrial use and as a result of industrial reorganisation is reflected in the loss in this region of Dunsfold, Hatfield, Langley, Leavesden, Radlett, Weybridge, Wisley and Woodley.

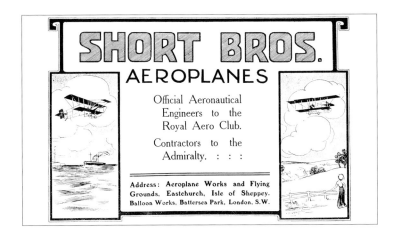

1
Pioneers
(1908–1914)

Flying in Europe began in France in 1906, with the flights of Santos Dumont in October and November of that year. By 1908, practical machines were being flown in France by such pioneers as Farman, Voisin and Blériot. The Wright brothers astounded their audiences with the performance and controllability of their craft when it was publicly displayed at Le Mans in the autumn of 1908. The time was now right for Britain's pioneers to take to the air.

A.V. Roe had been experimenting for some time at Brooklands, but his short flights of 8 June 1908 failed to achieve official recognition. S.F. Cody flew at Farnborough in October 1908, J.T.C. Moore-Brabazon flew at Eastchurch at the end of April 1909, and by July 1909 A.V. Roe's triplane was performing well at Lea Marshes. In February 1909, the Short brothers took a licence to manufacture Wright biplanes for the Aero Club, setting up a factory at Leysdown on the Isle of Sheppey. Britain now possessed an aircraft industry. The pioneering period prior to the First World War was marked by adventure, experiment and innovation – the techniques of building and of flying aeroplanes were not yet understood. There was no right or wrong solution to any aspect of design, and consequently almost every possible configuration was attempted and many blind alleys were explored. Potentially good designs were let down by poor detail design, inadequate control arrangements, or heavy, inefficient and unreliable engines.

Learning often came slowly: A.V. Roe advertised throughout the First World War that he was the pioneer of the tractor biplane, although, with his initial interest in the triplane configuration, it was 1911 before his Avro D flew. F. Warren Merriam, instructor at the Bristol School, remarks on how long it took to understand that a seat belt could save lives. In a number of cases, lives were lost because pilots simply fell off their machines. Quite trivial landing accidents could also cause death and injury as a result of the pilot being thrown from an aircraft that was otherwise little damaged. It also took a considerable time before the importance of pointing into wind for take-off and landing was understood. In the technical arena incorrect assumptions were commonplace: for example in the inadequate stressing of monoplanes against down loads. Even *Flight* is found in May 1913 expressing great surprise that the Eastbourne Aviation Company monoplane should have adopted ailerons for lateral control when wing warping has 'become almost standard practice'.

The pioneer aircraft that have been included in this volume are, in the main, those that are known to have flown successfully. In some cases, where the fact of flight is not entirely certain, aircraft have been included which at least have the appearance that they might have flown successfully (e.g. Fritz monoplane, Brooklands, 1911). Known freaks have been excluded (e.g. the Aerial Wheel monoplane which was entered in the 1912 Military Trials at Larkhill).

The main flying locations prior to the First World War were Brooklands, Eastchurch, Hendon and Shoreham. This volume therefore includes three of the four most important centres of pioneer activity, Hendon having been covered in the first volume of *British Built Aircraft*, which presents activities within Greater London.

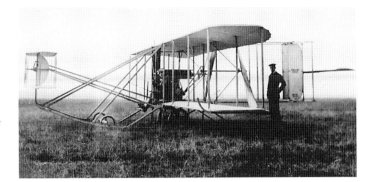

In 1909 the Short brothers manufactured six Wright biplanes under licence at Leysdown. This is the third of those machines, owned by Mr F.K. McClean. (Bombardier Aerospace, Belfast)

Although later to describe himself as the pioneer of the tractor biplane, A.V. Roe found initial success with his series of triplane designs. (Brooklands Museum Trust)

In addition to the major activity at the sites mentioned above, other significant pioneer activity in South East England includes:

- José Weiss and others experimenting at Fambridge.
- The Eastbourne Aviation Co. at Eastbourne.
- White & Thompson building Curtiss derived flying boats at Middleton on Sea.
- The Westlake monoplane at Clacton.
- Alec Ogilvie and Howard Wright at Camber Sands.
- Vickers Ltd experimental test flying at Joyce Green.

Enthusiasm for flying resulted in the establishment of a number of flying schools, notably at Brooklands, Shoreham, Larkhill and Hendon. The schools necessarily became adept at the repair, modification and rebuilding of aeroplanes. As a result, even where their school machines were initially of standard types, many were later modified, adapted, re-engined etc. to become new variants.

By the outbreak of the First World War, the Short Brothers, A.V. Roe, C.R. Fairey, Frederick Handley Page, The British and Colonial Aeroplane Company (later to become The Bristol Aeroplane Co. Ltd), Vickers Ltd, T.O.M. Sopwith, Harry Hawker and Geoffrey de Havilland were already active in the industry. Despite the diversity of the pioneering efforts, and the many bizarre and unsuccessful designs, the seeds of today's configurations, and of today's industry, were sown during this period of adventure. Great fruit was to be harvested once these seeds found the fertile ground of warfare.

2
First World War Mass Production (1914–1918)

The First World War saw an exponential growth in aircraft production, which is reflected in this survey of aircraft production in South East England. The importance of the aeroplane during the First World War, and the reasons for the rapid growth in production demand are therefore discussed in some detail below.

The Aircraft as a Machine of War

At the outbreak of the First World War, the utility of the aeroplane had only just begun to be appreciated by the Services. It was then slow, fragile and unarmed; moreover, very few were available. Thus the Royal Flying Corps (RFC) had a total of only sixty-three first-line aeroplanes, with a further thirty-nine landplanes and fifty-two seaplanes available to the Royal Naval Air Service (RNAS).

The war developed into static trench warfare, with major actions or 'pushes' preceded by artillery barrages. An early use was found in reconnaissance and artillery observation, and this role became the cornerstone of military aviation. General von Below is quoted by Maurice Baring, in *Flying Corps Headquarters 1914–1918*, as stating in a memorandum: 'The main object of fighting in the air is to enable our photographic registration and photographic reconnaissance to be carried out, and at the same time to prevent that of the enemy.' The use of fighters to prevent reconnaissance operations was therefore a natural development, followed by the application of the aeroplane to bombing operations, anti-submarine patrols and operations against airships.

Changing operational roles and the rapid development of aircraft and armament meant that existing in-service types were rapidly rendered obsolete. New designs were essential, and had to be rushed into large-scale production. Aircraft were flown intensively, and losses were high through both enemy action and accidents. A large-scale training activity was required to maintain a supply of pilots to the operational squadrons, giving rise to its own losses of both men and machines.

All of this required a rapid expansion of production of all types, a process hampered by the fact that many of the potential workforce were enlisting in the Services. This problem could only be solved by bringing into the production effort industrial enterprises that had no prior experience of aircraft manufacture; the furniture and motor trades were both critical in this respect. Similarly, the workforce needed to be augmented, and many women entered the production lines of the munitions factories (including the aircraft industry) for the first time.

The types that were most widely contracted out included the designs of the Royal Aircraft Factory (such as the BE2, BE12, RE8, FE2 and SE5A); training aircraft (notably the Avro 504 and DH6); Felixstowe designed flying boats; patrol seaplanes (Short 184); and successful combat aircraft (Sopwith Pup, Camel, 1½ Strutter and Snipe; Bristol F2B Fighter; AIRCO DH4, DH9, DH9A). Toward the end of the First World War significant orders were placed for the contract manufacture of long-range bomber types, such as the Handley Page O/400 and Vickers Vimy. Many of these orders were cancelled following the Armistice.

Loss Rates

The expansion of production during the First World War was, in truth, an enormous enterprise. Because of its significance, it is worth reflecting on some of the facts and figures associated with this accelerated production programme. As background, one needs to appreciate the intensity of air operations, and of the high rate of loss and materiel consumption involved, as indicated by the following contemporary data:

'The average life of an aeroplane at the battlefront is not more than two months. To keep 5,000 aircraft in active commission for one year it is necessary to furnish 30,000. Each machine in the period of its activity will use at least two motors, so that 60,000 motors will be required.' (M. Flaudin, head of the Allied Air Board (quoted in the American magazine *Flying*, September 1917).) These figures seem extraordinary, but closely match the levels actually achieved by the end of the conflict.

Aircraft losses in late 1918 were running at some 200 per month. In fact, aircraft destroyed by the enemy, and in training accidents, together with those that had to be scrapped as being obsolete, represented some 60 per cent of the total constructed during the war. Sadly, training exacted a heavy toll. A question in Parliament during the 1918 Air Estimates debate revealed that during 1917 more men were lost at the training schools than were lost flying on all fronts. Winston Churchill also spoke in Parliament on 4 April 1917 on the subject of the heavy losses being suffered by the RFC during training.

Data published in 1919 (in *Flight* and elsewhere) indicate that the total casualties over the whole period of the war were 6,166 killed, 7,245 wounded and 3,128 missing. 330 British airmen lost their lives in April 1917, the so-called 'Bloody April'. At this time, the expected operational life of an RFC pilot was no more than 17½ flying hours. Peter King in *Knights*

The intensity of production during the First World War is dramatically illustrated by this photograph of Snipe production at the Richmond Road Works at Ham. (BAE SYSTEMS plc)

of the Air indicates that losses in every month of 1918 were equal to the entire strength of the RFC at the start of the First World War.

The demands imposed by these short service lives and high attrition were considerable; how were the resultant production needs to be met?

Expansion of the Production Programme

Production at existing aircraft companies was rapidly expanded, and contracts were placed with established industrial concerns, particularly in the motor car and furniture trades, to boost supply. Many new companies were also founded specifically to meet this growing demand, and to provide a subcontract infrastructure. The resultant explosion of industrial activity was truly amazing, and has been inadequately recorded.

In May 1917, less than three years after the outbreak of the First World War, the position was summarised by the 'British Comptroller of Aeronautic Supplies' in a statement to the Board of Governors of the Aero Club of America. He stated: 'there are 958 firms in England engaged on work for the British Directorate of Aeronautic Supplies, 301 of which are direct contractors and 657 are sub-contractors.' The report further states that 'the total number of hands employed by the 50 firms of most prominence is 66,700. [...] The present British budget for aeronautics in the present year totals $575,000,000.' (reported in *Flying* magazine (June 1917)). These are impressive figures by any standard.

The *Aviation Pocket-Book of 1919–20* listed 148 aeroplane manufacturers and many other suppliers, and commented on the adequacy of its Gazetteer thus: 'It does not pretend to include the names of all who are accustomed to making aeroplane parts, for many firms were doing so for the period of the war only – in fact there is hardly a motor car or motor car accessory or wood-working firm that was not fully occupied with aviation work at the time of the Armistice. [...] Possibly, however, some names are not included that ought to be, since it is not an easy task, when compiling a directory of this nature, to ensure its being absolutely complete.' The author must echo these sentiments in respect of the present work.

Manufacture was split between aircraft manufacturers, with their own design teams, capable of producing original designs; contractors, who built established designs to order; and component suppliers. With the dispersion of production to many enterprises, it was found necessary to create a number of regional Acceptance Parks, to which contractors delivered their aircraft for inspection and acceptance. Contractors in some cases delivered wings, tail and fuselage separately by road or rail to the acceptance aerodromes, prior to assembly and flight test.

Within the area covered by this volume, the most significant aircraft manufacturing concerns were: Martinsyde Ltd at Woking and Brooklands; The Norman Thompson Flight Co. Ltd at Middleton on Sea; Short Brothers (Rochester & Bedford) Ltd at Rochester; The Sopwith Aviation Co. Ltd at Kingston (flying conducted at Brooklands); and Vickers Ltd at Joyce Green and Brooklands.

Smaller concerns included:

- Blériot & SPAD Manufacturing Co., Addlestone.
- Cowper-Coles Aircraft Co., Sunbury on Thames.
- Marine Experimental Aircraft Depot, Port Victoria, Isle of Grain.
- South Coast Aircraft Works, Shoreham.
- Wycombe Aircraft Constructors, High Wycombe.

Production Quantities

The achievements of the rapidly expanding industry were remarkable. This is illustrated rather graphically by the following statement made by Winston Churchill, Minister of Munitions, speaking in Parliament on 25 April 1918, when presenting the Estimates of the Ministry of Munitions:

> *We are now making in a single week more aeroplanes than were made in the whole of 1914, in a single month more than were made in the whole of 1915, and in a single quarter more than were made in the whole of 1916.*

The total British production during the First World War is widely reported as 55,093 airframes (other figures are also quoted, see below), with an additional 3,051 purchased abroad. Very significant production was also undertaken in France and the USA, with American production running at around 12,000 aircraft per year by the end of the war. Data published after the First World War (as a Parliamentary Paper on 24 April 1919) gave the following figures for British production.

First World War Aircraft Production

Period	Duration (months)	Aircraft built	Aircraft per month
August 1914 – May 1915	10	530	53
June 1915 – February 1917	21	7,137	340
March 1917 – December 1917	10	13,521	1,352
January 1918 – October 1918	10	26,685	2,669

(Note: This gives a total of 47,873, some 7,200 fewer than is given by more recent sources.)

The expansion in production is also reflected in the numbers of aircraft on charge with the RFC and RNAS, as follows: August 1914 272; January 1917 5,496; January 1918 11,091; October 1918 (RAF) 22,171. These figures, from the same source as the production numbers, show that in four years the aircraft establishment of the flying services had been increased more than eighty-fold, with the production rate increasing more than fifty-fold. To provide a comparison with United Kingdom production, one should acknowledge that this enormous acceleration in the field of aviation was evident among all combatants.

Production Difficulties

Significant production difficulties were encountered (and encountered again in the Second World War) due to the difficulty of building up production among a large number of dispersed and sometimes inexperienced contractors. The requirement to accelerate production was hampered by the steady depletion of the workforce as more and more were called up for service in France. There was near-continuous industrial unrest as a result of the heavy demands on the individual, and the Defence of the Realm Act was much used to maintain stability in the munitions industries.

Engine suppliers had great difficulty maintaining pace with airframe manufacture. Early in 1915 a serious shortage of 90hp RAF engines occurred, leaving Armstrong Whitworth with no fewer than 100 engineless BE2 machines hanging three or four deep from the ceiling. Similarly, in January 1918, no fewer than 400 SE5A were waiting for engines. The lower-than-expected performance of the Siddeley Puma proved to be a problem for the DH4. Martinsyde F.3 production was reduced because of the need for Rolls-Royce Falcon engines to power the Bristol Fighter. The lack of availability of Falcon engines resulted in the Bristol Fighter being flown (with variable success) with 300hp Hispano-Suiza, Siddeley Puma and Sunbeam Arab engines. Production of the FE2D was also constrained by the shortage of supply of its Rolls-Royce Eagle engine. The 200hp Hispano-Suiza engine fitted to the Sopwith Dolphin suffered from frequent connecting-rod failures. The supply of engines was further hampered by the need to create a new industry to supply magnetos, the manufacture of which, until the outbreak of the First World War, had been almost exclusively the province of German industry.

At the end of the First World War, engine orders were running at around 65,000 per year, more than 8,500 of these orders being for the disastrous ABC Dragonfly. F. Warren Merriam comments: 'There is no doubt that at this late stage in the War, our aero engines were becoming less and less reliable.' Shortages affected nearly every type. Standardisation was absent; in early 1918, Mr Pemberton Billing pointed out that forty-four different types of engine were in use. Ironically, the attempt to standardise on the Dragonfly also was an ignominious failure. In 1918, with vast numbers of engines on order from thirteen contractors, the Dragonfly was achieving a typical engine life of only 2½ hours before failure.

Scarcity of Resources

The needs of aircraft production resulted in a tremendous drain on resources, and even had an impact on the agricultural landscape, through the demand for flax to supply the need for aircraft linen. In July 1917, Dr Addison, Minister of Munitions, gave a specific indication of the strategic requirements of the aircraft industry, as follows:

> *The fact that no fewer than 1,000 factories are engaged on some process or other connected with the construction and equipment of the flying machine proves the magnitude of the work we have in hand. The needs of the aeroplane programme are enormous, almost passing belief. For our present programme of construction, more spruce is required than the present annual output of the United States, more mahogany than Honduras can supply – and Honduras is accustomed to supply the requirements of the World. Besides this, all the linen of the type required made in Ireland, the home of the linen industry, and the whole of the alloyed steel that England can produce can be used. As for flax, the Government has actually to provide the seed from which to grow the plant essential for its purposes.*

Flax seed was supplied free to growers, who were further encouraged with significant subsidies and guaranteed prices. The scheme was administered by the Flax Production Branch of the Board of Agriculture. Further financial assistance to growers was offered in July 1918 as a result of the Flax Companies (Financial Assistance) Bill. So successful were these measures that by the time of the Armistice, production of aircraft fabric was running at 7 million yards (nearly 4,000 miles) per month. By April 1919, the Ministry of Munitions had in stock and available for disposal no less than 31,970,725 yards of linen. In mid-1919, the total surplus (by now 40 million yards, or nearly 23,000 miles of fabric, in sixteen varieties and widths of 25–72 inches) was sold to one individual, Mr J.L. Martin, for about £4 million.

The Government requested in late 1917 that farmers carry out a census of ash trees, where potential supply problems were causing some concern. In supporting this request it was stated that 'the Government requirements for the next 12 months [i.e. 1918] are expected to exceed 200,000 trees'. In all, about a third of the volume of timber standing at the outbreak of war was felled, much being used in aircraft manufacture.

Overall, perhaps the most striking feature of the First World War mass production effort was that the entire enterprise, involving more than a thousand companies, was created within ten years of the construction of Britain's first aeroplane.

Foundation of the SBAC

On 23 March 1916, the main constructing firms came together to form an interest group through which to voice their common concerns. This was the Society of British Aircraft Constructors (SBAC), an organisation that continues to be a spokesman for the industry today. The founder members include a significant number of firms that are less than familiar today. The initial list of forty founder members, as published in April 1916, was as follows:

Aircraft Manufacturing Co. Ltd
Airships Ltd
The Austin Motor Co. (1914) Ltd
Wm. Beardmore & Co. Ltd
The Blackburn Aeroplane & Motor Co. Ltd
Boulton & Paul Ltd
The Brush Electrical Engineering Co. Ltd
The Coventry Ordnance Works Ltd
The Daimler Co. Ltd
Darracq Motor Engineering Co. Ltd
Wm. Denny & Brothers

The Dudbridge Iron Works Ltd
The Grahame-White Aviation Co. Ltd
Hewlett & Blondeau Ltd
Jouques Aviation Works
Mann & Grimmer
Martinsyde Ltd
Mann, Egerton & Co. Ltd
D. Napier & Son, Ltd
Handley Page Ltd
Phoenix Dynamo Manufacturing Co. Ltd
Parnall & Sons
A.V. Roe & Co. Ltd
Robey & Co. Ltd
Ruston, Proctor & Co. Ltd
Fredk. Sage & Co. Ltd

S.E. Saunders Ltd
Short Bros.
The Siddeley-Deasy Motor Car Co. Ltd
The Standard Motor Co. Ltd.
The Sunbeam Motor Car Co. Ltd
The Norman Thompson Flight Co. Ltd
Vickers Ltd
Westland Aircraft Works
J. Samuel White & Co. Ltd
G. & J. Weir Ltd
Wells Aviation Co. Ltd
Whitehead Aircraft Co. Ltd
Wolseley Motors Ltd.

This group of companies, plus a few others which joined the SBAC shortly thereafter (such as Sir W.G. Armstrong, Whitworth & Co. Ltd) made up the aircraft industry at the end of the First World War. Not one survives today as a wholly British aircraft manufacturer, although Shorts (as a subsidiary of Bombardier) and AgustaWestland are honourable near-survivors.

3
Collapse and Re-birth Between the Wars (1919–1939)

The inter-war period was marked by the near-complete collapse of the military aircraft market, and the return of the majority of contractors to their original products and markets. The larger companies were restructured to avoid excess profit duty, and they all faced competition from their own products now being marketed by the Aircraft Disposal Company. Military sales were very limited in number, although within this region H.G. Hawker Engineering Ltd (with its influential Hart family, flown from 1928 onward) and Vickers Ltd (with its successions of Vimy-derived products followed by the Vildebeest, Vincent, Wellesley and Wellington) were cushioned from the worst of these problems.

In the 1930s, the light aircraft movement resulted in expansion of civil production, and many new concerns were established, only to be cut off at the start of the Second World War. The de Havilland Aircraft Co. Ltd found a sustained civil market with a succession of designs following on from the ground-breaking DH60 Moth. Phillips & Powis/Miles and Percival Aircraft Ltd both prospered and were able to make a valuable contribution to Britain's efforts during the Second World War. Military rearmament began in 1935, and provided a lifeline for the main manufacturers.

Post-war Collapse

What brought about the collapse? Quite simply, the need for aircraft evaporated virtually overnight. Once the war stopped, the country had neither the resources, nor the need, to sustain the aircraft production juggernaut. Many orders were cancelled, and the enormous stock of war surplus aircraft was sold on favourable terms to the Aircraft Disposal Company at Croydon. In consequence, any firm attempting a new aircraft venture during the immediate post-war period inevitably found itself competing with its own, or its

The Vildebeest, and its development the Vincent, were important inter-war products for Vickers Ltd. This is the first production Vildebeest I, S1707. (BAE SYSTEMS plc)

After the First World War, many companies entered a period of decline, their survival depending on diversification into new products. This is a Martinsyde motorcycle dating from 1923. (Author)

competitors', second-hand products. When this difficulty was combined with the effects of excess profits duty, it is not surprising that wholesale reorganisation took place. Most of the subcontractors either went into liquidation or returned to their former trades. The prime contractors also reorganised, slimmed down, or went into liquidation; many flirted with the motor trade and other forms of diversification.

Examples in this area include: Shorts making aluminium bus bodies, barges and electric canoes; Martinsyde producing motorcycles; and Sopwith selling ABC motorcycles, as well as becoming involved in coachbuilding, and the manufacture of furniture and kitchen utensils. A number of firms that entered voluntary liquidation emerged in new, fitter, guises to carry on in the aircraft business. The survivors drew the protective cloak of the SBAC tightly around themselves.

The scale of the contraction after the Armistice was incredible. On 11 November 1918, 25,000 aircraft were on order. The Air Ministry sought to shut down production of all obsolete types immediately, and only accept delivery of those contracts from which they positively could not extricate themselves. Those obsolete types that could not be cancelled were sent directly to store. By cancellation of these orders, the number of aircraft that the Ministry was obliged to accept was reduced to 13,432. Scrapping for the recovery of useful parts proved not to be very economic, and it was recommended that greater savings would be made if the engine were to be removed, and the rest of the machine burned.

Hilary St George Saunders, in *Per Ardua – The Rise of British Air Power*, indicates an establishment at the end of the First World War of ninety-five squadrons and seven flights in France, Belgium and the Rhineland; thirty-four squadrons and eight flights in other theatres; and a Home establishment of fifty-five operational and no fewer than 199 training squadrons, for a grand total of 383 squadrons and fifteen flights. Within eighteen months, this was reduced to eighteen squadrons overseas, eight in India and seven in the Middle East, plus only two Home squadrons. Manpower was correspondingly reduced to some 10 per cent of the numbers engaged at the time of the Armistice.

By the end of 1920, AIRCO, British & Colonial Aeroplane Co. Ltd, Nieuport, Martinsyde, Central Aircraft, Grahame-White and Sopwith had variously closed, entered receivership or reorganised. By June 1922 only ninety-seven British civil aircraft had Certificates of Airworthiness, down from 240 in 1920. By the mid-1920s, the industry had reduced to sixteen major manufacturers – Sir W.G. Armstrong Whitworth Aircraft Ltd, A.V. Roe & Co.

Hawker's outstanding product of the inter-war period was its family of aircraft based on the Hart day-bomber. This is the last of three Hind aircraft supplied to Latvia in 1938. (BAE SYSTEMS plc)

Ltd, The Blackburn Aeroplane & Motor Co. Ltd, Boulton & Paul Ltd, The Bristol Aeroplane Co. Ltd, The de Havilland Aircraft Co. Ltd, Fairey Aviation Ltd, The Gloucestershire Aircraft Co. Ltd, Handley Page Ltd, H.G. Hawker Enginering Co. Ltd, George Parnall & Co. Ltd, S.E. Saunders Ltd, Short Brothers (Rochester & Bedford) Ltd, The Supermarine Aviation Works Ltd, Vickers Ltd and Westland Aircraft Works (Branch of Petters Ltd).

Military Production in the 1920s and 1930s

From this point onwards, military aircraft manufacture was effectively reduced to the modification and development of the existing in-service types, and the development of a smattering of prototypes. The prototype activity was spread across the industry and just about sustained the industrial base. The lack of active operations meant that only small production volumes of largely obsolescent aircraft were required to fulfil the needs of the RAF. Shorts, for example, built fewer than forty aircraft during the whole of the 1920s.

Fairey Aviation was a significant exception to this bleak scene, as the Fairey IIIF, Gordon, Seal, Fawn, Flycatcher, Swordfish and Battle ensured continuous production through this difficult period. Another successful military manufacturer was Hawker at Kingston upon Thames and Brooklands, which, after a period of limited production in the early 1920s, found production success and stability with the Hawker Hart and its subsequent long line of variants, eventually leading to the Fury and the Hurricane. As indicated earlier, Vickers Ltd also fared comparatively well during this period.

One measure of the desperation of the industry was that key military requirements, likely to lead to significant production contracts, would lead to a rash of official and private venture prototypes being produced. A good example is provided by requirement G.4/31 for a general-purpose aircraft capable also of carrying and dropping a torpedo (a requirement subsequently changed to the ability to conduct dive-bombing). The aircraft that were built for this complex and demanding requirement were as follows:

- Armstrong Whitworth AW19 (private venture, A3).
- Hawker G.4/31 (private venture, IPV4).

- Blackburn G.4/31 (private venture, B-7).
- Parnall G.4/31 (K2772).
- Bristol Type 120 (private venture, R-6).
- Vickers G.4/31 (K2771), declared the eventual winner, but no production contract was placed.
- Fairey G.4/31 (private venture, F-1).
- Westland G.4/31 (private venture, PV7).
- Handley Page HP.47 (K2773).

With no production contract forthcoming, and with six of the nine types flown having been constructed on a private venture basis, the design teams must have found this an expensive and frustrating waste of time and effort. The naval requirement N.21/26 produced an even larger response, attracting ten prototypes. At least on that occasion a production contract was placed, in favour of the Hawker Osprey.

The military market remained stagnant until tension rose within Europe during the late 1930s, leading to progressive rearmament from 1935. From this point onward, the military manufacturers saw increasing orders and the use of contract and dispersed production to increase capacity. This is discussed in the next chapter.

Civil Production and the Light Aeroplane Movement

Immediately after the First World War, there were limited attempts to generate an air transport market, with A.V. Roe & Co. Ltd (Avro Transport Service), Blackburn (North Sea Aerial Navigation Co. Ltd), Handley Page (Handley Page Transport Ltd) and AIRCO

The Handley Page HP42 prototype G-AAGX (yet to acquire its Imperial Airways name Hannibal) makes a stately progression across the sky whilst under test from Radlett. (Handley Page Association)

Thirty-one S.23 'C-Class' flying boats were built, followed by nine S.30 and two S.33, all collectively referred to as 'Empire' Flying Boats. S.23 Caledonia was first flown at Rochester in September 1936. (Bombardier Aerospace, Belfast)

Hawk fuselages are seen here in initial assembly at Phillips & Powis (Aircraft) Ltd. (Museum of Berkshire Aviation via Julian Temple)

(Aircraft Transport & Travel Ltd) all starting airline services, mainly using converted military aircraft. These efforts were unsuccessful and, although small numbers of commercial aircraft were sold to independent airlines, there was no real demand for air travel. Even after the formation of Imperial Airways, airliner production in Britain was restricted to modest production runs from Armstrong Whitworth, de Havilland, Handley Page and Shorts. The appearance of the de Havilland Dragon (1932) and Dragon Rapide (1934) saw production quantities increase. However, it is fair to say that, with the exception of de Havilland and Empire flying boat production at Shorts, military aircraft production dominated the affairs of most companies. Another exception was Airspeed Ltd, whose Envoy flew in 1934. Eighty-two were built, and the type was developed into the Oxford trainer.

While the Lympne Light Aircraft Competitions generated much publicity for the potential of privately owned aircraft, the competing aircraft themselves were not a great success. The appearance of the de Havilland Moth and the availability of subsidies for flying schools radically changed this picture. New companies emerged and prospered, including the famous names of Airspeed (at York and then Portsmouth), de Havilland (initially at Stag Lane and then Hatfield), General Aircraft (Croydon and then Hanworth), Percival (Gravesend and then Luton), and Miles (then as Phillips & Powis (Aircraft) Ltd, at Woodley). Much of this activity was concentrated in and near London, as flying gained popularity as a fashionable pastime.

A new phenomenon also arose in the form of the craze for the Flying Flea sparked by the design of the tandem wing *Pou de Ciel* by Henri Mignet. Although ultimately (and in some cases tragically) unsuccessful, the Flea served to legitimise the eccentric British habit of constructing home-built aircraft. This had originated in the pioneering period by the enthusiasm of the likes of Mr Jezzi at Eastchurch, being continued after the First World War by such characters as F.H. Lowe at Heaton, and the Blake brothers at Winchester. This tradition has been carried on to this day in Britain by individuals such as John Isaacs, John Taylor, Ivan Shaw and many others, now under the very professional administration of the Popular Flying Association, based at Shoreham for many years and recently moved to Turweston, Northamptonshire.

4
Second World War Mass Production (1939–1945)

Rearmament and the Shadow Factory Scheme
The expansion of the aircraft production programme against the threat of war built up gradually from 1935 and is inseparably linked to the Second World War aircraft production effort. While to many eyes the rearmament of Britain's forces came perilously late, moves began some five years before the Second World War broke out. The first step was the adoption of an expansion plan in July 1934, known as Scheme A, to increase the size of the Royal Air Force. Under this scheme the Metropolitan Air Force was intended to grow to 1,252 operational aircraft by the spring of 1939.

Hitler had become Chancellor in January 1933, but his repudiation of the Treaty of Versailles, reoccupation of the Rhineland, the Austrian Anschluss, the annexation of Czechoslovakia and the Nazi-Soviet Pact were still years ahead. It is clear, therefore, that some early positive decisions were made and as a result the armaments industry began to grow. The real difficulty lay in the lack of investment in modern designs and technology, combined with the drastic reduction in production capacity caused by the lean years of the 1920s and early 1930s.

The pace of rearmament in the aircraft industry quickened with Scheme C, which was instituted in May 1935 and which brought about further significant increases in both the size of the RAF and the production of new aircraft types. From October 1936 the need for increased production led to the formation of the shadow factory scheme. New factories were constructed using public funds and were owned by the Government but run by private industry. The shadow factories were used initially to boost the production of (initially) aero engine components, where the shortfall in production capacity was even more marked than in the airframe industry. The contractual complexities of the shadow factory scheme introduce uncertainty in some instances over the precise responsibility for site management and aircraft production/assembly at particular sites. This is an area that would benefit from further research.

In addition to Bristol (whose engines were to be produced), the five companies initially involved in the shadow factory scheme were Austin Motor Co. Ltd, The Daimler Co. Ltd, Rootes Securities Ltd (Humber), The Rover Company Ltd and the Standard Motor Co. Ltd. In February 1937 the scheme was extended to allow Austin and Rootes to construct airframes as well as engines. Despite this early recognition that engine availability was critical to the acceleration of airframe production, there were periods, as in the First World War, when engineless airframes were in plentiful supply.

The early expansion schemes favoured light day bombers such as the Fairey Battle and Vickers Wellesley. Unfortunately, the concept of the light day bomber proved to be a blind alley, with the Battle, in particular, suffering from high operational losses while trying to stem the Blitzkrieg across the Low Countries during 1940. (Fairey Battle losses between 10 and 14 May 1940 were sixty aircraft, out of the 108 deployed operationally, during attacks against troop

The Vickers Wellesley, together with the Fairey Battle, was the subject of the RAF's initial expansion plans as tension rose in Europe prior to the Second World War. The Wellesley pioneered the Barnes Wallis geodetic construction that was later to be famously employed by the Wellington bomber. (Brooklands Museum Trust)

This fine photograph of a Tiger Moth is a 1950s period piece. The type remains a classic trainer, whether of basic flying skills, or the need for precision in aerobatics. (H.E. North)

concentrations and the Albert Canal bridges). From 1936 onward types such as the Blenheim, Wellington, Hurricane and Spitfire began to be ordered in quantity through parent and shadow factories. Later on, the focus switched to heavy bomber production (particularly the Halifax and Lancaster), anticipating the need for a bomber offensive against Germany.

Wartime saw an increase in activity across South East England, paralleled by the establishment of additional production capacity elsewhere in Britain. Hawker capacity was increased with operations at Langley supplementing those at Kingston and Brooklands. Gloster Aircraft Ltd was used to provide additional Hurricane production capacity and to take responsibility for the Henley and Typhoon. Tiger Moth production was transferred to Morris Motors at Cowley to allow the de Havilland Aircraft Company to concentrate its resources on the Mosquito. Vickers Wellington production at Brooklands/Weybridge was supplemented by factories at Broughton (Chester) and Blackpool. The London Aircraft Production Group (at Aldenham and Leavesden) and the English Electric Co. Ltd (at Preston/Samlesbury) added to the output of Halifax bombers produced by Handley Page Ltd at Radlett. The heavy bomb damage sustained at Rochester resulted in production of the Short Stirling at Swindon and South Marston and the setting up of a production line at Short & Harland Ltd in Belfast. Production of the Miles Master was also undertaken at South Marston.

Production Difficulties

Large-scale orders were one thing; production proved to be quite another problem. Production difficulties were encountered with the accelerating demands placed on both airframe and engine manufacturers, particularly as the British industry was only just accommodating retractable undercarriages, variable pitch propellers, and all-metal stressed skin monoplanes. In contemporary reports one finds reference to:

- Poorly organised initial production by Supermarine at Woolston, with mismatched wing and fuselage production rates.
- Similar problems at Filton with the Blenheim, with thirty-two fuselages produced before any wings appeared.
- The initial inability of the Morris-run Castle Bromwich shadow factory to get the Spitfire into production.
- Miles Master development and production dictated by availability of particular engine types.
- Master, Oxford and Tiger Moth airframes dispersed into storage to await their engines.
- Fairey's problems of excessive dispersal of its factories, including delays to the Albacore due to problems with its Taurus engine. The delays to Albacore production lead to a further delay of about a year in establishing Firefly production. A delay of two years to the Barracuda was attributed to priority being given to other types in production by Fairey at Heaton Chapel and Errwood Park. Sir Stafford Cripps intervened to introduce new personnel and re-organise project management at Fairey Aviation.
- Bristol's engineless Beaufighters towed by road from the factory at Filton to Whitchurch to await completion.
- Production levels in 1937/38 running at around a third of those planned for the Battle and Blenheim, and virtually zero for the Spitfire.
- Slow production build up for the Halifax by the London Aircraft Production Group, delaying output from the assembly line at Leavesden.
- Dozens of Typhoons at Brockworth without engines being ferried to maintenance units using 'slave' engines. The engines were then removed, sent back to the Gloster factory, and refitted to the next aircraft for its delivery.

The setting up of the shadow factory scheme was, itself, a drain on the resources of the parent firms, due to their need to produce additional drawings and tooling, and to provide oversight of the expansion factories. One should not, however, forget the scale of the task, and the depleted production resource initially available for the effort.

Production Quantities and Standardisation

Despite all these difficulties, expansion in the immediate pre-war period was more successful than has been widely acknowledged. In 1935 893 military aircraft were produced. This figure was more than doubled in 1936, and by 1939 reached 7,940, a nearly nine-fold increase in only five years. In 1941, the figure was more than 20,000, and by 1944 it exceeded 26,000.

The main production effort during the Second World War was split between the following organisations:

- The main design firms of A.V. Roe & Co. Ltd, Sir W.G. Armstrong Whitworth Aircraft Ltd, Blackburn Aircraft Ltd, Bristol Aeroplane Co. Ltd, the de Havilland Aircraft Co. Ltd, the Fairey Aviation Co. Ltd, Gloster Aircraft Co. Ltd, Handley Page Ltd, Hawker Aircraft Ltd, Short Brothers (Rochester & Bedford) Ltd, Vickers-Armstrongs Ltd and Westland Aircraft Ltd.
- Shadow and dispersed factories controlled either by aircraft industry parent firms, or by the motor industry (Rootes Securities Ltd, the Austin Motor Co. Ltd, Morris Motors Ltd, Standard Motor Co. Ltd, etc), mainly in the Midlands and the North West of England. This activity includes contract production by the English Electric Co. Ltd at Preston and Samlesbury (Hampden, Halifax and Vampire), London Aircraft Production Group at Leavesden (Halifax) and Short & Harland Ltd in Belfast (Bombay, Hereford, Sunderland and Stirling).
- Smaller companies such as Airspeed (1934) Ltd, Cunliffe-Owen Aircraft Ltd, Folland Aircraft Ltd, Heston Aircraft Ltd, Phillips & Powis (Aircraft) Ltd/Miles Aircraft Ltd, Percival Aircraft Ltd, and Taylorcraft Aeroplanes (England) Ltd.
- Firms within the Civilian Repair Organisation such as AST at Hamble; manufacturer's repair organisations such as SEBRO at Cambridge, and RAF maintenance units such as Henlow and Kemble. Many aircraft that were nominally repaired and returned to service were substantially new airframes by the time that 'repair' had been completed.

The risk of bomb damage to main factory sites led every firm to set up dispersed operations. As in the First World War, large numbers of firms were involved and, as early as mid-1939, some 1,200 companies were involved in subcontract aircraft production. Peak production in the Second World War reached 2,715 aircraft per month (March 1944) with, in addition, more than 500 aircraft per month returned to service after repair.

Unlike during the First World War, there was a general policy of limiting the number of types in production. The increased efficiency and production volume that resulted off-set the

Regarded by many as the supreme example of piston-engined fighter design, production of the Martin-Baker MB5 was blocked as a result of wartime standardisation policies. (Martin-Baker Aircraft Ltd)

loss of some potentially outstanding designs (such as the Martin-Baker MB5), the production of which was blocked. As production gathered momentum, a number of companies were diverted from building their own types, in favour of the standardised designs.

The main Second World War production types are summarised in the following table:

Main Second World War Production Types

Fighter	Bomber	Trainer/Liaison	Other
Defiant	Hampden	Tiger Moth	Swordfish
Hurricane	Battle	Oxford	Sunderland
Spitfire	Blenheim	Master	Firefly
Typhoon	Wellington	Magister	Seafire
Tempest	Stirling	Anson	Walrus
Beaufighter	Halifax	Auster	Lysander
	Lancaster	Proctor	Beaufort
	Mosquito	Dominie	Barracuda

By about 1941, most of the production capacity for front-line machines had been grouped on the Stirling, Halifax and Lancaster bombers, the Beaufighter, the Mosquito, the Spitfire and the Barracuda. The reduced number of types produced reflects the technical maturity of the industry; it was no longer possible for the enemy to produce a new design that would comp-

The Sunderland was a mainstay of Coastal Command during the Battle of the Atlantic. (Bombardier Aerospace, Belfast)

The first of the four engine heavy bombers to fly was the Short Stirling. The type was produced at Rochester and South Marston by Short Brothers, and by Austin Motors at Longbridge. (Supplied by Medway branch RAeS)

Above: *Standardisation limited the number of aircraft and engine types in production during the Second World War. More than 50,000 of these four famous Merlin-powered types were built.* (Author)

Left: *The Second World War saw the return of the female population to aircraft production, as shown by this classic propaganda photograph of Halifax fuselage production by the London Aircraft Production Group.* (Handley Page Association)

letely change the balance of air power overnight. The Messerschmitt Me 262 might have had such an effect, had it been available earlier and in larger numbers, but in general it was found that progressive improvement of existing designs could keep pace with new enemy designs. Thus, the Spitfire was able to maintain its operational utility, through progressive engine, carburation and airframe developments, in the face of the Focke Wulf Fw190 and its developments.

Figures released at the end of the war by the Ministry of Aircraft Production stated that wartime production totalled some 125,000 complete aircraft, largest numbers being (in sequence) Spitfire, Hurricane, Wellington, Anson, Lancaster, Mosquito, Halifax, Beaufighter, Blenheim and Oxford (all 5,000 aircraft or more). (Note that the published list does not include non-operational types such as the Tiger Moth, more than 8,800 of which were built.)

It is also worth noting, in the light of the post-war domination of the industry by the USA, that although starting later, the US industrial machine outstripped United Kingdom production by a comfortable margin. The US built some 360,000 aircraft during the Second World War, nearly 96,000 of them in 1944 alone.

5
Post-war
(1945–1960)

When peace came the various shadow factories were no longer required for aircraft production, and were closed or converted for car and engine manufacture. The aircraft industry set about meeting the challenges that it faced. These were the relatively unfamiliar demands of the commercial market, and the race to exploit the new technologies of war as tensions mounted between the West and the Soviet Bloc. The industry's efforts were made more difficult by the weakness of Britain's war-shattered economy. Although the conditions facing the industry were not as drastic as those that obtained after the First World War, some companies still found themselves diversifying into new products. Examples include the production of pre-fabricated housing by a number of concerns, Vickers-Armstrongs Ltd supplying cabin furnishings for other manufacturers and Folland Aircraft Ltd manufacturing boats, motorcycle parts and refrigerators. Miles Aircraft Ltd diversified into the production of the Miles Photocopier and the famous 'Biro' ball-point pen. In some respects, the move of Westland, Fairey and Bristol into helicopter manufacture can also be seen in this light.

Commercial Aircraft Developments

A key decision which has shaped the post-war commercial aircraft industry was that wartime transport aircraft production was allocated to the United States of America. As a result, the excellent C-47 Dakota or DC-3 was immediately available for opening up the post-war air routes, with longer-range services provided by the DC-4 (C-54 Skymaster), the later DC-6 and the Lockheed Constellation. Not only were these excellent aircraft in their own right, but they also proved capable of development into a line of successful derivative aircraft.

What then of Britain? New aircraft types were needed – Britain's pre-war airliners had, after all, not exactly led the world in their performance or technology. Despite the strain on the economy, an attempt was made, through the Brabazon Committee, to identify and develop a fleet of new aircraft covering a wide range of commercial applications. Unfortunately, these designs could not be created overnight, and, in the short-term, stop-gap designs and converted bombers were all that was available to compete for airline markets. Worse was to follow, as when the new types appeared, they were (with a couple of notable exceptions) not well suited to the prevailing market conditions. One common fault seems to have been the specification of too few passenger seats. Perhaps this reflected the view that few people could afford to fly, and those that could would expect a suitably civilised environment!

To modern eyes, and admittedly with the benefit of hindsight, the first post-war commercial offerings from British Industry seem brave but, in many cases, doomed from the outset.

Above: *Although developed into a robust and long-lived design, the structural failures of the initial Comet 1 meant that Britain's opportunity to gain a world lead in air transport was lost.* (Marshall Aerospace Ltd)

Right: *(© BAE SYSTEMS plc)*

Below: *The Vickers VC1 Viking, with the military Valetta and Varsity, proved to be a successful, if unglamorous, product line for Vickers-Armstrongs Ltd. The combined production total for these three types was 575 aircraft.* (Brooklands Museum Trust)

Among these were:

- The hurriedly converted bombers – the Lancastrian, Halton, and Stirling V.
- Britain's only true transport of the war, the Avro York – itself a development of the Lancaster bomber.
- The Sunderland flying boat conversions and developments – the Hythe, Sandringham and Solent.
- Non-starters – Armstrong Whitworth Apollo, Bristol Brabazon, Cunliffe-Owen Concordia, Portsmouth Aerocar, Percival Merganser, and Saunders-Roe Princess.
- The honourable exceptions – the new designs which reached production. These were the Airspeed Ambassador, Avro Tudor, Bristol Freighter, Bristol Britannia,

de Havilland Comet, de Havilland Dove, Handley Page Hermes, Handley Page (Reading) Marathon, Vickers Viking and Vickers Viscount.

Sadly, the vast majority could not compete with the operational economics of the American designs, nor the economies of scale afforded by the US industrial machine. Of British commercial aircraft in the immediate post-war period, only the de Havilland Dove and the Vickers Viscount were unqualified successes. It is indeed tragic that the Comet, which could have achieved a generation of British leadership in the skies, proved to be unexpectedly flawed. Although redesign of the Comet eventually produced a robust and successful aircraft, the moment had been lost as far as British domination of the commercial air transport market was concerned.

Military Aircraft Programmes

On the military side, the defeat of Germany and Japan brought peace, but no reduction in tension, because of the development of the Cold War with the Soviet Union. The end of the war had seen the development of long-range surface-to-surface rockets, jet- and rocket-propelled aircraft, and the atomic bomb. German technical progress with the development of the thin swept wing had also opened the door to much higher speeds, and the prospect of supersonic flight. Britain, and indeed the whole developed world, therefore plunged into a race to develop and exploit these technologies in the military field.

Britain's brilliant lead in jet-engine technology saw operational fruit with the Meteor and Vampire, but was rapidly surpassed by the pace of development in both the USA and the USSR. In these nations, the significance of German swept-wing developments was better understood and acted upon, resulting in the superlative F-86 Sabre and Mikoyan & Guryevich MiG 15/17. Despite 'super-priority' programmes, Britain was unable to bring its own Swift or the Hunter quickly into service, and had to suffer the indignity of the interim operation of the F-86 Sabre in order to preserve a credible operational capability. Naval aviation relied upon the propeller-driven Sea Hornet, Sea Fury and Wyvern, with jets being introduced in the form of the Attacker, Sea Venom, Sea Hawk and DH110 Sea Vixen. As the 1950s came to an end, Dunsfold saw the beginnings of a new form of fighting aircraft with the development of the experimental V/STOL P.1127, which was to lead via the Kestrel to the Harrier. The P.1127 made its first tentative tethered hover in October 1960.

The Sea Fury was the last piston-engine fighter for the Royal Navy. This aircraft is seen sharing an Exeter dispersal with three Spitfires. (H.E. North)

The outstandingly successful Hunter was followed by V/STOL experimentation by Hawker Aircraft Ltd, with the P.1127 and Kestrel. Both types were developed at Dunsfold, Surrey.
(BAE SYSTEMS plc)

The grace and elegance of the Victor at altitude. The crescent-winged Victor was the last of the V-bombers to retire from service, having provided the RAF with nuclear deterrent, strategic reconnaissance and air-to-air refuelling capability.
(Handley Page Association)

In the field of bombers, the superb Canberra was flown in 1949 and continues in RAF service in 2004. The Canberra was followed by the challenging V-Bomber programme, which demonstrated that Britain could indeed produce world-class designs. How extraordinary, however, that after all its deprivations in the Second World War, the country could actually afford to carry all three V-Bombers – the Valiant, Victor and Vulcan – into production in the face of the Cold War threat.

Transport and training aircraft programmes also delivered some long-serving types including the Beverley, Chipmunk, Devon, Hastings, Pembroke, Prentice, Provost, Valetta and Varsity.

Westland made the transition to the manufacture of helicopters based upon the licence-built construction of Sikorsky designs, initially in the form of the WS-51 Dragonfly, and the WS-55 Whirlwind. A wider rotorcraft industry developed with a range of home-grown designs from Bristol (Sycamore and Belvedere), Fairey (Ultra-Light, Gyrodyne and Rotodyne) and Saunders-Roe (Skeeter and P.531).

Re-structuring of the Industry

As the 1950s came to a close, it was clear that an industry where every company built every type of aircraft could not be sustained. The Government recognised that this situation was unacceptable, and put great pressure on the industry to rationalise.

Duncan Sandys' 1957 Defence White Paper of 4 April 1957, *Outline of Future Policy*, has become somewhat notorious for its suggestion that missile technology was now maturing at such a rate that it would supplant manned aircraft in many roles. It stated that in view of 'the good progress made towards the replacement of the manned aircraft of RAF Fighter Command with a ground to air missile system, the RAF are unlikely to have a requirement for fighter aircraft of types more advanced than the supersonic P1, and work on such projects will stop'. Development of a supersonic manned bomber was not to be started, emphasis being switched to atomic weapons and guided missiles.

Clearly great changes in the aircraft industry were becoming inevitable. The first step was the formation of the British Aircraft Corporation Ltd in January 1960, the Government having indicated that it would only support the TSR.2 programme if it were to be produced by a single company. This resulted in the aviation interests of Vickers, Bristol and English Electric joining forces, with Hunting Aircraft following shortly afterwards. In parallel, the companies in the Hawker Siddeley Group – Armstrong Whitworth, A.V. Roe & Co. Ltd, Blackburn, Gloster and Hawker – found themselves being progressively joined by new bedfellows. These consisted of Folland (1959), de Havilland and its Airspeed Division (1960), and Blackburn (1960). In July 1963, this group was further reorganised to generate Hawker Siddeley Aviation Limited.

Thus was created what *Aviation Week* has called the 'Society of Both Aircraft Companies'. This was something of an exaggeration, as Short Brothers & Harland continued in Belfast, as did Scottish Aviation Ltd at Prestwick, Handley Page Ltd at Radlett and Auster at Rearsby. The helicopter industry was the subject of a similar Government-dictated rationalisation, in which Westland acquired the helicopter interests of its competitors: Saunders-Roe Ltd (1959), Bristol (1960) and Fairey Aviation (1960).

Above: *The Fairey Ultralight was one of a series of Fairey designs to feature a tip-driven rotor. G-AOUK is seen here in its initial configuration with a single vertical laid surface.* (Fairey Aviation, via Westland)

Right: *The TSR.2 was to have a fundamental role in the reshaping of the British aircraft industry in 1960.* (Author)

6
Rationalisation – The BAC and Hawker Siddeley Years (1960–1977)

Market Trends: Commercial and General Aviation

BAC and Hawker Siddeley inherited a civil market that was struggling to break out from American domination. It is unfortunate that during the initial post-war period, a unique British ability to market the wrong products had resulted in the commercial market for piston-engined aircraft being dominated by the USA. It was doubly unfortunate, then, that despite the success of the Viscount, the Comet disasters opened the door to the Boeing 707 and DC-8.

The BAC One-Eleven never matched its rival, the DC-9, in terms of sales. G-AYWB is seen here immediately after take off from Bristol Airport. (Author)

The death knell for Concorde was sounded with the announcement on 10 April 2003 that Concorde services would end at the end of October 2003. (Author)

XS765 was the first production Beagle B206R Bassett CC.1, and is seen here at Cranfield. (Author)

One glance at the shape of the Skyvan brings to mind the phrase once used by C.G. Grey, the editor of The Aeroplane, *to describe the Hamble River, Luke & Co. HL1: 'it strikes one at once as being undoubtedly for use, and not for ornament'.* (Author)

If possible, worse was to follow. Myopic specifications from Britain's nationalised airlines (BEA and BOAC) and political indifference to the commercial aircraft industry undermined the potential of the Vanguard and VC10, BAC One-Eleven and Trident. The technically brilliant Concorde was economically, politically and environmentally flawed, particularly after the oil price shock of the 1970s, and the on-off-on development of the HS146 (later the BAe 146 and Avro RJ family) appeared to be driven by pure politics.

In a significant move for the future, the Hatfield Division of Hawker Siddeley entered into an agreement to develop wings for the new European consortium Airbus Industrie. This followed inter-governmental agreement to support Airbus project definition, signed in September 1967. From May 1969, the United Kingdom government withdrew from further project funding, but Hawker Siddeley took the decision to continue in the project on a purely commercial basis.

In the field of general aviation, the 1960s scene seemed more positive; Beagle (British Executive and General Aviation Limited) was set up in October 1960, drawing upon the creative abilities of Auster at Rearsby and F.G. Miles at Shoreham. New designs emerged in the shape of the Beagle Pup, the twin engine Beagle 206, and the Bulldog military trainer. De Havilland had seen the value of the executive jet market and designed their DH125, initially known as the Jet Dragon, which was taken up and marketed by Hawker Siddeley as the HS125 with great success worldwide.

At Bembridge, Isle of Wight, John Britten and Desmond Norman had, through their operation of agricultural aircraft in some of the more basic areas of the world, identified the need for a simple robust utility aircraft capable of operation from short airstrips in all climates. The design that resulted, the Islander, fulfilled the designers' concept in every respect. On a larger scale, Shorts were also successful in bringing the utilitarian Skyvan into production for both civilian and military users.

In the helicopter arena, Westland Helicopters Limited built a solid base from its manufacture of Sikorsky products under licence. The Whirlwind and Wessex attracted large-scale orders, and the Saunders-Roe P.531 was developed successfully into the Scout and Wasp. Westland boomed in the 1970s as the Anglo-French helicopter deal came to fruition, with WHL building its own Lynx, and the Aérospatiale-designed Puma and Gazelle. Simultaneously, the company secured large national and export orders for the Sea King helicopter, which it built under licence from Sikorsky in the USA.

Commercial Casualties

Handley Page Ltd, having achieved only modest sales with the HPR.7 Dart Herald, conceived a twin turboprop feeder liner, the Jetstream. The Jetstream was greeted with enormous enthusiasm in the marketplace, with significant sales achieved before its first flight. This sales success was in large measure dependent upon the aircraft delivering its declared performance, within its FAA certification limited maximum weight of 12,500lb. In the event, this could not be achieved.

Handley Page Ltd had invested in tools and facilities for large-scale production, and was now faced with a difficult and expensive development programme while bearing the costs of their unfulfilled production expectations. The company proved unable to withstand the

Although not as successful as its chief competitor, the Fokker Friendship, the durable Herald first flew in 1955 and remained in service until 1999. This is G-BAZJ, photographed on the approach to Southampton Airport. (Author)

The troubled Handley Page Jetstream is seen here in early production at Radlett. Although the type brought Handley Page to its knees, it was subsequently successfully developed by British Aerospace at Prestwick as the Jetstream 31. (Handley Page Association)

financial pressures and entered voluntary liquidation in August 1969, ceasing to trade in June 1970. The subsequent development of the aircraft by British Aerospace shows that this was regrettably another case of that British trait, most familiar in the field of sport, of defeat snatched from the jaws of victory.

Similar difficulties were encountered at Beagle. Here, despite the sale of nearly 400 Pup aircraft, the Government withdrew financial support to the company in December 1969. Beagle eventually produced 152 Pup aircraft and eighty-five Beagle 206. Even the hugely popular Islander suffered from the problems brought about by sales success. Although the aircraft survived and remains in limited production, the company suffered a series of financial crises, including a number of periods in receivership.

Military Developments and Collaborative Ventures

In the military field, an almost mortal blow was struck when BAC, having been drawn together to produce the TSR.2, saw it cancelled by Denis Healey in April 1965. BAC military efforts were then concentrated on the completion of Lightning production, supplemented by export Canberra refurbishment and the development of the pressurised Jet Provost T. Mk 5, and the BAC167 Strikemaster. BAC then moved on to the collaborative development of the Jaguar.

In the late 1960s, the RAF identified the requirement to reduce its number of front line types, while achieving the following aims:

- The progressive replacement from the late 1970s of the Canberra and the V-bomber fleet.
- To establish the capability to carry out the low-level penetration roles that were to have been the province of the TSR.2.

ZA254 is the prototype Tornado F.2 – an interim step in the development of the RAF Tornado F.3 interceptor. (Author)

- In the longer term, to phase out the Lightning and Phantom from their air defence roles.
- Also in the longer term, to replace the Buccaneer in its low-level strike, reconnaissance and maritime strike roles.
- With all these objectives in mind, a further collaborative project emerged known as the Multi-Role Combat Aircraft, or MRCA – later named Tornado. BAC joined with MBB and Aeritalia to form Panavia to produce the Tornado, which first flew in 1974.

Hawker Siddeley faced its own political traumas, with the cancellation of the supersonic V/STOL P.1154 project, the Royal Navy variant being cancelled by Peter Thorneycroft in February 1964. The RAF P.1154 version followed under the Healey axe of 1965, which also saw the cancellation of the HS.681 V/STOL transport. Despite these difficulties, Hawker Siddeley prospered on the strength of the products that it had inherited from its parent companies. Of particular note were the Harrier from Hawker, the HS.748 from A.V. Roe & Co. Ltd, and the HS125 from de Havilland. Other work included the Buccaneer (ex-Blackburn), the Nimrod maritime patrol aircraft, Hunter refurbishment, and production of the Trident.

During this period Hawker Siddeley designed what may prove to be Britain's last purely home-grown military aircraft, the HS.1182 Hawk trainer, which first flew in 1974, and continues to be one of the world's most successful trainer aircraft. In 1977, the next major stage in the development of the British aircraft industry took place; the creation of British Aerospace – the 'Single British Aircraft Company'.

7
Modern Times

The Nationalisation and Privatisation of British Aerospace

British Aerospace (BAe) was formed as a nationalised corporation in April 1977, as a result of the Aircraft and Shipbuilding Industries Act 1977. In January 1981, BAe converted from a nationalised corporation to a public limited company (plc) in preparation for privatisation. The United Kingdom Government sold 51.57 per cent of its shares in February 1981, and all but a single £1 'golden share' in May 1985. When BAe was founded, it employed some 50,000 people on eighteen sites – Bitteswell, Brough, Chadderton, Chester, Christchurch, Dunsfold, Filton, Hamble, Hatfield, Holme-on-Spalding Moor, Hurn, Kingston, Preston, Prestwick, Samlesbury, Warton, Weybridge and Woodford.

Throughout its existence, BAe (now BAE SYSTEMS) has developed an ever more international flavour. The BAC collaboration on Jaguar was followed by the tri-national Tornado programme. Tornado production for Saudi Arabia has now ended, and BAE SYSTEMS has started production of Eurofighter, in partnership with Spain, Italy and Germany.

Something of a defining moment for the industry came on 24 December 1998 when the new-build Sea Harrier FA.2 NB18 was bought off by the Royal Navy customer. The completion of this aircraft was said by BAe to mark the last delivery of an all-British fighter aircraft to the UK armed services. February 2002 saw the announcement of the plan to withdraw the Sea Harrier FA.2 from service by 2006. One national programme, the Hawk, continues to go from strength to strength. Private venture developments of the Hawk 100 and Hawk 200 have allowed the type to remain effective, and it continues to be selected as the preferred training and light attack aircraft of many armed forces around the world.

By the time of the merger of British Aerospace with Marconi Electronic Systems to form BAE SYSTEMS on 30 November 1999, the number of sites manufacturing aircraft components was down to eight – Brough, Chester, Chadderton, Filton, Prestwick,

A Sea Harrier FRS.2 development aircraft under test at the British Aerospace factory and airfield at Dunsfold. (J.S. Smith)

Left: The export success of the Hawk was illustrated by this formation of aircraft flown at the SBAC Show. BAe had painted each aircraft with the flag of a different customer nation to emphasise the worldwide usage of the type. (Author)

Below: BAE SYSTEMS' transatlantic programmes include the T-45 Goshawk and AV-8B Harrier II with McDonnell Douglas (now Boeing) and the F-35 JSF with Lockheed Martin. The US Navy plans to acquire a total of 234 T-45, developed from the Hawk. (BAE SYSTEMS plc)

Samlesbury, Warton and Woodford – less than half the number of sites taken over in 1977. By this time, only Dunsfold remained as a major site of aircraft manufacture in South East England, and that under notice of closure.

Further ahead is the JSF programme, with BAE SYSTEMS teamed with Lockheed Martin to produce the supersonic CTOL/ASTOVL F-35 multi-role strike fighter for the USAF, US Navy, US Marine Corps and the RAF. Other transatlantic military co-operations include the T-45 Goshawk for the US Navy and the AV-8B Harrier II and II Plus with McDonnell Douglas (now Boeing). Development work is underway on an extensively modified Nimrod, the MRA.4 (with new wings and engines), to preserve Britain's maritime patrol capability.

BAe/BAE SYSTEMS Commercial Programmes

In the civil field, the establishment of the Airbus consortium has at last introduced a note of success into Britain's involvement in commercial aviation. Much against many observers' expectations, Airbus has proved to be a worthy rival to Boeing, achieving initial market penetration with the A300 and A310. These types have been followed up by the smaller, and hugely successful, A320 family, and the A330 and A340 long-haul transports. Airbus has now launched its super-wide body project, the A380, and is also the nominated project management organisation for a joint European military transport project, the Future Large Aircraft A400M.

Elsewhere, the civil market has not proved a happy experience for British Aerospace/BAE SYSTEMS. Corporate jet activity was continued with production of the BAe125 (previously HS125, previously DH125). The aircraft has been extensively developed throughout its production life, the final BAe production versions being the Hawker 800 and Hawker 1000. BAe sold its corporate jet business to the Raytheon Corporation in June 1993.

BAe's regional turboprop products were the Jetstream and the Advanced Turbo-Prop, or ATP, a stretched and re-engined development of the Avro/HS 748. The ATP was manufactured at Woodford until October 1992, when production was transferred to Prestwick, and the aircraft relaunched under the designation Jetstream 61. At Prestwick, meanwhile, a growth version of the Jetstream, the Jetstream 41, was launched. Market conditions proved initially unfavourable due to production over-capacity in this sector. BAe responded by forming an alliance with Aérospatiale and Alenia known as Aero International (Regional), AI(R), with a view to rationalising product lines. An early casualty was the

A typically spirited start to its flying display at the SBAC Show by Airbus A300 F-BUAD. (Author)

The ATP has its origins as a stretched and re-engined HS748. The type found only limited market success, with sixty-five being built at Woodford and Prestwick. (Author)

ATP/Jetstream 61, which, together with the original Jetstream 31, was not taken up by the AI(R) consortium. BAe continued with the Jetstream 41, but announced in May 1997 that the production line would close by the end of 1997. The AI(R) consortium was itself disbanded in 1998.

In the regional jet market, BAe produced the 146, taken over from Hawker Siddeley. Although produced in significant numbers (219 aircraft), initially at Hatfield, and then at Woodford, the 146 was not a financial success for BAe. Production costs were high and many aircraft were leased on terms that ultimately proved unprofitable to BAe. The aircraft was relaunched as a family of types known as the Avro RJ (Regional Jet) series.

Unfortunately, the terrorist attack on the New York World Trade Center on 11 September 2001 sounded the death knell for the RJ/RJX programme. On 27 November 2001, BAE SYSTEMS announced that it would be withdrawing from the construction of commercial aircraft at Woodford and would close the RJ and RJX programmes, with a consequential loss of 1,669 jobs. This decision, following the earlier suspension of the Jetstream 41 and 61 programmes at Prestwick, marked the end of BAE SYSTEMS' construction of complete aircraft for the civil market.

The Wider Industry

Outside BAe/BAE SYSTEMS, Shorts produced the SD330 and 360 developments of their 'ugly-duckling' Skyvan, and went on to supply the RAF with an extensively developed version of the Embraer Tucano for basic training. The last SD360 was built in 1991, and the last Tucano in 1992. Purchased by Bombardier in 1989, the company has become increasingly centred upon aerospace component manufacture and assembly. It is unlikely that the company will ever build another complete aircraft.

The boom that Westland experienced in the late 1970s could not last. Partly as a result of its ill-starred WG30 civil helicopter venture, Westland found itself in financial difficulties in 1986. A huge political row erupted over whether WHL should accept a possible European rescue package, or one offered by Sikorsky. After much acrimony, including the resignation of the Defence Secretary Michael Heseltine from the cabinet, the Sikorsky option was taken.

AgustaWestland produces the EH101 military, naval and civil transport helicopter. Italian Utility prototype I-LIOI is seen here displaying at Middle Wallop. (Author)

The Slingsby T.67M Firefly is an all-composite development of the Fournier RF6. The type is operated as a preliminary trainer by many air forces around the world. (Author)

Westland, like BAe, has taken an increasingly international route to secure its future. This has centred on the EH101 helicopter developed with Italy. WHL was purchased by GKN in 1994. During 1998, GKN announced its intention to combine its helicopter operations with those of the Italian company Agusta SpA. This merger has resulted in the formation of a new company, AgustaWestland, which has a mix of civil and military products, and involvement in both the EH101 and NH90 programmes. In the UK, the company has the EH101 and the WAH-64 Apache in production. The Lynx also remains in production, having gained export success in the form of the Super Lynx 300. The worldwide helicopter marketplace still suffers from over-capacity, and AgustaWestland will continue to need good penetration in export markets to secure its long-term future.

In the general aviation sector, the almost immortal Islander continues in limited production. Private aircraft have, for the most part, remained a bleak area for the British industry. Success has, however, been achieved by three products – the Slingsby T.67 Firefly, the CFM Shadow and the Europa.

- Slingsby redesigned the wooden Fournier RF6 (T.67A), adopting an all composite structure and installing increased power to produce a highly successful fully aerobatic trainer, which has found favour at entry level with a number of air forces around the world.
- The CFM (Cook Flying Machines) Shadow was designed by David Cook of Leiston, Suffolk. More than 400 of these aircraft have been built in a number of variants, including the high-performance Streak Shadow which flies at up to 105kt on its 64hp. The Shadow and Streak Shadow have been sold in more than thirty-six countries, and have completed many notable flights, including from England to Australia. As with so many British aircraft manufacturers, there have been trading difficulties along the way. CFM Metal Fax Ltd went into liquidation in November 1996 and was taken over by CFM Aircraft Ltd in 1997. CFM Aircraft Ltd was itself in receivership in autumn 2002, before being taken over by CFM Airborne Inc. of Texas who announced in November 2002 the setting up of a UK facility, CFM Airborne (UK) Ltd.

- Ivan Shaw's all-composite Europa, designed for the homebuilt and kit construction market, first flew in September 1992. Within seven years, more than 900 kits had been sold in thirty-four countries, and more than 300 aircraft were flying.

Future Prospects

Where does the future of the British industry lie? Shrinking defence markets have forced rationalisation in the USA. To some extent, this was also the engine for the creation of Hawker Siddeley and BAC, and subsequently the formation of British Aerospace and BAE SYSTEMS. With an increasing trend towards collaborative projects, and as a result of the large-scale investment required to launch new projects, aerospace is rapidly moving towards being a global business.

Lockheed, Martin Marietta, General Dynamics (Fort Worth Division), IBM, Loral, and Vought have already coalesced into a single corporation. Northrop and Grumman have merged to become Northrop Grumman; Boeing, McDonnell and Douglas have merged under the Boeing title. Faced with these giant businesses, European restructuring became inevitable. British Aerospace took a 35 per cent share in Saab of Sweden and spent a period in ultimately unsuccessful restructuring discussions with DaimlerChrysler Aerospace of Germany (DASA).

On 19 January 1999, BAe and GEC announced that they had reached agreement on the merger of BAe with the GEC defence interests (Marconi Electronic Systems). This merger, effective from the end of November 1999, created BAE SYSTEMS, then Europe's largest defence company, ranking at third largest in the world with a workforce of nearly 100,000 employees. In response to the creation of BAE SYSTEMS, DaimlerChrysler announced in June 1999 that they were acquiring the Spanish company CASA, thereby strengthening their position for future restructuring discussions. An agreement with Aérospatiale Matra followed, leading to the formation of EADS (European Aeronautic Defence and Space Company), on 10 July 2000. EADS is the world's third largest defence organisation, behind Boeing and Lockheed Martin, displacing BAE SYSTEMS from this position.

With transatlantic projects such as JSF looking to secure global export markets, overtures from the major players in the USA may not be long delayed. A future global aerospace business may yet be created by one of the major US defence conglomerates acting in partnership with BAE SYSTEMS and/or EADS. In ten years' time, it is hard to believe that the current structure of the industry will not have seen further upheaval – we will have to wait and see. By that time, indeed, it may seem almost quaint to refer to the British aircraft industry.

8
The Genealogy of British Aerospace/BAE SYSTEMS

The preceding narrative has charted the evolution of the British aircraft industry. Much of the manufacturing capacity of the industry is now in the hands of only two companies; BAE SYSTEMS, previously British Aerospace plc, manufacturing military fixed wing aircraft and commercial aircraft components, and AgustaWestland (previously GKN Westland Helicopters Ltd), manufacturing military helicopters.

The narrative has shown how political and commercial imperatives led to progressive restructuring of the industry. The impact of these changes is best appreciated when presented in the form of a family tree. BAE SYSTEMS came into being with the merger between British Aerospace and the defence interests of GEC, Marconi Electronic Systems (MES). As MES did not include any UK aircraft manufacturers in its heritage, the following family tree represents only the British Aerospace heritage that passed into BAE SYSTEMS. Three diagrams are presented:

1. British Aerospace: The Big Picture
2. BAe: Hawker Siddeley Companies
3. BAe: British Aircraft Corporation and Scottish Aviation

While in many respects these diagrams speak for themselves, a few observations are worth making:

- British Aerospace was formed in 1977 by the merging of three companies: Hawker Siddeley Aviation Ltd, the British Aircraft Corporation (BAC) and Scottish Aviation Ltd. Short Brothers & Harland were the only major fixed wing aircraft manufacturer that remained independent of this group.
- Because Scottish Aviation Ltd had acquired the rump of the Beagle Aircraft Ltd and Handley Page Ltd activities, they effectively brought with them into the BAe family tree the heritage of these firms. This encompasses (via Handley Page Ltd) Martinsyde Ltd and Phillips & Powis/Miles Aircraft Ltd, and (via Beagle) Auster Aircaft Ltd and Taylorcraft Aeroplanes (England) Ltd.
- Hawker Siddeley Aviation Ltd (HSAL) added Blackburn and General Aircraft Ltd, the de Havilland Aeroplane Co. Ltd and Folland Aircraft Ltd to the group of Hawker Siddeley companies that had already been merged in 1935, although continuing to trade under their original identities (A.V. Roe & Co. Ltd, Hawker Aircraft Ltd, Gloster Aircraft Company Ltd, and Sir W.G. Armstrong Whitworth Aircraft Ltd).
- The less familiar antecedents of HSAL include H.H. Martyn & Co. (via Gloster), William Denny & Bros Ltd, General Aircraft Ltd and CWA Ltd (via Blackburn) and

Airspeed Ltd, May Harden & May and Wycombe Aircraft Constructors (via AIRCO/de Havilland).
- Only four companies were grouped into BAC, these being English Electric Aviation Ltd, Bristol Aircraft Ltd (previously the Bristol Aeroplane Co. Ltd), Vickers-Armstrongs (Aircraft) Ltd and Hunting Aircraft Ltd (previously Percival Aircraft Ltd). The Vickers-Armstrongs heritage includes the Supermarine Aviation Works Ltd and Pemberton-Billing Ltd. The aircraft interests of the English Electric Co. Ltd were originally formed by merging the aircraft activities of Coventry Ordnance Works, Phoenix Dynamo Co. Ltd and Dick, Kerr & Co. in December 1918.
- Between 1919 and 1921 many company names were changed, and a number of new companies were founded following the closure of closely linked predecessors. This reflects the impact of taxation imposed after the First World War on companies that were considered to have made excess profits.

BAe – The Big Picture

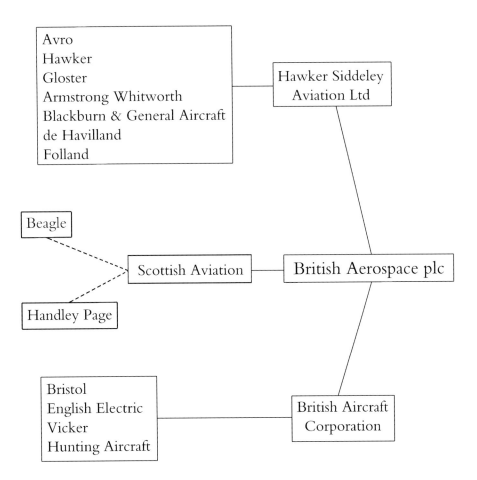

British Aerospace – Hawker Siddeley Companies

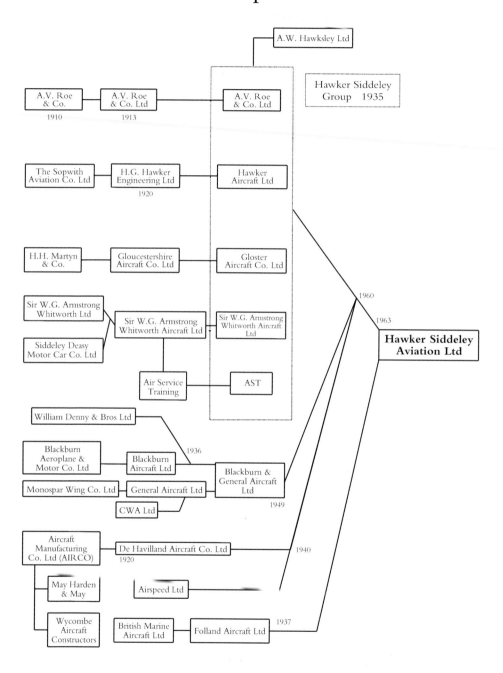

BAe: British Aircraft Corporation & Scottish Aviation

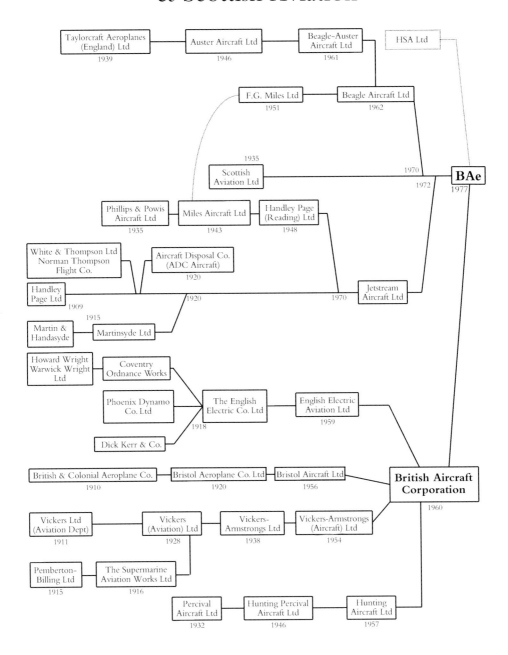

The Aircraft Manufacturers of South East England

Berkshire

Aldermaston

The Fairey Aviation Co. Ltd. The Fairey GR.17/45 (Gannet) prototype VR546 was towed by road from Hayes to Aldermaston for its first flight on 19 September 1949. Fairey Aviation also operated at Hamble, Hayes, Harmondsworth, Heston, Northolt, Stockport and White Waltham.

Vickers-Armstrongs Ltd. The airfield at Aldermaston was used for the assembly and flight test of Supermarine Spitfire aircraft manufactured by the companies that formed the Reading Spitfire dispersed production organisation.

Above: *G-FIRE is a Spitfire Mk.XIVC that was assembled at Aldermaston with RAF serial number NH904. This aircraft is currently flying in the USA as N114BP* (Author)

Right: *The long-winged AMF Chevvron microlight is a quiet two-seater and has proven to be a safe and successful design.* (Author)

British Airways' smallest aircraft ever, perhaps. G-AXVK is an upgraded Campbell Super Cricket. (Author)

Hungerford and Membury

AMF Aviation Enterprises Ltd (previously **Microflight Ltd**) built the Chevvron at Membury airfield. The Chevvron is a successful 'three-axis' microlight with a high aspect ratio 44ft-span wing and two-seat side-by-side seating. With its three-blade propeller, the Chevvron is one of the quietest microlights flying. The type has had an impeccable safety record.

The prototype Chevvron was first flown in 1983 from Bidford gliding site near Evesham, type certification being achieved in 1987. Production has comprised a single Chevvron 2-32A (without flaps), eighteen 2-32B (with split flaps), and twenty-one 2-32C with drag flaps. Some twelve of the 2-32B aircraft were subsequently converted to the 2-32C version. A single seaplane version was built, winning the first prize at the Nice Cavalere Seaplane Festival in 1986.

The company was formed in 1976 and initially manufactured glider trailers. The company was re-formed in December 1997 as **Aviation Enterprises Ltd** and is active in development and production of a wide range of products including composite propellers and wind tunnel blades, ducted vectored drive systems, glider and aircraft trailers, and lightweight composite structures. Aviation development continues with a long-term project to develop a high-performance light aircraft, the Aviation Enterprises Magnum, to full Certificate of Airworthiness standards.

The Magnum is a two-seat side-by-side, all-composite, low-wing monoplane, with a retractable tricycle undercarriage. The design features an efficient wing design that incorporates a sophisticated Fowler flap system. A cruise speed of 160kt is predicted using a Rotax 914 Turbo rated at 100hp maximum continuous power. By late 1999, extensive development had led to the construction of major structural components for the prototype, allowing the conduct of undercarriage retraction trials. Steady development continued over the next four years, leading to a first flight of the prototype, G-61-2, from Membury on 5 June 2003.

Campbell Aircraft Ltd of Everland Rd, Hungerford, built some fifty Campbell-Bensen, Cricket, Super Cricket, and Cougar gyroplanes between 1967 and 1973. Sadly Mr and Mrs Campbell were killed in a commercial airline crash in late 1967. After this, the Bensen-based design was substantially redesigned to result in the Cricket series. The first Cricket G-AXNU flew in November 1969, the type being assembled and flown at Membury. Cricket production ceased in 1971 after the manufacture of some forty-two airframes, not all of which were assembled or registered.

In 1975 the company reformed as **Campbell Gyroplanes Ltd**, at Boxford near Newbury, producing the single Super Cricket G-AXVK. The Cougar G-BAPS was a two-seat version built at Weston-super-Mare which first flew on 25 April 1973, but which did relatively little flying, and did not enter production.

The **Chilton** DW1 Monoplane was designed and built by the Hon. A. Dalrymple and A.R. Ward, previously of the de Havilland Technical School. The aircraft was built in the grounds of Chilton Lodge, just to the north of Hungerford, where A.R. Ward lived. Work on the type began in 1936, with **Chilton Aircraft Ltd** being formed in May 1936. The DW1 was a delightful single seater of clean lines and sparkling performance. The first aircraft G-AESZ was test-flown at Witney in April 1937 by Ranald Porteous (later a famous exponent of the Auster, and also previously of the DH Technical School). This Ford-engined prototype was fitted with a throttle that worked in the reverse sense to the norm – this provoked some comment at the time! The Chilton performed well in air races, particularly with the Train and, later, Mikron engines. The Train-engined DW1A G-AFSV won the 1939 Folkestone Trophy at 126mph – highly creditable on 44hp. Four aircraft were built, all of which survived the war. In 1939, the sale price quoted for a Chilton Monoplane was £315.

During the Second World War, Chilton Aircraft carried out sub-contract manufacturing work. Sadly, Mr Dalrymple was killed in the crash of a Fieseler Storch aircraft near Hungerford on Christmas Day 1945, on his first flight after the end of the Second World War.

In 1997 a home-built Chilton Monoplane G-BWGJ was cleared for flight, having been built by T.J. Harrison.

Maidenhead

D.M.K. Marendaz Ltd/Marendaz Special Cars Ltd (formed May 1932) set up a company in April 1937 known as **International Aircraft & Engineering Ltd** at Cordwallis Works, Maidenhead, with a view to entering the aircraft industry. Unfortunately, the works were destroyed by fire in June 1937.

The single-seat Chilton Monoplane was a sporting ultralight with sparkling performance and delightful handling. Only four were built. (Author)

The surviving Marendaz Special No. 1 bears witness to the statement made by The Aeroplane *that 'the company are known as makers of custom-built sports cars'.* (Author)

The first Marendaz design was the Marendaz Special Monoplane, described in *The Aeroplane* of February 1936. A general arrangement drawing showed this to be a two-seat side-by-side low-wing cabin monoplane with a fixed spatted undercarriage and a Pobjoy engine. The type had rectangular wings of 28ft span, with a tip shape that was cut back to give a reduced length to the trailing edge compared with the leading edge. The standard version was to feature wire-braced wings, with a full cantilever version available at extra cost. In overall configuration the type resembled a rectangular wing version of the Aeronca LB or Ryan SCW. Ord-Hume reports that this machine was not proceeded with solely because Captain Marendaz neglected to acknowledge the role of G.N. Wikner in the design of the aircraft when it was initially publicised.

The Aeroplane commented that 'the company are known as makers of custom-built sports cars that are comfortable to drive and easy to handle.' Captain Marendaz was the owner of the Bedford School of Flying at Barton le Clay and, after the destruction of the Cordwallis Works, further development continued at Barton le Clay.

The second type to be built was the Marendaz III low-wing cabin monoplane with retractable undercarriage. The first prototype was destroyed as a result of the fire at the Cordwallis Works, but the type nevertheless emerged in the form of G-AFGG, which was displayed (statically) at the Royal Aeronautical Society Garden Party at Harmondsworth in May 1938. G-AFGG was built at Barton-le-Clay, in the same works used by Luton Aircraft Ltd, and is widely believed never to have flown, although there is no conclusive evidence in this regard.

International Aircraft & Engineering entered receivership in June 1938, following which a further company, **Marendaz Aircraft Ltd**, was established. This company constructed a Cirrus Minor-powered, low-wing, tandem two-seat, open-cockpit aircraft, the Marendaz Trainer, G-AFZX, which was briefly flown in late 1939 before being given to the Air Training Corps Squadron at Halton.

Newbury

Geoffrey de Havilland carried out early experiments at Seven Barrows Field near Beacon Hill to the south of Newbury, assisted by Frank Hearle. The actual site of these experiments was close to the village of Whitway, in the neighbouring county of Hampshire, and these trials are covered in Volume 2 of this series (South West & Central Southern England).

Elliotts of Newbury, Albert Works, Albert Road, Newbury. The factory was located right in the centre of Newbury, off the main shopping street, but the area has now been redeveloped. The Elliotts company was a long established joinery and furniture manufacturer that constructed transport gliders as part of the group organised by Harris Lebus Ltd during the Second World War. From 1939, Elliotts built aircraft components for such types as the Tiger Moth, Mosquito, Oxford, Spitfire, Martinet and Hamilcar. Most notably, they were responsible for a substantial volume of Airspeed Horsa production, and also were involved in manufacture of the powered Hamilcar.

This involvement in glider production during the Second World War led to Elliotts becoming one of the UK's major glider manufacturers. The company initially built primary gliders, together with some fifty EoN Baby gliders, a version of the well-known Grunau Baby. The company moved on to the higher-performance sailplanes, with its extensively developed Olympia series, which originated from the German DFS Meise. The prototype Olympia first flew in January 1947 and the final, most highly developed, version was the Olympia 463, which flew in April 1963. Elliotts built more than 250 sailplanes and more than sixty primary gliders before production ceased in 1965.

Elliotts' only powered aircraft design was the Newbury Eon G-AKBC which first flew on 8 August 1947 at Welford. (Eon stood for Elliotts of Newbury.) Design of the Newbury Eon was carried out by **Aviation and Engineering Projects** of Feltham. The aircraft was of all-wooden construction, with a smooth surface finish being achieved by plywood skinning, exploiting Elliotts' experience of glider manufacture, although this gave the rear fuselage a slightly corpulent appearance, similar to that of the German Putzer Elster. The modernity of the design was emphasised by the use of a tricycle undercarriage. The prototype required an increase in power from its initial Cirrus Minor, and this was provided by installation of a 145hp Gipsy Major to produce the Eon 2 which first flew on 26 June 1948. The Eon was not put into production, and the prototype was destroyed in a pilotless take-off at Lympne (with a glider in tow) in April 1950.

Reading (Woodley)

Manufacturing activities at Woodley have been dominated by the activities of Phillips & Powis Ltd and its successors. This entry presents a chronological review of the Phillips & Powis and Miles activity, followed by an alphabetical listing of other aircraft types to have been built and/or flown at Woodley.

Genesis: Between the Wars

Woodley airfield was owned by **Phillips & Powis Ltd**, and opened in spring 1929. Phillips & Powis Ltd were motor dealers in Reading who became involved in light aircraft by becoming sales agents for the Simmonds Spartan and the DH60 Moth. The company were also interested in flying training, and purchased an Avro 504 and a DH Moth in the autumn of 1928. The company is recorded as having re-engined Avro 504K G-EBWO with an Anzani radial engine at Woodley in 1928.

In the light of these interests, Phillips & Powis developed the airfield at Woodley, which was in use by Easter 1929. **Phillips & Powis Aircraft (Reading) Ltd** was registered on 19 March 1929 with share capital of £5,000, and the Phillips & Powis School of Flying was set up with an expanded fleet of DH Moth aircraft.

Mr F.G. Miles, who began aircraft construction with Southern Aircraft Ltd at Shoreham, designed the Miles Satyr (which was built at Yate), and then the Miles Hawk. The M.2 Hawk was built with the help of Charles Powis, thereby establishing the connection between **Miles** and **Phillips & Powis.**

The Miles M.2 Hawk prototype G-ACGH first flew at Woodley on 29 March 1933. The Hawk proved to be a pivotal design, from which was developed a wealth of derivatives, resulting in an alphabetically challenging series of variants running (with almost no gaps) from the M.2A to the M.2Z. The success of the Hawk and its variants established Phillips & Powis as an important manufacturer of private touring, training and racing aircraft. The company used participation in air races as a promotional activity from the outset, the results achieved fully justifying this decision.

The main pre-war production types of the company are tabulated below.

Type	First Flight/Prototype	Comments
M.2 Hawk	29 March 1933, G-ACGH	Initially sold at £395, forty-eight built with Cirrus IIIA engine.
M.2D	4 February 1934, U1	Three-seat variant. Six built.
Hawk Speed Six	28 June 1934, G-ACTE	Gipsy Six powered racing variant, built in a number of versions including M.2E (one), M.2L (two) and M.2U (one). See additional comments below.
Hawk Major	23 June 1934, G-ACTD	Gipsy Major powered. Main production variants M.2E (eighteen built), and M.2H (version with flaps, forty-seven built). Other versions included the M.2G, M.2M, M.2P, M.2S and M.2T.
Hawk Trainer I and II	31 July 1935	A number of trainer derivatives were built, including the M.2R (four aircraft), M.2W (twelve), M.2Y (eight) and M.2Z (ten for Romania).
M.3 Falcon	23 September 1934, U3/G-ACTM	First cabin derivative, the prototype being followed by thirty-six production aircraft built in five versions. The most important versions were the M.3A (G-ADBF first flown 16 January 1935, nineteen built) and the M.3B Falcon Six (G-ADLC first flown on 20 July 1935). See additional comment below.
M.4/4A Merlin	24 March 1935, U8	Five-seat cabin monoplane. Four aircraft built
M.5/5A Sparrowhawk	19 August 1935, G-ADNL	Single-seat open cockpit racing air-craft. Five built.

Type	First Flight/Prototype	Comments
M.7/7A Nighthawk U5/G-ADXA	26 October 1935,	Two-seat cabin monoplane for instrument training. Five built.
M.8 Peregrine	12 September 1936, U9	Twin-engine eight-seat aircraft, similar in concept to a wooden version of the Dove. Powered by Gipsy Six II engines driving variable pitch propellers. Two only built, the second aircraft L6346 being used for boundary layer control research.
M.9 PV Trainer	3 June 1937, U5	This Kestrel powered training aircraft was subsequently developed into the prototype Miles M.9A Master. The development of theMaster, and its production history is discussed below.
M.11, M.11A Straight and Whitney Straight	3 May 1936, G-AECT	The prototype M.11 Straight was developed developed into the production Whitney Straight two-seat touring aircraft. Some fifty were laid down, but not all were completed.
M.12 Mohawk	22 August 1936, G-AEKW	A single aircraft built to the requirements of Charles Lindbergh.
M.13 Hobby	4 September 1937, U2	A small single-seat racing aircraft, later registered as G-AFAW.
M.14/14A/14B Hawk Trainer III and Magister	20 March 1937, U2/G-AETJ	The definitive trainer variant of the Hawk, which led to Phillips &Powis achieving major production success with its adoption as the standard RAF basic trainer. A total of 1,281 aircraft were built of all M.14 variants. See additional comments below.
M.16 Mentor	5 January 1938	Three-seat communications aircraft, forty-five built.
M.17 Monarch	21 February 1938, G-AFCR	Three-seat development of the M.11 A Whitney Straight; eleven built.
M.18	4 December 1938, U2	Intended as a Magister replacement, only four aircraft were built. See additional comments below.

The total number of M.2 and M.2-derivative types built was 173 aircraft. The Miles M2L Hawk Speed Six G-ADGP first flew at Woodley on 6 June 1935, and was raced extensively from the late 1940s until the 1960s. Its most notable success came in 1950 with the establishment of a world 100km closed circuit record in Class C1b of 192.83mph.

The Miles Falcon was an outstanding tourer and record-breaking aircraft with a high cruising speed and slow landing speed due to its effective flaps. It did, however, have a rather restricted view and a very noisy cabin. The type was advertised in February 1936 as 'Fastest in its Class – The Miles Falcon has been supplied to many owners in this country as well as in Africa, Australia, Austria, China, Egypt, France, Germany, Holland, Italy, Palestine and Spain.'

M.11A Whitney Straight G-AERV refuelling at Exeter. (HE North)

An advertisement promoting the success of Miles aircraft in the 1935 King's Cup Air Race read: 'Everybody claims Speed, Comfort and Value. Here is positive proof that the Miles Falcon Six is UNEQUALLED in these Qualities – King's Cup Race: First T. Rose Miles Falcon Six, 176.2 mph, 2nd and 3rd Miles Hawk Trainers. The Miles Falcon Six has a cruising speed of 160mph and sells for £1,325, flaps £60.' In this event, Miles became the first company to fill the first three places of the King's Cup Air Race with its products.

Major production success came with the Magister (the M.14 Hawk Trainer III adapted for RAF use). 1,230 Magisters were built for the RAF, the type being the service's first monoplane training aircraft. Although ultimately highly successful, the M.14 had early problems with its spinning characteristics. Three of the early Hawk Trainer aircraft were lost in spin trials, leading to the adoption of anti-spin strakes ahead of the tailplane on the M.14A. M.14 production comprised two prototypes, 1,224 Magister I, six Magister II powered by the Cirrus Major engine, twenty-three civil M.14/M.14A Hawk Trainer III, three civilian M.14B, and twenty-three export M.14/14A. In addition, Miles Aircraft Ltd subsequently modified some 234 ex-service Magister aircraft for civilian use.

Although not technically adventurous in its original design, the Miles M.18 (a proposed Magister replacement) gave rise to an advanced high-lift research machine. This was the M18 Mk IV, U11/JN703, which was fitted with full span slots of 20 per cent chord, and full span flaps of 40 per cent chord. The ailerons were incorporated as surfaces inset into the outer flap, and a tailplane of increased area was fitted. The aircraft was used for test flying in support of development of the Supermarine S.12/40 Seagull, and achieved the very high maximum lift coefficient of $CL_{MAX} = 3.2$ during flight trials.

A number of changes were made in the company's trading name as it developed and evolved. **Phillips & Powis (Aircraft) Ltd** was formed on 5 March 1935, with share capital of £125,000, to take over the aircraft construction business of **Phillips & Powis Aircraft (Reading) Ltd**. The transfer of control took effect from 1 November 1934, the company adopting the telegraphic address 'Hawk, Reading'. On 5 October 1943, the company was renamed **Miles Aircraft Ltd**. After the collapse of **Miles Aircraft Ltd** in 1948, that portion not taken over by **Handley Page (Reading) Ltd** became the **Western Manufacturing Co.** and then, in 1955, **Adamant and Western Co. Ltd** (subsequently becoming **Adwest plc**).

Second World War Production

The Miles Master advanced trainer was developed from the Miles M.9 Private Venture Trainer, the Master prototype N3300 being first flown on 31 March 1939. 475 M.9B Master I were built, followed by 400 M.9B Master IA with reduced wing span. A further version, the M.24 Master Fighter, was produced as an emergency fighter with six-gun armament, flying in mid-1940; twenty-five were built. The next version of the Master was the M.19 Master II, production comprising two prototypes converted from Master I, and 1,249 production aircraft built at Woodley, 488 at South Marston and ten at Doncaster. The last Woodley-built Master was delivered on 15 December 1942. 190 aircraft due to be produced at Doncaster (supported by additional facilities at Sheffield) were transferred to the South Marston production unit. The final version was the Master III, which was built exclusively at South Marston. A prototype, converted from a Master I, was followed by 602 production aircraft. Ultimately, some 3,250 Master aircraft of all versions were built, including the sole M.31 Master IV.

Two prototypes and 1,722 production examples of the M.25 Martinet were built to serve in the unglamorous role of target tug, the first (LR241) flying on 24 April 1942. A number of these aircraft were subsequently to become targets themselves, being converted to Queen Martinet targets. A further sixty-five M.50 Queen Martinet aircraft were built from the outset for target use. A second specialist target tug, the Miles M.33 Monitor, was first flown (NF900) on 5 April 1944, the two prototypes being followed by twenty production aircraft. Many of the Queen Martinet aircraft, along with the production examples of the Miles Monitor, were delivered directly to store and did not enter operational service.

Miles created a number of innovative prototypes during the Second World War, one of the more striking being the M.20, which was intended as a low-cost fighter and built largely from 'non-strategic materials' (i.e. from wood). Two aircraft were built, the first being flown as M.20/2 U9 (later AX834) on 15 September 1940, only sixty-five days after design work was started. A second aircraft, M.20/4 U-0228/DR616, incorporating a range of modifications, was flown on 8 April 1941.

Miles constructed a series of unauthorised prototypes during the war years at its Liverpool Road works. The first example was the Miles M.28 Mk 1 (or LR1) U-0232/HM583. This was a cabin two-seat light aircraft with twin fins and a retractable undercarriage that had a strong influence on the design of the later Messenger and Gemini aircraft. The M.28 Mk 1, also known as the Miles Mercury, was first flown on 11 July 1941. This first aircraft was followed by five further M.28 in three- and four-seat versions. The M.28 prototype was adapted to become the M.28/38, this being a development prototype for the M.38 Messenger. This aircraft was first flown from Woodley on 12 September 1943, bearing the marks U-0223. The type was built as an unauthorised private venture as a short take-off and landing liaison aircraft, but it did not, initially, find favour with the Air Ministry. The first true prototype did not fly until February 1944, and by the end of hostilities only twenty-one of the 250 military aircraft eventually ordered had been delivered. Development continued after the war and is discussed further below.

Miles also built the unconventional M.35 and M.39 tandem-winged aircraft. The tiny M.35 'Libellula' U0235 (20ft long and 20ft span) flew on 1 May 1942 and was powered by a single Gipsy Major. The M.35 was another unauthorised private venture. The M.39B U-0244 was intended as a sub-scale test aircraft for a projected bomber design, the B.11/41. Powered by two Gipsy Major 1C engines, the M.39B flew on 22 July 1943. Both these prototypes were built in the experimental department at Liverpool Road, acquiring in consequence the alternative designations LR2 and LR3.

The M.39B gained some official recognition when the RAE adopted it for research purposes with serial number SR392. The M.39B was a most attractive design, despite its unconventional configuration. There is little doubt, however, that Miles' unorthodox approach, both in terms of configuration and in its attitude to bureaucracy, militated against the success of these projects.

Above: *A wartime photograph of the prototype Messenger U-0223, one of a number of new designs built at Miles Aircraft's Liverpool Road works.* (Museum of Berkshire Aviation via Julian Temple)

Right: *An impressive production line of Miles Monitors at Woodley.* (Adwest Group via Ken Ellis)

After the Second World War two Martinet aircraft were converted to act as prototypes for the M.37, an unnamed advanced trainer. The M.37 featured a prominent raised rear cockpit for the instructor with a bubble canopy. The first aircraft JN275 was flown on 11 April 1946, but the type did not enter production.

During the Second World War a large number of Spitfire aircraft were overhauled at Woodley by Phillips and Powis within the Civilian Repair Organisation. The company handled some 2,000 aircraft, many of these being under subcontract from Morris Motors Ltd at Cowley. Marketing was surprisingly aggressive: 'Monoplane Pilots Need Monoplane Training', 'More Milestones in Aviation' (a horrible pun referring, in 1945, to the Master, Messenger and Marathon).

Post-war Hopes and Collapse

Post-war production focused on the Messenger, Gemini, Aerovan and Marathon, with additional work in the form of civil and export conversions of the Magister. In 1946 no less than 148 Magister aircraft were prepared for export to Argentina. Production totals for the Messenger, Aerovan and Gemini are somewhat confused by the sudden collapse of the company in 1948. The data presented here (including production numbers and first flight dates) are based on those cited by Julian Temple in his excellent history of Phillips & Powis and its successors, *Wings over Woodley*.

The Messenger continued in production throughout the post-war life of Miles Aircraft Ltd, being built both at Woodley and in Northern Ireland. The total production of the Messenger comprised the prototype, twenty-one Messenger 1 (eleven at Woodley, five at Danbridge and five at Newtownards), sixty-five Messenger 2A, three Messenger 4 and one each of the Messenger 2B, 2C, 3 and 4A. Nineteen additional Messenger 4A were produced by conversion of ex-military aircraft. Other production figures can be found elsewhere.

The Miles M.57 Aerovan 1 (or LR4) U-0248/G-AGOZ, which was flown on 26 January 1945, was yet another unauthorised prototype to emanate from Liverpool Road. The main advantages of the Aerovan are summed up in contemporary advertising: '1.7 cu ft of cargo capacity for every horsepower.... This outstandingly versatile aircraft is readily adaptable as

Opposite: *One of the least well known of the Liverpool Road prototypes, this is the Miles M.30 X-Minor U-0233, which was first flown in February 1942.* (Museum of Berkshire Aviation via Julian Temple)

Above: *The Miles Gemini was a neat and economical twin. Unfortunately, it did not survive in Britain's post-war climate of austerity.* (Author)

freighter, passenger plane, air ambulance, emergency operating theatre, flying caravan, mobile workshop, aerial shop or showroom.'

A creditable total of at least fifty-six Aerovan aircraft were built, the main production version being the Aerovan 4, of which forty-five were built. (Production figures quoted for the Aerovan differ in some sources – not all aircraft were necessarily completed and flown. Based on allocated serial numbers, it would appear that fifty-three were built by Miles, and three aircraft allocated serial numbers by Handley Page (Reading) Ltd, but not flown.)

The remarkable lifting ability of the Aerovan was demonstrated by a flight in July 1947 in which an especially lightened aircraft (stripped to an empty weight of 2,683lb) was successfully flown at an all-up weight of 6,228 lb – a payload equal to 132 per cent of the empty weight.

One unsuccessful design was the M.64 tricycle undercarriage side-by-side trainer, U-6/U-0253, which was built at Liverpool Road (as LR5) and flown at Woodley on 3 June 1945. Aerodynamic problems were encountered and the type suffered from an inadequate climb rate and excessive buffet at low speeds; development was quickly abandoned.

The Gemini was more successful. One of the first new designs to fly after the end of the Second World War, the prototype Gemini G-AGUS first flew at Woodley on 26 October 1945. Like the Messenger, the first aircraft was built at Liverpool Road, Reading (as was the initial production batch). Production was then transferred to Woodley, a total of 150 being laid down for production. Of these, Miles Aircraft Ltd completed 139. This number was increased after the collapse of Miles Aircraft by two further examples completed by Handley Page (Reading) Ltd as Gemini 1A. Six additional Gemini airframes, ten sets of wings (some of which were used for Messenger aircraft) and large quantities of spares were sold at this time to Ron Paine at **Wolverhampton Aviation Ltd**. The Ron Paine Gemini aircraft were constructed as Gemini 3A. Three further aircraft were purchased by F.G. Miles who took them to Redhill for completion by his new company **F.G. Miles Ltd**, these aircraft eventually appearing as a single Gemini 1A and two Miles M.75 Aries.

With its box-like fuselage, the Aerovan might have been thought sufficiently unorthodox in appearance, but for two even more extreme developments built and flown during 1948 immediately before the demise of the company. These were:

- The M.68 Boxcar or 'Pantechnicon' G-AJJM, which was flown on 22 August 1947, powered by four 100hp Cirrus Minor engines and featuring a removable freight pod fuselage.
- The M.71 Merchantman U21, flown on 7 August 1947. This was a larger all-metal aircraft powered by four Gipsy Queen engines and having a conventional passenger fuselage. The M.71 was designed, built and flown in only ten months.

The final Miles design to enter production was the Miles Marathon, an attractive four-engine, twenty-seat feeder line aircraft which suffered from protracted development and inadequate sales. The prototype U10, later G-AGPD, was first flown on 19 May 1946. Twenty-five were ordered by the Ministry of Supply, and a further twenty-five (intended to be powered by two Mamba turboprops) by BEA. The second prototype G-AILH flew in February 1947. The

The Mamba Marathon G-AHXU is seen here bearing the Handley Page insignia and RAF markings, as VX231. (BAE SYSTEMS plc)

loss of the Marathon prototype in an accident near Boscombe Down on 28 May 1948 added to the difficulties that the company was already facing.

Phillips & Powis (Aircraft) Ltd and its successors built some fifty types and sub-types to the designs of Mr and Mrs F.G. Miles. Sadly, the glue that Miles used in their wooden aircraft, like that of the Percival Proctor, did not stand the test of time, and many of these fine aircraft were consigned to the scrap heap and the bonfire in the 1950s and '60s.

Handley Page (Reading) Ltd was formed when the Miles company was taken over on 5 July 1948. The background to this change was the severe financial pressure facing Miles Aircraft Ltd by the end of 1947. Miles Aircraft Ltd issued the following statement to their shareholders on 14 April 1948: 'Arrangements have been completed whereby Handley Page Ltd will proceed with the building of the Miles Marathon. Handley Page will help to build the Marathon; they will find all the finance (and Miles Aircraft will have a small share of the profits); and will give the benefit of their advice and assistance in dealing with the listed assets shown on the balance sheet.' Miles were reported to have sustained a loss of £967,700 in the first ten months of 1947. The arrangement with Handley Page was also contingent upon Government ratification of orders for the Marathon. The Mamba-powered M.69 Marathon II G-AHXU was flown for the first time on 23 July 1949 under the control of Handley Page (Reading) Ltd.

BEA cut back its order to seven Mk 1 Marathon, and eventually a total of forty production aircraft were built, many without customers. The BEA order was finally cancelled in February 1952 and thirty aircraft were diverted to the RAF. These served as navigation trainers for about five years.

Handley Page (Reading) Ltd went on to design the Herald, which was initially flown at Radlett on 25 August 1955 as the HPR.3 G-AODE with four Leonides Major engines. The same aircraft was modified (as the HPR.7 Dart Herald) with two Dart turboprops, and flew at Woodley in this configuration on 11 March 1958. Woodley production comprised the aircraft listed below. It is not clear whether all of these aircraft were flown from Woodley; the Berkshire Museum of Aviation suggests that G-APWA was the last to fly from the airfield.

Registration	Type	Comments
G-AODE	HPR.3/HPR.7	Prototype built at Woodley and flown from Radlett. Later re-engined to become the prototype Dart Herald. Crashed following engine fire on 30 August 1958.
G-AODF	HPR.3/HPR.7	Second aircraft, converted to become second Dart Herald. Later modified to become prototype Herald Srs 200, flying in this form on 8 April 1961. Reregistered as G-ARTC.
G-APWA	Herald Srs 100	Prototype flown at Woodley on 30 October 1959.
G-APWB-D	Herald Srs 101	Three production aircraft for BEA.
G-APWE	Herald Srs 201	First production Srs 201 Last aircraft to be built at Woodley.

One other Handley Page (Reading) design to fly was the HPR.2 trainer, powered by an Armstrong Siddeley Cheetah AS17. The prototype, WE496, flew on 1 May 1950 at Woodley and competed unsuccessfully with the Percival Provost for an RAF trainer contract. The Mamba Marathon was re-engined in 1955 with Alvis Leonides Major engines to become the HPR.5 test aircraft in support of the HPR.3 Herald programme. The HPR.5 VX231 first flew on 15 March 1955.

The Herald production line was transferred to Radlett and Cricklewood, the Woodley site finally closing on 31 March 1963. Despite its unhappy beginnings in the wreckage of Miles Aircraft Ltd, Handley Page (Reading) Ltd continued aircraft manufacture at Woodley for some fifteen years. Handley Page (Reading) Ltd built some fifty complete aircraft with HPR designations, and 150 Canberra tail units under subcontract. The company also completed nine Messenger, two Gemini, three Aerovan and the M.69 Marathon 2, while capitalising the assets of Miles Aircraft Ltd. One of the last aircraft to be built at Woodley (Dart Herald G-APWA) is preserved at the excellent Museum of Berkshire Aviation, to the south of the airfield site, which is now a large housing estate.

A small glider named the Broburn Wanderlust was constructed and flown at Woodley, by **Broburn Sailplanes Ltd**. T.E. Brown and K.W.R. Radburn registered this company on 12 November 1946, Broburn being a composite derivative of their surnames.

The **Carden-Baynes** Scud III Auxiliary powered glider (later registered as G-ALJR) was first flown at Woodley on 8 August 1935. It was derived from the Scud glider, a number of which were built at the **Abbott-Baynes** Works at Farnham.

The **Somers Kendall** SK1 racing aircraft was assembled and flown at Woodley, initial construction having been begun at Hugh Kendall's home in Church Road, Woodley. The design was a clean V-tail wooden stressed-skin monoplane powered by a Turbomeca Palas jet engine mounted above the fuselage, behind the cockpit. The design gained third prize in the racing aircraft class of the Royal Aero Club Design Competition of 1952. First flown on 14 October 1955, the SK1 G-AOBG was of truly delightful appearance. An engine failure in July 1957 brought an end to its flying career.

Vickers-Armstrongs Ltd. Reading was a centre of the Supermarine Spitfire dispersed production scheme. Wings were built at the **Great Western Garage**, **Vincents Garage** undertook fuselage manufacture, and fuselage assembly took place at Caversham Works. Assembly and flight tests were conducted at Aldermaston and Henley. The Reading group of factories produced the Spitfire PR.IV, XI, XIX, and Mk IX and XIV.

Slough

Mr J.F. Benton of Chalvey (on the southern edge of Slough) is reported in *British Aircraft Before The Great War* to have built two biplanes, the Benton B.I and B.II with the assistance of Mr J. Allen of Maidenhead. These were unsuccessful. A series of tractor biplanes, the B.III to B.VII, followed. These were of workmanlike design – the B.VII being similar to an AIRCO DH6 – and flew successfully at Chalvey between 1912 and 1914.

CW Aircraft was formed in 1936, with works on Montrose Avenue, Slough Trading Estate, to develop an all-metal two-seat light aircraft, the CW Cygnet. This type was designed by the company's founders, Mr C.R. Chronander and Mr J.I. Waddington. The prototype Cygnet G-AEMA was first flown at Hanworth in May 1937.

CW Aircraft ceased trading in March 1938, the rights to the Cygnet being sold to General Aircraft Ltd. GAL modified the design, initially by adopting a twin fin and rudder empennage, and then by the introduction of a tricycle undercarriage.

ML Engineering Co. Ltd, later **ML Aviation Co. Ltd**, operated from United Building, Slough Trading Estate, see White Waltham for further details.

PD Cowl, of Slough Trading Estate, manufactured aircraft dinghies and fuel tanks for the Spitfire, Halifax, Lancaster and Mosquito during the Second World War.

The **Tipsy Aircraft Co. Ltd** had premises at 183-7 Liverpool Rd, and 798 Weston Rd, Slough Trading Estate from 1939. The company's main operations were conducted at Hanworth, in Greater London.

Welford

Elliotts of Newbury: The Newbury Eon G-AKBC was first flown at Welford on 8 August 1947; for further details see Newbury.

White Waltham

The Fairey Aviation Co. Ltd lost the use of their flight test facilities as a result of the requisitioning of Heathrow and its subsequent development as London's international airport. After a period when flight testing was conducted at Heston, Fairey Aviation transferred these operations to the large grass airfield at White Waltham, making use of buildings originally erected by the de Havilland Aircraft Co. Ltd. Production at White Waltham included the later marks of Firefly, together with the Fairey Gannet shipboard anti-submarine and airborne early warning aircraft.

Gannet AS.1 WN369 displaying its lowered arrester hook. (Fairey Aviation via Ken Ellis)

Three prototypes and 349 production Gannet aircraft were built with production split between Hayes and Stockport (where eighty-eight were built – sixty-four AS. Mk 1, twenty-four AS. Mk 4). The type was exported to Indonesia (18 aircraft), Australia (36) and West Germany (16) in addition to its use by the Fleet Air Arm. The first Gannet prototype VR546 was flown at Aldermaston on 19 September 1949. The first two prototypes were constructed as two-seat aircraft, the third prototype, WE488, being the first to fly in the production three-seat configuration on 10 May 1951. The Gannet T. Mk 2 prototype WN365 was flown at Northolt on 16 August 1954. This aircraft was subsequently modified to T. Mk 5 standard and operated from White Waltham as G-APYO. XJ440, the first of forty-four Gannet AEW.3, was first flown on 20 August 1958. The Gannet AEW.3 was fitted with the AN/APS-20A radar previously fitted to the Douglas Skyraider. Later, a number of these same units were transferred to the Shackleton AEW.2 aircraft, which replaced the Gannet after the withdrawal of the Royal Navy's conventional aircraft carriers. In March 1958, Fairey were advertising as follows: 'FAIREY GANNET Shore-based or carrier borne, the Fairey Gannet is the most sophisticated concept of an anti-submarine aircraft in the world.'

White Waltham was used for Fairey Aviation rotorcraft activities, which were centred on the development of the Gyrodyne and Rotodyne concepts under the leadership of J.A.J. Bennett, previously of the Cierva Autogiro Co. Ltd.

The first of the Fairey rotorcraft to fly was Gyrodyne G-AIKF, which was flown at Heston on 7 December 1947. In the Gyrodyne, rotor torque was reacted not by a tail rotor but by a tractor propeller mounted at the end of a stub wing, which also served to unload the rotor

The unconventional Rotodyne was a courageous attempt to develop a new advanced rotorcraft configuration. Performance, weight and noise problems frustrated development, however. (Author, and Fairey Aviation via Ken Ellis)

The diminutive Fairey Ultralight was intended for Army observation duties, but did not enter production. (Westland)

in forward flight. G-AIKF achieved a Class G helicopter speed record of 124.31mph on 28 June 1948, but was destroyed in a fatal accident on 17 April 1949.

The Jet Gyrodyne G-AJJP/XJ389 was a modification of the second Gyrodyne, specifically intended to explore technical developments in support of the much larger Rotodyne project. The Jet Gyrodyne eliminated gearbox torque by using compressed air expelled from the tips of the two rotor blades to rotate the rotor without the need for a mechanical gearbox. Fuel was pumped to the rotor tip, mixed with the compressed air and ignited to provide additional power to the rotor. In cruising flight, propulsion was transferred to two pusher propellers installed at the wing tips, and the main rotor allowed to autorotate.

The Jet Gyrodyne thus differed visually from the Gyrodyne by its use of a two (rather than three) blade rotor and twin pusher (rather than single tractor) propellers for propulsion. The first tethered flights were made at White Waltham in January 1954, with the first transition from helicopter to autogyro flight being made on 1 March 1955.

The Jet Gyrodyne provided data to support the larger Rotodyne transport design. The Rotodyne XE521 was assembled at White Waltham and first flew on 6 November 1957, with the first transition between rotor- and wing-borne flight being made on 10 April 1958. The aircraft had a boxy transport fuselage and a shoulder-mounted wing on which were mounted Eland engines driving tractor propellers. Air was tapped from the engines and ducted to the rotor tips, where it was mixed with fuel to provide hot gas drive to the rotor. The type met with developmental difficulties in achieving the required payload/range performance, and with high external noise. The noise problem was the subject of comment in the aviation press; in August 1958, *RAF Flying Review* said: 'Fairey's Rotodyne […] and – my goodness – what a noise!' This was further expanded on with the description of the sound as being 'reminiscent of a paddle steamer mixed with a pile-driver'.

Commenting upon the prospects for the Rotodyne, the Bristol sales department in a sales report noted that 'Considerable tribulation has been the lot of the Rotodyne in its brief history. Noise is one of the chief deterrents to would be purchasers […] previous selling has been hampered by shortcomings in capacity and performance.' With the harsh judgement of hindsight, these remarks appear to have been entirely accurate. Nevertheless, the Rotodyne succeeded in setting a world speed record over a 100km closed circuit of 190.9mph (307.22km/h) at White Waltham on 5 January 1959. The end of the project came when, on 26 February 1962, the Minister of Aviation, Mr Peter Thorneycroft, announced that Government aid would no longer be available for the Rotodyne programme.

The diminutive Fairey Ultralight of 1955 retained tip jet drive, but was a pure helicopter without a lifting wing, or propeller(s) to provide propulsion. Six were built, but the type did not enter production. The first prototype XJ924, flew at White Waltham on 14 August 1955.

On 31 March 1959, the Fairey Aviation Co. Ltd was re-styled **Fairey Aviation Ltd**, a subsidiary of the **Fairey Co. Ltd**. This move came shortly before the announcement that the company's aircraft and helicopter interests were to be merged with Westland Aircraft Ltd, this enforced merger taking effect on 2 May 1960. For details of subsequent helicopter activity at White Waltham, see the Westland entry, below.

White Waltham was used for a series of ventures based on the construction, in the UK, of versions of the French Piel Emeraude design. The design was given the name Linnet, and examples were built by **Garland-Bianchi**, **Garland Aircraft Ltd**, and **Fairtravel Ltd**.

Garland-Bianchi Linnet G-APNS was the first of a limited production run of anglicised variants of the Piel Emeraude, which were built at White Waltham and Blackbushe by Garland Aircraft Ltd and Fairtravel Ltd. (Author)

The first Linnet to be built, G-APNS, was constructed by P.A.T. Garland and D.E. Bianchi as the Garland-Bianchi Linnet. G-APNS was built at White Waltham and first flown at Fairoaks on 1 September 1958. Garland Aircraft Ltd was set up to continue production and completed G-APRH and a third Linnet airframe, which was subsequently sold to Fairtravel Ltd.

Fairtravel Ltd completed the Linnet taken over from Garland as G-ASFW, it being flown on 20 March 1963 as the Fairtravel Linnet II. Two further Fairtravel built aircraft were built and flown at Blackbushe. The Fairtravel company addresses were at Boyne Hill Road, Maidenhead, and Dale House, Clewer Green, Windsor.

Hants & Sussex Aviation Ltd purchased all the spares holdings for the Auster series of aircraft, disposing of them in 1972. The company also operated at Portsmouth.

Helmy Aerogypt IV. The Aerogypt was built at Heston in 1938 in a trimotor configuration, and was modified to a twin-engine (Continental A65) configuration at White Waltham in 1943, also acquiring a tricycle undercarriage. G-AFFG was flown in this configuration at White Waltham for the first time (straight hops) on 12 January 1946, with fully successful flights from 17 February. Intending to fly the aircraft to Egypt, Mr Helmy flew it to Northolt on 26 November 1946 to clear customs. Unfortunately, the aircraft was damaged on landing, and then further damaged when accidentally dropped from a crane, which was being used to move it. The fuselage still existed in 1960, albeit in use as a hen-house, near White Waltham.

The **ML Aviation Co. Ltd**. ML Aviation experimented during the Second World War with a rotor attachment to allow Jeep vehicles to be towed behind aircraft. This device, designed by Raoul Hafner, was known as the Rotabuggy, or Rotajeep, and was technically successful, although it did not enter production. The Rotabuggy was constructed by **R Malcolm Ltd**, this company becoming the **ML Aviation Co. Ltd**. Flight testing was carried out at Sherburn-in-Elmet.

The ML Utility was an inflatable-wing light aircraft designed by Marcel Lobelle. The first aircraft, XK784, was flown at White Waltham in August 1955 and was initially powered by a 40hp McCulloch engine. Two further aircraft were built, XK776 and XK781. A number of different engines were fitted to the three examples flown, including a Walter Mikron III derated to 38hp. The individual aircraft also differed in constructional detail. The Mikron powered Utility had a wing span of 35ft, a wing thickness of some 4½ft (!) and an all-up weight of 1,000lb.

ML Aviation Co. Ltd subsequently manufactured a range of items including ejector release units, weapon ground-handling equipment, aircraft handlers, test equipment and many other products.

Personal Plane Services constructed a number of replicas for film use, both here and at Booker (High Wycombe). These included:

- A Vickers Type 22 monoplane.
- Three Demoiselles for *Those Magnificent Men in their Flying Machines*.
- A Pfalz DIII G-ATIF for *The Blue Max* (at Booker).
- A Fokker EIII G-AVJO.
- A Morane Saulnier N monoplane, G-AWBU.
- A Manning-Flanders MF1, first flown on 1 March 1974.

Slingsby Aviation Ltd built a number of replica aircraft for use in films. One such was Sopwith 1F.1 Camel replica G-AWYY (the Slingsby T.57), which was flown for the first time at White Waltham during March 1969.

The **Taylor** Monoplane prototype G-APRT was built by John Taylor in Ilford, but first flown from White Waltham on 4 July 1959. At the time of the twenty-fifth anniversary of its first flight, about 100 of these aircraft had been built and flown, including a significant population of the type in New Zealand.

Westland Aircraft Ltd: The merger of the aircraft and helicopter interests of Fairey with Westland Aircraft Ltd took effect on 2 May 1960. Subsequent Westland activity at White Waltham is summarised below.

Above left: *G-AWBU is a replica Morane Saulnier Type N monoplane, one of a number of replica aircraft built by Personal Plane Services Ltd for display flying and film work.* (Author)

Above right: *Camel replica G-AWYY masquerades as a Sopwith-built 1F1 Camel. This particular replica was built by Slingsby as the Type 57, and was first flown at White Waltham in March 1969.* (Author)

Above: *G-APRT is the original prototype of John Taylor's highly successful Taylor Monoplane. G-APRT was built in Ilford and first flew at White Waltham in 1959.* (Author)

Left: *This Wasp HAS.1 XT417 was photographed at Yeovil. It was later to be exported for service with the Royal New Zealand Navy.* (Westland)

The first pre-production Westland Scout AH.1 XP165 was flown at White Waltham on 4 August 1960. Eight development aircraft and 141 production machines were built at Hayes for UK service, with limited additional aircraft exported. The first production aircraft, XP846, was flown on 6 March 1961. The first Westland Wasp HAS1 XS463 was flown at White Waltham on 28 October 1962. The two pre-production aircraft (XS463 and XS476) were followed by ninety-eight production machines built for the Royal Navy at Hayes, with aircraft exported to Brazil (three), the Netherlands (twelve), New Zealand (three), South Africa (seventeen) and Indonesia.

Windsor

Sir Sidney Camm was born at 10 Alma Road, Windsor, on 5 August 1893. His association with Windsor was commemorated by a plaque installed by the Royal Borough of Windsor and Maidenhead, which was unveiled on 12 March 1986, the twentieth anniversary of his death. Sidney Camm (later Sir Sidney) was Hawker's famous chief designer from 1925 to 1959, when he was appointed chief engineer. Camm oversaw the design of a succession of incomparable fighters including the Fury, Hurricane, Typhoon, Tempest, Sea Fury, Hunter and Harrier.

Vickers-Armstrongs Ltd. Smith's Lawn polo ground in Windsor Great Park was used by Vickers during the Second World War as a dispersed assembly facility for Brooklands, particularly for the Vickers Warwick. Warwick aircraft were delivered from Smith's Lawn, often to Kemble, by the Air Transport Auxiliary. Training aircraft also used Smith's Lawn as a relief landing ground.

G-BCWH is probably one of the best known of the Practavia Sprites. This aircraft was built and flown at Warton. (Author)

Wokingham

C.F. Taylor (Metalworkers) Ltd of Molly Millars Lane, Wokingham, was a sub-contractor that produced components for a wide range of aircraft. These included airframe components for the Herald, Carvair, TSR.2, One-Eleven, Viscount, Devon and VC10. The company produced the fuselage spine for the BAC Lightning; galley units for the VC10 (for RAF use) and Concorde; empennage test units for the Trident; ducting for the Nimrod; and the tail rotor assembly for the Canadair CL-84 V/STOL prototype.

Buckinghamshire

Booker/High Wycombe

Croydon Aviation & Engineering Co., had a business address of 35 Queens Res., High Wycombe; nothing else is known.

The late Doug Bianchi's **Personal Plane Services** is located at Booker and has constructed a number of film replicas (mainly at White Waltham, Berks). Personal Plane Services is responsible for the restoration and support of a number of historic aircraft. The company is now run by Doug Bianchi's son, Tony.

Plans for the 'Pilot' Sprite were marketed by **Practavia Ltd**, based at High Wycombe, which also provided support to constructors of the type. The design was publicised through *Pilot* magazine and at least three of these aircraft have been completed in the UK, these being G-BDDB at Sherburn-in-Elmet, G-BCVF at Elstree, and G-BCWH at Blackpool. An Irish version, the Murphy Sprite, EI-BOY has also been flown. The aircraft is an all-metal low-wing monoplane with side-by-side seating and tricycle undercarriage. The individual aircraft built to date have shown some marked differences in configuration.

Wycombe Aircraft Constructors Ltd, of 57 London Road, High Wycombe, was set up by G. Holt Thomas of AIRCO, and F.H. Payne, previously of Grahame-White, in October 1917. The company was sub-contracted from AIRCO to provide additional capacity for wing manufacture. Additional works were located as follows: stores and yard at High St, High Wycombe; timber yard at Oxford Road, High Wycombe. Wycombe Aircraft Constructors advertised as 'Contractors to HM Government'.

Denham Airfield

The Hafner ARIII autogyro G-ADMV was designed by **ARIII Construction (Hafner Gyroplane) Ltd** at Hanworth; was built at the Martin-Baker works, at Denham; and was flown at Heston and Hanworth, Greater London.

Hordern-Richmond Aircraft Ltd was set up at Denham to market and develop the Autoplane, although these plans were to come to nothing. The Autoplane was first flown at Heston in Greater London (see *British Built Aircraft, Volume 1, Greater London*) and the company subsequently operated at Thame (see below). The company was registered on 29 April 1937.

Luton Aircraft Ltd was based at the Phoenix Works, at Gerrard's Cross, close to Denham, and produced the Luton LA.4 Minor. This small parasol monoplane has become a popular type for home construction. The company originated at Barton-le-Clay, near Luton, moving to Gerrard's Cross in 1936.

The Luton LA.4 was a development of the single LA.3 G-AEPD, which was built at Gerrard's Cross and flown at Heston on 3 March 1937. The first LA.4 G-AFBP was also flown in 1937, a small number of the type being built by amateur constructors prior to the outbreak of the Second World War.

After the Second World War, the type was refined, and plans issued for the Luton LA.4A, which has been built in significant numbers. The machine is cold and extraordinarily draughty, but a sheer delight to fly – albeit requiring considerable contortions to enter and leave the cockpit, threading oneself through the flying wires and under the wing centre section. The modifications that resulted in the LA.4A were the responsibility of C.H. Latimer-Needham and Mr Arthur W.J.G. Ord-Hume. Plans for the Luton LA.4A were distributed by **Phoenix Aircraft Ltd**, this company being named after the Luton Aircraft works at Gerrard's Cross, which were destroyed by fire in 1943.

Take off in the Luton Minor. This particular aircraft, which was photographed at East Pennard, is the slowest and draughtiest aircraft that the author has ever flown. (Author)

HB-YAH is a rare example of the Luton LA.5A Major. (Author)

Luton Aircraft Ltd also built an enlarged design, the LA.5 Major, the Walter Mikron-powered prototype G-AFMU being flown at Denham on 12 March 1939. Despite the attractions of an enclosed cabin and two seats, only a limited number of the LA.5A Major have been built, and the type has not attained the popularity of the Luton Minor.

The **Martin** Monoplane G-AEYY was built by Luton Aircraft and flown at Denham in October 1937. The type had its origins in the earlier **Clarke** Cheetah (flown at Brough, East Yorkshire), from which it used the upper wings (originally from a DH53) and the fuselage. The Martin monoplane was of low-wing configuration with inverted V bracing struts, resulting in an uncanny resemblance to the DH53. Following a crash on its second flight, Airwork Ltd rebuilt the Martin Monoplane at Heston, with a new fuselage.

The Martin Monoplane and the Luton Buzzard, Minor and Major, were all designed by C.H. Latimer-Needham, previously of the Halton Group. Mr Latimer-Needham founded the Halton Aero Club in 1924 and designed the Halton HAC.1, HAC.2 and HAC.3 during the period 1924 to 1929. He was the chief designer of Luton Aircraft Ltd, and was also well known for his extensive gliding and soaring activities. Mr Latimer-Needham subsequently became the Chief Engineer of Flight Refuelling Ltd.

The Martin-Baker Aircraft Co. Ltd was registered on 17 August 1934 and based at Higher Denham, Bucks. The company founders were Mr James Martin and Capt. Valentine Baker. This company could have been as well known for fighters as it is now for ejection seats, had its MB2, MB3 or MB5 designs (which combined ease of maintenance, excellent cockpit layout and high performance) reached production.

The Martin-Baker MB1 G-ADCS was a clean two-seat low-wing monoplane, which was built at Denham and first flown from nearby Northolt during March 1935. The company then turned its talents to the design of a series of high performance fighter aircraft that set new standards for ease of maintenance and servicing. The MB2 (M-B-1/G-AEZD/P9594) first flew at Harwell on 3 August 1938; the MB3 R2492 first flew at Wing on 31 August 1942; and the MB5 at Harwell on 23 May 1944. Sadly, the MB3 crashed following engine failure on 12 September 1942 fatally injuring Capt. Baker.

The MB5 R2496 was displayed publicly at Farnborough in June 1946 by Jan Zurawoski and 'presented one of the most brilliant flying demonstrations of the day and was outstanding for

Above: *Martin–Baker's majestic MB5 is seen here at Hatfield for de Havilland propeller testing.* (BAE SYSTEMS plc.)

Below left: *The bare frame of the Martin-Baker MB1 under construction in 1935.* (Martin-Baker Aircraft Ltd)

its speed range and manoeuvrability'. The Boscombe Down assessment report stated: 'It is considered that the general design and layout of the Martin-Baker 5 is excellent, and is infinitely better – from the engineering and maintenance aspect – than any other similar type of aircraft.'

In its early days the company manufactured airfield equipment, advertising in February 1936 'The Martin patent all-steel wind indicator for day or night flying.' This was a giant illuminated 'T' for indicating wind direction, measuring 50ft by 30ft.

Although long absent from the business of aircraft production, credit must be given to the flight safety contribution of Martin-Baker in developing and refining aircraft ejection seats. By late 2002, no fewer than 6,957 lives had been saved in ejections using Martin-Baker seats and more than 68,000 seats had been delivered for use in 79 countries. On 11 June 2003, an ejection from a Sea Harrier FA.2 brought the toal number of lives saved by Martin-Baker ejection seats to 7,000. Denham is used for seat manufacture and environmental testing. Flight test activities in support of ejector seat development were initially undertaken at Oakley (near Thame), before transferring to Chalgrove, Oxfordshire.

Halton (near Aylesbury)

The **Halton Aero Club** built two light aircraft at RAF Halton technical training school in the 1920s. The first was the Halton HAC1 Mayfly G-EBOO, a two-seat biplane, distinguished by its 'X'-shaped interplane struts, designed by C.H. Latimer-Needham, Education Officer at RAF Halton, for the 1926 Light Aircraft Competition. Unfortunately, the Mayfly was not ready in time, and it was first flown at Bicester on 31 January 1927, participating enthusiastically and successfully in a number of air races, pageants and air shows in 1927.

The Halton HAC.2 Minus was a modification of the Mayfly, it being converted in 1928 from a two-seat biplane to a single-seat parasol monoplane to improve its performance. The Minus retained the same registration as the Mayfly, despite the drastic change to its configuration. The discarded wings and interplane struts were reused by the 1929 Clarke Cheetah G-AAJK, which was flown at Brough, East Yorkshire. Like the Mayfly, the Minus was raced successfully, winning the 1928 Wakefield Trophy at a speed of 95mph.

Mr Latimer-Needham later designed the Luton series of aircraft – notably the Luton Minor – and was also the designer of the Martin Monoplane, which made use of DH53 and Clarke Cheetah components. The entry for Denham provides further details of his career, together with information on the Luton Minor and Martin Monoplane.

Langley Airfield (close to the junction of the M4 and M25)

Hawker Aircraft Ltd, Sutton Lane, Langley. The pre-war expansion of the RAF led to the decision in 1936 that a shadow factory and airfield should be constructed at Langley for the manufacture of Hawker aircraft. Langley was used for Hurricane production and for the development of the Typhoon, Tempest and Fury series. The airfield site at Parlaunt Park Farm was purchased in 1939 and used in wartime and the early post-war years for fighter

Tempest production in full swing at the Langley factory of Hawker Aircraft Ltd. (Brooklands Museum Trust)

testing and manufacture. The availability of Langley enabled Hawker Aircraft Ltd to leave Brooklands early in the Second World War.

Some of the key developments and first flights made at Langley are summarised below:

Type	Serial, first flight date	Comments
Tornado	P5219, 6 October 1939	Vulture II.
Typhoon	P5212, 24 February 1940	Most of the subsequent production was carried out by **Gloster.**
Hurricane	1940 & 1941	First prototypes of the Hurricane Marks IIA, IIC and IID.
Tornado	HG641, 23 October 1941	Centaurus powered – a key to the development of the Tempest II.
Tempest V	HM595, 2 September 1942	Sabre II.
Tempest I	HM599, 24 February 1943	Sabre IV.
Tempest V	JN729, 21 June 1943	first production aircraft, more than 800 of this variant produced.
Tempest II	LA602, 28 June 1943	Centaurus. 414 built by Hawker, plus thirty-six by the Bristol Aeroplane Company.
Tempest VI	HM595, 9 May 1944	Sabre V, re-engined Tempest V prototype. 142 built.
Fury F.2/43	NX798, 1 September 1944	Centaurus XII. First flight date also reported as 2 September 1944.
Fury F.2/43	LA610, 27 November 1944 NX802, 25 July 1945	Prototypes powered by various engine and propeller combinations – LA610 (Griffon 85, later Sabre VII); NX802, Centaurus XV.

Above: *The Fury F.2/43 or Tempest III LA610 was flown with different engine and propeller combinations as part of the development leading up to the Sea Fury.* (BAE SYSTEMS plc)

Opposite above: *An impressive photograph of the fast and potent Tempest V. The type saw valuable service against the flying bomb threat and in ground attack missions in Europe.* (BAE SYSTEMS plc)

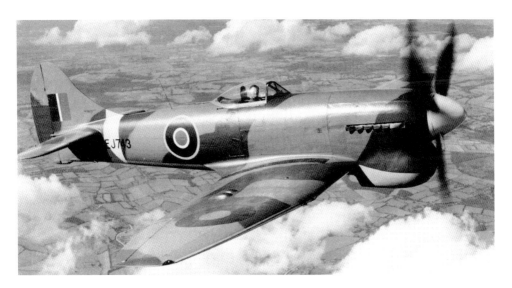

Although not adopted for RAF use, the Fury became the last British front-line piston-engined fighter when adopted/adapted for use by the Fleet Air Arm as the Sea Fury. Like the Fury, a number of engine and propeller combinations were flown on Sea Fury prototypes. First to fly was the 'semi-navalised' SR661 on 21 February 1945 powered by the Centaurus XII, followed by the 'fully-navalised' SR666 on 12 October 1945. The first production Sea Fury Mk X TF895 flew on 7 September 1946. 665 were built for the Royal Navy and twenty-two aircraft were built under licence in Holland. In addition, the Royal Navy purchased sixty two-seat trainers, designated Sea Fury T. Mk 20, the first of which, VX818, flew on 15 January 1948. Significant exports were also achieved, with users including Iraq, Netherlands, Canada, Pakistan (ninety-three Mk 60, five Mk 61 two seaters and five reconditioned FB. Mk XI) and Egypt (twelve). Reconditioned surplus aircraft were sold to Burma (eighteen single seat and three T Mk 20 two seaters), Cuba (fifteen FB. Mk XI and two T. Mk 20) and West Germany, the latter for use as target tugs. Including all variants and operators, the production total was 860 aircraft.

In 1947, eighty-nine surplus RAF Tempest II were reconditioned at Langley for Indian use. These aircraft were followed by some twenty-five aircraft for Pakistan.

With the arrival of jet prototypes in the late 1940s, and the increasing levels of traffic at Heathrow, it was clear that Langley would be unsuitable in the longer term. The Hawker jet prototypes of this period (P.1040, P.1052, P.1072, P.1081 and Hunter) were typically first flown from Boscombe Down, and then returned for company test flying from either Farnborough or Dunsfold, of which Hawker became tenants in 1950. Langley was eventually closed, being occupied by Ford commercial vehicles in 1959.

Airflight Ltd carried out a Lincolnian freighter conversion, G-ALPF, at Langley for Surrey Flying Services Ltd. This aircraft was used as a tanker in the Berlin Airlift.

Langley was also the engineering base of **British South American Airways Corporation** (BSAA). Avro Tudor 5 aircraft were converted at Langley for use as tanker aircraft in the Berlin Air Lift.

Alan Muntz & Co. Ltd (Aircraft Division). This company, which is more familiarly associated with Heston, was operating at Langley in the early 1950s.

Milton Keynes

David Mickleborough of Milton Keynes has produced a new design for home construction, the L107 Sparrow. The aircraft is a single-seat low-wing monoplane of composite construction powered by a 1,834cc Volkswagen engine. Construction started in April 1993, with the type receiving a PFA award in 1994 for best new aircraft design for home construction. By December 1997, the fuselage was essentially complete, the engine was running with a solid state ignition system, and wing construction was underway.

Thame (Aylesbury and Thame Airport between Oxford and Aylesbury)

Thame was used by the Air Transport Auxiliary as a training school from 1943, the aircraft used being the Proctor and Harvard. The RAF used gliders based here for radar research, the tow aircraft including some of the oldest aircraft in RAF service, including eleven Hector, three Hind, twelve Tiger Moth and two Avro 504N, the latter still being in use at the end of 1941.

Airtech Ltd converted twelve Stirling V for civil use by the Belgian operator Trans-Air from May 1947 onwards. Work was also carried out on freighter conversions of the Halifax (e.g. G-AJPK, G-AKGN and F-BCJR/G-AHVT), Lancaster and Lincoln (RE290/G-ALPF), using large bomb bay panniers. G-AGUM was one such Lancaster, modified for use by BSAA ferrying engines. This aircraft was test flown at Thame in April 1949.

Halifax aircraft were prepared at Thame for export to the Pakistani Air Force and included G-AKUT/RG736 and G-AKUU/RG813; other Pakistani Halifax aircraft were prepared and delivered from Stansted by LAMS. Airtech fitted a very large under-fuselage pannier to a BSAA Handley Page Halton, for the purpose of carrying a complete Humber Hawk car from Bovingdon to Madrid on 7 May 1948.

Airtech's own advertising of 1948 sets the scene:

> *Airtech – for fully comprehensive aircraft service. We specialise in:*
> - *Halifax Freighter modifications*
> - *Dakota Passenger Conversions*
> - *Consul, Rapide, Fairchild and Proctor C of A and repairs*
> - *Cheetah, Gipsy and Cirrus complete overhauls*
> - *Radio and radar repairs*
> - *Early delivery of Halifax Freighter Aircraft and spares*

Airtech Ltd also operated at Bovingdon and Croydon

Hordern-Richmond Aircraft Ltd (Hydulignum Works, Haddenham, Bucks) was set up at Denham in April 1937, moving to Haddenham, near Thame, with the intention of manufacturing the Hordern-Richmond Autoplane. The prototype Autoplane G-AEOG was test flown at Heston in late 1936.

No production actually took place, and the company turned to the production of laminated compressed wood products (Hydulignum – high-duty wood material) used

Above: *The clean lines of the short-lived Martin-Baker MB3. The sole example, R2492, was first flown at Wing on 31 August 1942.* (Martin-Baker via Ken Ellis)

particularly in propellers for such aircraft as the Spitfire, Hurricane, Seafire, Halifax, Whitley, Tiger Moth, Oxford and Magister. Hordern-Richmond was taken over by Rotol in 1945. The rotor blades for the Bristol 171, and the tail rotor of the Westland WS-51 were manufactured by Hordern-Richmond Ltd.

Martin-Baker Aircraft Co. Ltd carried out initial flight test work at Oakley airfield (near Long Crendon, Thame), using initially a Boulton Paul Defiant, with an ejection seat fitted in the turret position of the Defiant. The company's first Meteor III EE416 was delivered to Oakley on 6 November 1945, together with EE415 for use as a photographic platform. Meteor III EE479 followed on 28 February 1946 for intended cockpit installation trials, but was, in the event, not put to use. By mid-1946, flight operations had transferred to Chalgrove, Oxfordshire, where they remain to this day. Oakley was a satellite station of 11 OTU at Bicester.

Wing

Martin-Baker Aircraft Co. Ltd. Wing airfield, south of Milton Keynes, was used for flight-testing the Martin-Baker MB3 R2492. The first flight took place on 31 August 1942, but the aircraft was destroyed in an accident on 12 September 1942, killing Capt. Baker. The company's main operating base is at Denham, with flight operations at Chalgrove and additional test facilities in Northern Ireland.

Essex

Ashingdon (Canute Air Park)

The **Canute Air Park** of Lower Canewdon Road, Ashingdon, was used by Messrs Chadwick and Gordon to carry out aircraft maintenance. Chadwick and Gordon also planned to manufacture Mignet Flying Flea aircraft at Ashingdon and subsequently set up **Premier Aircraft Constructions Ltd** at Harold Wood, this company building three Gordon Dove aircraft, which were flown at Maylands.

The **Phoenix Aircraft Construction Co.** was resident here (4 miles north of Southend) in the 1930s. Nothing else is known.

Audley End

Historic Flying Ltd has been responsible for the restoration of a number of vintage fighter aircraft, and ex-RAF gate guardian Spitfires in particular. Major restoration projects are tabulated below:

Type	Serial	Comments
Spitfire LF. Mk XVIe	RW382	G-XVIA, first flight after rebuild 3 July 1991. Previously gate guardian at RAF Leconfield.
Spitfire Mk IX	TE566	G-BLCK, first flown after rebuild on 2 July 1992. Recovered from a kibbutz in Israel.
Spitfire FR. Mk XVIIIe	TP280	G-BTXE, first flown after rebuild on 5 July 1992. Aircraft recovered from India.
Spitfire LF. Mk XVIe	TD248	G-OXVI, previously the gate guardian at RAF Sealand, flown on 10 November 1992.
Mosquito	RR299	In 1992, Historic Flying obtained the contract to renew the fabric on British Aerospace's historic but ill-fated Mosquito.
Spitfire Mk XIV	NH799	G-BUZU, first flown after rebuild on 21 January 1994. Aircraft recovered from India.
Spitfire Mk XIV	SM832	G-WWII, first flown after rebuild on 22 May 1995. Aircraft recovered from India.
Spitfire LF. Mk Vb	EP120	G-LFVB, first flown after rebuild on 12 September 1995.
Spitfire PR.XIX	PM631	Winter overhaul 1995/6 for the Battle of Britain Memorial Flight.
Hurricane	LF363	Rebuilt for the Battle of Britain Memorial Flight following accident. Flown on 29 September 1998.
Spitfire Mk Vb	BM597	G-MKVB, ex-RAF gate guardian at Hednesford, Bridgnorth, Church Fenton. First flown after restoration 17 July 1997.
Spitfire Mk Vc	AR614	G-BUWA, returned to the UK from Canada. Flown at Audley End on 5 October 1996.
Spitfire FR. XVIIIe	SM845	G-BUOS, ex-Indian Air Force HHS687. First flown after restoration 7 July 2000.
Spitfire Vb	AB910	Refurbished in late 1996/early 1997 for the RAF Battle of Britain Memorial Flight.
Seafire LF. IIIc	PP972	Survey only.
Spitfire LF. Mk IXc	MK912	Flown after restoration on 8 September 2000, G-BRRA.
Spitfire Mk Vc	JG891	Awaiting restoration 2002.
Spitfire Mk XIV	RN201	G-BSKP, first flight after restoration 24 April 2002, Duxford.

Type	Serial	Comments
Spitfire Tr.IX	IAAC 161/ PV202	G-TRIX under rebuild after major accident damage at Goodwood. 15 September 1996.
Spitfire IX	'UB424'	Ex-Burmese aircraft awaiting restoration 2002.

The work of Spitfire restoration continues (at Duxford, Cambridgeshire) with four to six aircraft likely to be under restoration at any time. Historic Flying Limited moved its operations to Duxford in April 2001.

Blackwater Estuary

British Deperdussin Co. Ltd. In July 1913 the British Deperdussin 'Seagull' was based at Osea Island, near Millbeach, but ultimately proved to be unsuccessful. A related entry can be found under Brooklands, Surrey, and the company also operated at Hendon, Highbury, London (Central) and Upper Holloway, all in Greater London.

Clacton

The **Fitch** biplane of 1911 was a re-engined version of the unsuccessful Laking biplane of 1909. *British Aircraft Before The Great War* records that this aircraft was flown from a field at Little Clacton by Mr A. Westlake (see below) on 4 July 1911, completing a short circular flight.

The **Westlake** monoplane was an elegant monoplane built in 1913 by Mr A. Westlake, characterised by the tailplane flaring out laterally from the fuselage, using the splayed upper longerons to form its leading edge. Performance was adequate only for straight flights due to the low installed power of 18hp. This machine had every appearance of having great potential given a more powerful engine. The works, which traded under the name **East Anglian Aviation Co. Ltd**, were situated at Clacton next to the waterfront. By September 1913, several 'straights' but no extended flights had been made. After initial trials with ailerons, it was reported that the machine was to be converted to wing warping.

Colchester

Three examples of the Robinson Redwing were built by **Redwing Aircraft Co. Ltd** at Blue Barns Aerodrome, Colchester. Robinson Aircraft, whose main operations were conducted at Croydon and Thornton Heath, established a number of Redwing 'service stations', including Blue Barns Aerodrome, with others at Croydon and at High Post. Colchester replaced Croydon Airport as the Redwing factory site in early 1932, with an official opening in March of that year. G-ABRM, G-ABRL and G-ABNX were built at Colchester, which was also used for overhaul and inspection of Redwing and other types of aircraft.

In May 1932 the company purchased the aerodrome at Gatwick (Lowfield Heath), where the company ran the Redwing Flying School. The works continued to be at Colchester, where the last aircraft to be built flew in early 1933. Redwing Aircraft Co. Ltd subsequently returned to Croydon Airport, the move being completed on 26 February 1934.

Note: contemporary photographs show prominent barns at the airfield – one would not be surprised to find that they were painted blue!

G-ABNX was the last of three Robinson Redwing to be built at Colchester and is, today, the only survivor. Nine aircraft had previously been built at Croydon Airport. (Author)

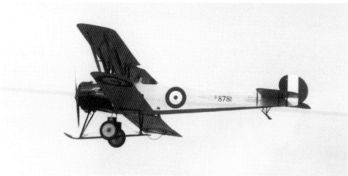

D8781/G-ECKE is an Avro 504K replica built by A3D Engineering and first flown at Cambridge in September 1994.

Earls Colne (Essex) and Milden (Suffolk)

AJD Engineering of Moat Farm, Milden, Suffolk, is run by Tony Ditheridge, whose initials give the company their name. AJD Engineering has links to **Hawker Restorations** of Earls Colne, Essex, and to **Euroair Technical Services** (ETS). These companies have constructed a number of very high-quality replicas of First World War aeroplanes (some of which are fully airworthy), and have repaired, restored and maintain a number of other historic aircraft. Earls Colne is used as the test airfield, aircraft being restored at Milden.

Examples of early aircraft replicas include a Bristol M.1C, a Blériot XI, and an Avro 504K commissioned by the Chilean Air Force Museum. The Bristol M.1C commemorates the use of this type for the first aerial crossing of the Andes on 12 December 1918. The replicas for Chile were delivered in February 1990.

Two SE5A replicas were built to the original drawings in early 1991, one for display in the Prince's Mead shopping centre in Farnborough, Hampshire, and the second for the Chilean Air Force Museum. A further SE5A replica was constructed for the RAAF Museum at Point Cook, Victoria, carrying the markings 'A2-31'. In late 1991, an original Avro 504 S-AHAA was under restoration for the Swedish Air Force Museum, and an Avro 504J replica 'C4451' was constructed for the Southampton Hall of Aviation. G-ECXE, an Avro 504K replica, was constructed to the original drawings, with the exception of the engine. G-ECXE 'D8781' made its first flight on 29 September 1994 at Teversham, Cambridgeshire. Avro 504K E3747 was built to flying condition for the RAAF Museum at Point Cook, Victoria.

AJD/ETS were contracted to perform the rebuild of the historic Percival Mew Gull G-AEXF after its accident at Old Warden in July 1991. G-AEXF was flown again on 1 November 1996 following a 5½-year rebuild. The year 1992 saw the construction of a Sopwith Camel G-ASOP/B6291 and Sopwith Pup replica 'A635', which was built in autumn 1992 for export to California. G-ASOP was flown for the first time at Old Warden on 27 July 1993.

Hawker Restorations was founded on 28 September 1994 and rebuilt Hurricane P3351/ZK-TPL and P2902/G-ROBT. In the case of P3351, Hawker Restorations rebuilt the airframe, with engine work to bring the aircraft to flying condition being carried out in New Zealand. Hawker Restorations have been undertaking restoration work on five additional Hurricane aircraft, reported to be G-BRKE/BW853, G-TDTW/5450, G-KAMM/BW881, G-HURY/KZ321 and G-TWTD/AE977 (Sea Hurricane). AE977 was first flown after restoration at RAF Wattisham in July 2000. Hurricane IV G-HURY/KZ321 was flown for the first time following restoration on 8 July 2003 at Earls Colne. Hurricane Z3174 (also quoted as 42025/RCAF5390) is under restoration for static display at the USAF Museum at Dayton, Ohio.

A listing of aircraft for which the three companies have been collectively responsible for maintenance, repair and/or overhaul includes: Seafire III G-BUAR/PP972, four Blériot, Sopwith Pup, Mew Gull, BE.2E A1325/G-BVGR, four Avro 504, Bristol M.1C, Spitfire PV202, Bf 109E G-BYDS/1342, Bf 109F-4 10132 and a number of other vintage and combat aircraft. The company also completed the restoration of Spitfire Vc AR614 in late 1999.

Fambridge

E.C. Gordon England joined forces with **Noel Pemberton Billing** to run an early flying ground here. The field was acquired by Mr Pemberton Billing expressly for flying, and extended to 3,000 acres, upon which two large hangars were erected. In an anticipation of the modern 'Air Park', twenty four-room bungalows were built to accommodate pilots, but the scheme was ahead of its time.

The **Macfie** monoplane of 1909 was tested by R.F. Macfie, an American who had recently moved to Britain, on an unsuitable field at Fambridge, and then at Maplin sands. Tested with limited success during September and October 1909, the monoplane was moved to Maplin in November, but did not fly again. Success came with the Empress biplane, which was flown in 1910 at Portholme and then at Brooklands, Surrey.

José Weiss carried out experimental testing at Fambridge in early 1910, and subsequently on sands to the west of Littlehampton. Weiss influenced the early ideas of Handley Page, who met him at Fambridge. E.C. Gordon England tested a José Weiss designed glider at Amberley Mount in 1909.

Howard Wright followed the example of Mr Macfie; the unsuccessful 1908 Howard Wright biplane was tested at Fambridge before further attempts to fly at Camber Sands. Howard Wright was later to move his flying operations to Brooklands, Surrey.

North Weald (Essex)

Mr Mike Woodley. During 1998, the rights to FLS Sprint, *née* SAH1, were purchased by Mike Woodley of North Weald. The SAH1 was initially developed at Bodmin, Cornwall, and was subject to further development by FLS at Hurn, Dorset. These locations are included in *British Built Aircraft Volume 2: South West & Central Southern England*.

Orsett (near Grays, Essex)

The **Essex Flying Club** built up two Avro 504K aircraft from spares (G-ABWK, G-ABYB) in a garage at Orsett in 1932.

Southend Airport (Rochford)

Aviation Traders (Engineering) Ltd of Stansted and Southend was formed in 1949, carrying out Handley Page Halifax and Percival Prentice civil conversions, and Avro Tudor freight conversions, before developing their own Accountant and Carvair designs. The company, throughout its life, also operated extensive commercial aircraft maintenance facilities. The full group comprised (in 1953) Aviation Traders Ltd – sales agents for aircraft, engines and ancillary parts; Air Charter Ltd – a charter airline operating eight York, three Tudor and one DC-3 for passenger and freight operations 'to anywhere in the world'; and Aviation Traders (Engineering) Ltd with repair and overhaul facilities at Southend, Stansted, Bovingdon and Blackbushe.

During 1949 and 1950, Aviation Traders handled large numbers of Halifax aircraft at Southend for conversion to civil use and/or preparation for export. More than thirty Halifax

The unique shape of the Aviation Traders Carvair is well shown here by a surviving example seen at Anchorage, Alaska. (Author)

The Prentice was an imposing, if uneconomic, private aircraft. This example is at the Popular Flying Association Rally at Cranfield. (Author)

A. Mk 9 aircraft were registered to Aviation Traders, nine of these being exported for use by the Egyptian Air Force carrying the serial numbers 1155 to 1163. Many other Halifax aircraft which passed through Aviation Traders' hands were eventually scrapped, mainly at Southend.

The company also purchased the ex-BOAC fleet of Halton aircraft for resale. Aviation Traders' advertising material reflected their extensive experience in Halifax conversions; in December 1948 they advertised: 'Halton aircraft complete with one year's certificate of airworthiness, zero-hour Hercules "100" grey-nose engines, radio and anti-icing equipment. 21 days delivery from date of order, freight or passenger versions available. We also hold the only complete stock of Halton spares.'

Aviation Traders acquired 252 Percival Prentice in 1956 for civil conversion, and about twenty were eventually sold on to the civil register.

Aviation Traders converted a total of twenty-one DC-4/C-54 aircraft into the bulbous-nosed Carvair car ferry/cargo aircraft for use by British Air Ferries and others. Initially named after famous bridges (in keeping with their 'air bridge' role), they acquired less complimentary names towards the end of their careers: *Fat Albert*, *Plain Jane*, *Big Joe*, etc. The Carvair could carry five cars and twenty-two passengers in its car ferry configuration. Operators included Aer Lingus, Ansett-ANA and Aviaco. The first Carvair conversion was G-ANYB, which first flew on 21 June 1961.

The single Accountant G-ATEL (an out of sequence registration for **Aviation Traders Engineering Ltd**) first flew as G-41-1 at Southend on 9 July 1957, but had a flying career of only six months before the programme was abandoned. The Accountant was a twenty-eight passenger twin turboprop monoplane powered by the Rolls-Royce Dart, and resembled the Grumman Gulfstream 1. The company advertised the type's virtues as: 'economy of operation; ease of maintenance; and low initial cost'. It was described, less glowingly, in the aviation press as 'having a somewhat utilitarian, sturdy appearance.'

Aviation Traders last major conversion programme comprised the modification of ten BEA Vanguard aircraft to freight configuration as the Vanguard Merchantman. The first of these, G-APEM, flew on 10 October 1969. The last flight of a Vanguard was the delivery of Merchantman G-APEP to Brooklands in October 1996, to join other Vickers types in the Brooklands Museum.

BAF (British Air Ferries), based at Southend, undertook a significant programme of engineering modifications from the late 1980s to provide a fifteen-year life extension to its fleet of Vickers Viscount aircraft.

John Taylor of 25 Chesterfield Crescent, Priory Wood, Leigh-on-Sea, designed and built the single-seat Taylor Monoplane and Taylor Titch. The Taylor Monoplane was first flown on 4 July 1959, and has become one of the UK's most successful home-built aircraft, with more than fifty being registered by the late 1980s. Mr Taylor's next design was the faster and more sophisticated Titch with its tapered wings and enclosed cockpit. The prototype Titch G-ATYO was first flown at Southend on 4 January 1967 (note: some editions of *Jane's All the World's Aircraft* give a date of 22 January 1967). The Titch design was placed second (to that of the Luton Group Beta) in the Rollason Midget Racer Design Competition of 1964. The Titch has also been widely constructed worldwide and is notably popular in the United States. See also White Waltham, Berkshire for further details related to the Taylor Monoplane.

Above: *This Taylor Titch was used (in a subsequent modified guise) to set a number of point-to-point speed records in its class.* (Author)

Left: *The Percival Prentice was built at Luton and Brough prior to modification for civil use by Aviation Traders Ltd.* (Author)

Stansted Airport

Stansted has been predominantly a charter and cargo airfield since the start of its civil use. One of its first occupants, from 14 December 1946, was London Aero & Motor Services (LAMS), who operated a large number of civil Halifax conversions. LAMS operated from Elstree prior to their occupation of Stansted.

Aviation Traders (Engineering) Ltd. Aviation Traders modified a number of Avro Tudor 4B to have double freight doors as the Super Trader (G-AHNI, G-AHNJ, G-AHNM, G-AHNO). Modification and conversion work on the Prentice, Halifax and other types was performed both at Stansted and at Southend. Aviation Traders at Stansted were responsible for manufacture of the wing centre section of the Bristol 170 Freighter.

Handley Page Ltd. The Handley Page HP.88 VX330 crashed at Stansted during flight trials on 26 August 1951, after a total of only twenty-eight flights.

Stapleford Tawney Airfield (near Abridge, Essex)

The **Eardley Billing** replica constructed for use in the film *Those Magnificent Men in Their Flying Machines* first flew here on 14 June 1964.

Edgar Percival Aircraft Ltd. The first prototype E.P.9 Prospector G-AOFU was flown at Stapleford Tawney on 21 December 1955. Used for utility and agricultural work, the

The Edgar Percival E.P.9 Prospector utility aircraft was built initially at Stapleford Tawney. Subsequently, the type was taken over by Lancashire Aircraft, at Blackpool and Samlesbury. (Author)

Prospector enjoyed only modest success, with a total of twenty airframes being completed at Stapleford. In 1957, the company was advertising:

> *Ordered for use in 8 countries, the versatile EP9*
> - *In Production*
> - *In Service*
> - *Early Delivery*
> - *Short Take Off*
> - *Short Landing.*

The company and design rights to the E.P.9 were sold to Samlesbury Engineering Ltd in October 1958, the type becoming known as the Lancashire Aircraft Prospector. After the sale to Samlesbury Engineering Ltd, further development was carried out at Blackpool and Samlesbury in Lancashire. When production ceased, a total of twenty-seven Prospector aircraft had been built.

Foster Wikner Aircraft Co. Ltd. Initial test-flying of the Wicko two-seat light aircraft was carried out at Stapleford, with the first flight of the prototype G-AENU taking place on 21 September 1936. Development continued at Eastleigh (Southampton Airport) and a total of eleven were built. The type was advertised at a price of £895 for a fully aerobatic machine with 'Dual Control (Two Sticks) Viceless Performance'.

Tawney Aircraft Ltd. The Tawney Owl G-APWU was a monoplane with a pusher engine and twin tailbooms. G-APWU flew only once (being damaged in the process) on 22 April 1960. The aircraft was built by **Thurston Engineering Ltd** at Stondon.

Hertfordshire

Ayot St Lawrence, Welwyn
CMC (Chichester Miles Consultants Ltd), designers of the CMC Leopard private jet, have a company address at Ayot St Lawrence. The Leopard was designed at Dilton Marsh, Wiltshire,

and was test-flown at RAE Bedford, with further development trials conducted at Cranfield, Bedfordshire.

Broxbourne (near Hoddestone)

Broxbourne was the home of the Herts and Essex Flying Club, and the London General Omnibus Co. Flying Club (LGOC). The opening flying meeting of the LGOC Club was held on 17 September 1931.

The **Deekay Aircraft Corporation** (previously **Anderson Aerocars Ltd**, registered in London EC3) was formed on 3 October 1936 and built the Deekay Knight, G-AFBA, which first flew in November 1937. G-AFBA was a two-seat, side-by-side, low-wing cabin monoplane with a fixed, trousered undercarriage. It featured a three-spar wing with external chord-wise stiffening, similar to that of the American Emigh Trojan. Power was provided by a 90hp Blackburn Cirrus Minor engine.

The Knight was built in wood, with a view to the later incorporation of plastic components. The Deekay Corporation became more interested in the development of plastics as such, changing its name to **Aeroplastics Ltd** in May 1939 and moving to Earl Haig Road, Glasgow, finally becoming a part of **The Fairey Aviation Co. Ltd**. The Deekay Knight remained unconverted from its original wooden construction, and was destroyed during the war.

During the Second World War, **Herts and Essex Aviation Ltd** managed a modification and repair activity at Broxbourne within the Civilian Repair Organisation. The wartime workforce grew to around 300, and Proctor aircraft were rebuilt at a rate of around two per week. Around twenty Caudron Simoun were modified for the Free French Air Force, and overhaul work was carried out on a very diverse range of (mainly) light aircraft types.

The Simoun aircraft were delivered in a dismantled state in two batches from December 1940. After their rebuild, these aircraft were flight-tested at Luton. At least two Simoun were converted to Gipsy Six engines, and fitted with Proctor undercarriages. A Caudron Goëland was overhauled in 1941, and Herts and Essex Aviation also prepared Canadian-built Harvard aircraft for RAF use.

Opposite: *Deekay Knight G-AFBA.* (Ken Ellis collection)

Right: *Fairfield Aviation Ltd was something of a Lysander specialist, being particularly associated with implementing Special Operations modifications on this type.* (Westland)

Elstree Airfield

Elstree (then known as Hog Lane, Aldenham) was used as the flight test airfield for **Fairfield Aviation Ltd** of Watford. The Fairfield activity was mainly concerned with transport conversions of Vickers Wellington bombers; special operations modifications to the Lysander; and miscellaneous work on the Miles Master, Bristol Blenheim, Hawker Hart variants and other types. By mid-October 1945, the company had handled 473 Wellington, 1,217 Lysander, sixty-seven Miles Master and fifty-two other types for a total of 1,809 aircraft. The last Wellington aircraft to be handled by Fairfield was MP534, a conversion to Wellington Mk XVII, with Hercules XVI engines and a radar nose. Fairfield Aviation Ltd was a subsidiary of Redwing Ltd of Croydon and Thornton Heath.

Six Handley Page Halifax aircraft were converted for civil use with under-fuselage panniers for **London Aero and Motor Services Ltd** (LAMS) of Elstree. LAMS took over the hangars previously used by Fairfield Aviation Ltd and subsequently moved to Stansted Airport, Essex.

London Aircraft Production Group. This group (see Leavesden) carried out dispersed production of the Handley Page Halifax, building a total of 710 aircraft. The London Passenger Transport Board provided a number of the production resources of the group, including the use of works at Aldenham (close by Elstree Airfield) for work on Halifax major assemblies. The responsibilities allocated to the Aldenham site comprised the front fuselage and complete centre section, including the installation of the engines. This major assembly was then moved to Leavesden by road to be joined in final assembly with the rest of the airframe, prior to flight test, acceptance and delivery.

Hatfield

Activity at this site has been dominated by the de Havilland company and its successors, which are described chronologically below.

The de Havilland Aircraft Co. Ltd. The Hatfield site was acquired in 1930 in response to the effects of house building, which was rapidly surrounding the de Havilland site at Stag

Lane. It was reported at the time that the de Havilland Aircraft Co. Ltd was 'at a loss' for an appropriate name for its new aerodrome at the junction of the Barnet bypass with the Hatfield–St Albans road. The company offered a free fifteen-minute flight in a Gipsy Moth for the best suggestion (entries to be received by 31 May 1930). The airfield at Stag Lane remained in use until 28 July 1934.

Hatfield was the home of some of the world's most beautiful aeroplanes. Notable examples are the Comet Racer, Albatross, Moth Minor, Mosquito, Hornet, Dove and the DH106 Comet. Hatfield first flights and production details are shown in the table below:

Type	Registration	Date	Comments
DH89 Dragon Rapide	E.4/CH-287	17 April 1934	The first new type to fly at Hatfield. Some 730 DH89 were eventually built, 392 by de Havilland, 335 by Brush, two rebuilt at Witney, and one in Canada.
DH87 Hornet Moth	E.6/G-ACTA	9 May 1934	Two-seat side-by-side cabin biplane. 165 built.
DH88 Comet	E.1/G-ACSP	8 September 1934	Twin-engine long-range racing aircraft. The type was originally constructed for the 1934 MacRobertson England to Australia International Air Race. Five built, including the race winner G-ACSS, which was flown from Mildenhall to Melbourne in 70hr 54min.
DH90 Dragonfly	E.2/G-ADNA	12 August 1935	Five-seat twin-engine executive touring aircraft. Sixty-seven built.
DH91 Albatross	E.2/G-AEVV	20 May 1937	Seven aircraft, two of which were mailplanes. A beautiful aircraft powered by four Gipsy Twelve engines in an outstandingly clean installation. The fuselage construction pioneered that later used on the Mosquito.
DH94 Moth Minor	E.4/G-AFRD	22 June 1937	Seventy-three built at Hatfield, with additional aircraft built in Australia

Opposite: *The works of the London Aircraft Production Group at Aldenham (close to Elstree) were used for the manufacture of the forward fuselage and complete centre section of the 710 Handley Page Halifax built by this industrial group.* (Handley Page Association)

Right: *DH89A Dragon Rapide G-AIDL is seen here celebrating sixty years of Shoreham as municipal airport* (Author)

The fine lines of the DH91 Albatross anticipated the wartime Mosquito and the Hornet, which made use of the same construction techniques. Only seven were built. (A.J. Rae)

Type	Registration	Date	Comments
			following the outbreak of the Second World War. The type failed to deliver its true potential, due in part to the protracted development required to achieve satisfactory spinning characteristics.
DH95 Flamingo	later G-AFUE	28 December 1938	Sixteen built, additional comments below.
DH98 Mosquito	E.0234, W4050	25 November 1940	Built at Salisbury Hall and first flown at Hatfield. More than 3,000 were built at Hatfield of a total of 7,781.
DH100 Vampire	LZ548/G	20 September 1943	Originally known as the DH Spider Crab. The Vampire F.3 was flown on 4 November 1946. See additional comments below. UK production

Type	Registration	Date	Comments
DH103 Hornet	RR915	28 July 1944	of single-seat fighter variants was 1,157, many by the English Electric Co. at Preston. Two prototypes plus 195 for the RAF, and three prototypes (from Hornet) plus 190 Sea Hornet for the FAA. Production total of 384 also quoted.
DH104 Dove	G-AGSS	25 September 1945	First flown on the twenty-fifth anniversary of the formation of the firm. Additional comments below.
DH106 Comet 1	G-5-1/ G-ALVG	27 July 1949	Britain's first jet airliner, additional comments below. Twenty-one built, including both Comet 1 and 1A variants.
DH112 Venom	VV612	2 September 1949	Prototype modified from Vampire with thinner wing and tip tanks. Built in large numbers and widely exported in both single- and two-seat variants. See also Sea Venom, below. Production included 375 FB.1, 150 FB.4 (first flown 29 December 1953), twenty-two FB.54 for Venezuela, seventeen FB.50 (Italy two, Iraq fifteen), with licence production of 250 FB.50/54 in Switzerland. Night fighter prototype G-5-3 flown 23 August 1950 – production included ninety NF.2, 129 NF.3, sixty-two NF.51 for Sweden.
DH113 Vampire NF.10	G-5-2	28 August 1949	Two-seat night fighter variant, developed as a private venture.

Prototype Vampire LZ548 in a screened off area at Hatfield (BAE SYSTEMS plc via Ken Ellis)

Type	Registration	Date	Comments
DH114 Heron Srs 1	G-ALZL	10 May 1950	149 Heron were built, operating in more than thirty countries. All but eight of these aircraft were built at Chester, the last Hatfield aircraft being the Srs.2 prototype.
Heron Srs 2	G-AMTS	14 December 1952	
DH115 Vampire T.11		15 November 1950	Two-seat trainer variant developed as a private venture. A total of 804 were built, including seventy-three Sea Vampire T.22 and extensive export sales, the type being operated by twenty air forces in addition to the RAF.
DH112 Sea Venom	WK376	19 April 1951	Naval Venom with side-by-side seating. 298 built – three prototypes, fifty FAW.20, 167 FAW.21, thirty-nine FAW.22 for the Royal Navy and thirty-nine FAW.53 for Australia.
DH110	WG236	26 September 1951	Built to specification F.4/48 and eventually developed into Sea Vixen.
DH106 Comet 2X	G-ALYT	16 February 1952	Avon-powered with increased fuel capacity and range. Seventeen built, two used by the Ministry of Supply, fifteen by the RAF.
DH106 Comet 3	G-ANLO	19 July 1954	Stretched fuselage and wing-pinion fuel tanks – one aircraft only.
Comet 4	G-APDA	27 April 1958	Definitive production version for BOAC. Seventy-four built comprising Comet 4 twenty-eight; 4B eighteen; 4C twenty-eight (plus two unsold aircraft for Nimrod development).
DH106 Comet 4B	G-APMA	27 June 1959	For BEA with reduced span, lengthened fuselage and no pinion tanks.

The elegant proportions of de Havilland's lovely Comet 3 are well shown in this evocative photograph. In the author's opinion, this was the most attractive of all the Comet variants. (BAE SYSTEMS plc)

Type	Registration	Date	Comments
DH106 Comet 4C	G-AOVU	31 October 1959	Comet 4B fuselage married to Comet 4 wing.
DH121 Trident 1	G-ARPA	9 January 1962	117 of all versions built, including twenty-four Trident 1C; for other variants, see below.
DH125	G-ARYA	13 August 1962	Outstandingly successful executive jet which remains in production with more than 1,000 sold. Production of marks up to the Srs 400 consisted of two prototypes, eight Srs 1, seventy-seven Srs1A/1B, twenty Dominie, sixty-five Srs 3A/3B and 100 Srs 400.
Trident 1E	G-ASWU, later 9K-ACF	2 November 1964	Fifteen Trident 1E.
Trident 2E	G-AVFA	27 July 1967	Fifty Trident 2E (Trident Two).
Trident 3B	G-AWYZ	11 December 1969	Twenty-six Trident 3B (Trident Three), and two Super 3B.
HS146	G-SSSH	3 September 1981	Last new type to make its first flight at Hatfield. Developed into the Avro RJ series.
BAe146-200	G-WISC	1 August 1982	Fuselage stretched by 7ft 10in to accommodate up to 109 seats.
BAe146-300	G-LUXE	1 May 1987	Modification of original BAe146 prototype G-SSSH. Further stretch of 10ft 4in compared with Srs 200 to seat up to 130 passengers.
BAe RJ85	G-ISEE	23 March 1992	This was the last aircraft to be built at Hatfield.

The Hornet Moth was being advertised in September 1935 with the glowing recommendation: 'The Pilot's View: The easiest machine to fly and land – even at night – that I have ever flown. It is really most exceptional.' By December 1936, the price had been reduced to £775 and the advertising had become even more expansive:

> *Owned and flown in Australia, Austria, Belgium, Canada, Denmark, France, India, Ireland, Kenya, New Zealand, Netherlands East Indies, Rhodesia, Straits Settlements, South Africa, Spain, Sweden, Switzerland, Yugoslavia.*
>
> *In winter or summer, dressed for leisure or the business of life, one may settle into the broad, soft seat of the Hornet Moth beside one's companion and set off across country with enough baggage for a fortnight, confident to be handling a machine which takes off with power to spare and lands so easily that every field can be considered an airport.*
>
> *A perfectly unobstructed view, air brakes for a steep approach, a special wing section for fault forgiving landings, and differential brakes for controllability on the ground all go to ease the mind and increase the pleasure of the pilot.*

The elegant tapered wings of the initial production DH87A proved to be unsatisfactory in terms of stalling characteristics. Consequently, all DH87A aircraft were retrospectively modified to adopt the rectangular wing planform of the later production standard, the DH87B.

The DH90 Dragonfly was sold as 'an airliner in miniature'. The advertising emphasised the type's long range and performance, including the following capabilities: five persons and luggage with a range of more than 600 miles; tankage for 885 miles; 10 miles to the gallon; all day cruising at 127–131mph.

The Fox Moth, Dragon, Express, Dragon Rapide, Dragonfly, Comet Racer and Albatross were all designed by Arthur E. Hagg, who went on to design the Heston Racer, before moving to de Havilland's Christchurch Division to design the Ambassador. Beautiful aircraft, one and all. Hagg was replaced at Hatfield by an equally great figure, R.E. Bishop.

The DH95 Flamingo was less successful than many de Havilland types, partially due to the outbreak of the Second World War. Built as a response to the inroads of the Douglas DC-2 and DC-3, and the Lockheed 10 and 14, only sixteen were built.

Hatfield's wartime production record comprised 3,054 Mosquito (production continuing after the war), 795 Tiger Moth (plus 1,150 pre-war), 110 Queen Bee (plus 210 pre-war), and 200 DH89A (plus 206 pre-war). In addition to types of their own design, de Havilland built 1,515 Airspeed Oxford at Hatfield (seventy-five of these prior to the outbreak of the Second World War), with production running as high as eighty aircraft per month in August 1941. The first de Havilland-built Oxford was N4270. In addition, 150 Hurricane and 1,252 Mosquito were repaired at Hatfield.

Like many other manufacturers, de Havilland found it essential to disperse many of its departments to local business premises. Some 400 subcontractors, many in the furniture industry, were involved in Mosquito production. An additional repair facility was established at Witney in Oxfordshire.

Examples of de Havilland post-war advertising included the following:

- *Sea Hornet:* '*Speed – with manoeuvrability, Power – with docility, Range – with striking power, Endurance – with fighter performance.*'

The DH95 Flamingo appeared shortly before the Second World War; only sixteen were built. (Ken Ellis collection)

Above: *Tiger Moth G-AJHS was built at Hatfield as N6866. Here it shows its classic lines to the camera over the Dutch countryside.* (J.S. Smith)

Left: *Various dispersed production facilities were controlled from Hatfield, including the Oxford wing shop at Welwyn Garden City.* (BAE SYSTEMS plc)

- Vampire: 'The Vampire with the de Havilland Goblin engine – unequalled all-round effectiveness in high-altitude interception.'
- Venom NF. 2: 'Unsurpassed in climb, in endurance, in manoeuvrability at altitude and in cockpit layout, the Venom 2 night fighter with the de Havilland Ghost jet engine materially advances the effectiveness of Britain's defence by night.'
- Chipmunk: 'The finest introduction to sound airmanship – The de Havilland Chipmunk basic trainer.'
- Heron: 'Extreme simplicity, Exceptional take-off, Engine out safety – de Havilland Heron.'

The Dove was advertised by de Havilland as 'The world's most advanced aircraft for feeder service and private travel. An 8–11-seater light transport bringing trunk-line standards of safety, comfort and economy to the subsidiary air routes.' 'Main liner amenities on tributary airways.' 'Dove – on all counts the most suitable aircraft yet produced for executive travel.' Two prototypes and 542 production aircraft were built, the type having its origins in the Brabazon Committee Specification 5B for a Rapide replacement. The last aircraft to leave the production line was G-AVVK, a Dove Mk 8 which was delivered in February 1968, marking the end of a twenty-three year production run. For once, the product was to live up to the advertising!

The de Havilland DH104 Dove was one of the relatively few outright successes of the immediate post-war period. (H.E. North)

Although the type was designed in Canada, Chipmunk aircraft for use by the RAF were built at Hatfield and at Hawarden. The prototype de Havilland Canada DHC1 Chipmunk first flew at Downsview, Ontario, on 22 May 1946, and was subsequently brought to Britain and registered G-AKEV. 1,283 Chipmunk were manufactured, 217 in Canada, 111 at Hatfield, sixty-six in Portugal, and 889 at Hawarden, for a UK total of exactly 1,000. (Other sources give 1,014 UK Chipmunk aircraft, and total production 1,292, but this figure is believed to include a number of 'ship-sets' built for use as spares.)

A hard runway was laid (with work beginning in November 1946) to allow Vampires to fly from a more suitable surface. The runway was ready for use from 12 May 1947. Production of the Vampire (and Venom) was initially sub-contracted to English Electric at Preston. The Vampire FB.5 was built at Hatfield, Preston and Hawarden (Chester/Broughton). The Vampire Trainer was produced at Christchurch. Large numbers of export and licence-built Vampire were sold worldwide and total production was 3,268 aircraft. On 23 March 1948, Vampire TG278 was flown to an altitude record of 59,446ft, perhaps justifying the advertising claim of '[......] unequalled all-round effectiveness in high-altitude interception'.

The de Havilland Comet first flew at Hatfield in July 1949 to usher Britain into the jet age, at least in respect of commercial air travel. Although it was to prove tragically flawed, the Comet was eventually developed into a successful and long-lived design. The last revenue flight by a Comet (Comet 4C G-BDIW) took place on 9 November 1980, and the type provided the basis of the Nimrod maritime patrol aircraft which looks set to serve the RAF well into the twenty-first century.

Eight Heron (seven Heron 1 and the prototype Heron 2, G-AMTS) were built at Hatfield, the remainder (forty-four Heron 1 and ninety-seven Heron 2) being built at Chester. The Heron 2 can be distinguished from the Heron 1 by its adoption of a fully retractable undercarriage, that of the Heron 1 being fixed.

The extent of the de Havilland enterprise in 1953 is summed up in the following advertising copy: 'De Havilland builders of aircraft, engines and propellers for the Queen's air forces and merchant service, and for export to the world markets. Hatfield, Leavesden, Edgware, Chester, Bolton, Christchurch, Portsmouth, Sydney, Toronto, Wellington, Johannesburg, New York.'

A summary of engine test-bed aircraft operated in support of de Havilland jet engine development is given below:

- H1 Goblin – Gloster F.9/40 (Meteor prototype) DG206/G, first flown Cranwell on 5 March 1943. Vampire VV454 used for Goblin afterburner testing.
- H2 Ghost – Lancastrian VM703 and VM729 (first of these flew at Hatfield in late July 1947); Vampire TG278, first flown on 8 May 1947; Venom VV612 Ghost afterburner trials. 425 hours of Ghost Lancastrian testing was carried out.
- Gyron – Short Sperrin VX158 (test-bed designation Short PD6), first flown with Gyron on 7 July 1955 at Aldergrove, but mainly operated from Hatfield.
- Gyron Junior flown in a Gloster Javelin test bed at Hatfield in January 1961.

One of many Lancasters, Lancastrians and Lincolns used for engine development, Lancastrian VM703 supported DH Ghost flight testing at Hatfield. (BAE SYSTEMS plc)

Spitfire XIV RB144 was one of a number of aircraft used for the flight-testing of de Havilland propellers at Hatfield. (BAE SYSTEMS plc)

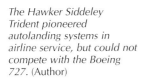
The Hawker Siddeley Trident pioneered autolanding systems in airline service, but could not compete with the Boeing 727. (Author)

Development of the HS125 was carried out at Hatfield, with production at Chester. N800BA is actually the BAe 125-800 prototype G-BKTF, which was first flown at Hatfield in May 1983. (Author)

In addition to the above, an Avro Lincoln RA678 was flown from Hatfield for trials of the de Havilland propellers for the Avro Tudor. A varied and active propeller test fleet included a wide range of operational types, together with second-line types adapted for test-bed use, including the Hawker Henley. A Handley Page Halifax provided with a nose-mounted icing spray rig was used for propeller de-icing/anti-icing trials.

Hawker Siddeley Aviation Ltd. The de Havilland Aircraft Co. Ltd became part of the Hawker Siddeley Group in 1960, and traded as Hawker Siddeley Aviation Ltd from 1964. The news of the impending merger was announced on 17 December 1959. This period coincided with early flying of the DH121 Trident (G-ARPA first flown 9 January 1962), which is therefore essentially a Hawker Siddeley product of de Havilland design. With masterful understatement, a Bristol Sales Department survey notes: 'Future prospects for the Trident were dealt something of a blow in December 1960, when the Boeing 727 design was announced.' Although never as successful as the Boeing design, the Trident had an important part to play in the introduction of automatic landing systems into routine commercial airline service. The DH125/HS125/BAe125/Raytheon Hawker executive jet first flew in 1962, and is therefore also a Hawker Siddeley product of de Havilland design.

British Aerospace. British Aerospace continued DH/HS125 development under **BAe Corporate Jets Ltd** at Hatfield, production being carried out at Hawarden. New versions of this type to be flown at Hatfield included: BAe125-800 G-BKTF, first flown on 26 May 1983, and BAe 125-1000 G-EXLR, first flown on 16 June 1990. In June 1993, BAe Corporate Jets Ltd was sold to the Raytheon Corporation.

BAe Regional Aircraft Ltd. The first BAe 146 G-SSSH flew at Hatfield on 3 September 1981. Despite an at times chequered history, particularly in its early days, the BAe 146 and its close relatives of the Avro RJ Series were delivered in larger numbers than either the BAC

One-Eleven, or the Sud Aviation Caravelle. Production of the 146 was subsequently transferred to Woodford, with the first Manchester-built example flying in May 1988. The type was then developed into the Avro RJ series. Further development to produce the RJX foundered following the terrorist attacks in the United States on 11 September 2001, which led to the cancellation of both the RJ and RJX programmes.

The last aircraft to fly from Hatfield airfield was Tiger Moth G-APLU on 4 April 1994, flown by Dick Bishop, son of the great de Havilland designer R.E. Bishop. The only Hatfield activity remaining after the closure of the manufacturing site was the jet sales and leasing arm of **BAe Asset Management Ltd**, which manages a portfolio of more than 500 jet and turboprop aircraft in which the company has a financial interest (mainly BAe146, ATP and Jetstream aircraft). The objectives of the Asset Management organisation are to sell these aircraft where possible, or lease to the highest quality operators at the highest possible rates for the longest possible time. After the merger of BAe and MES to form **BAE SYSTEMS**, the jet and turboprop asset management activities were combined and incorporated within **BAE SYSTEMS Regional Aircraft**.

The organisational history of BAe/BAE SYSTEMS Regional Aircraft activities is summarised in Volume 2 of this series, under Farnborough, Hampshire.

The **DH Technical School** was founded at Stag Lane and moved to Hatfield with the parent firm. The Technical School was eventually given its own permanent home in 1949, at Astwick Manor on the north side of Hatfield aerodrome. The school operated as an aircraft engineering training college for de Havilland technical apprentices and encouraged its students in the design and construction of light aircraft.

The de Havilland Technical School built DH9J G-ABPG, three Tiger Moth, G-ACPS, G-ADGO and G-AEVB and Moth Major G-ADIO. After this experience of building established production designs, the students turned their hand to the design of a number of original prototypes distinguished by their use of TK as a type designation.

The TK1 G-ACTK/E-3 flew at Stag Lane in June 1934 and was a conventional biplane seating two in tandem. (There are some uncertainties over the first flight date: Ord-Hume (in *British Light Aeroplanes*) and A.J. Jackson (in *British Civil Aircraft since 1919*) both give June 1934, but A.J. Jackson (in *De Havilland Aircraft since 1915*) also gives a first flight date of 14 November 1933.) The TK1 was subsequently converted to single-seat configuration, and was scrapped in 1936. The clean two-seat TK2 E-3/G-ADNO flew on 16 August 1935 and was an outstanding success, achieving a maximum racing speed of 189.7mph on its 140hp. Used as a communications aircraft during the Second World War, the TK2 continued flying until the end of 1947.

The Technical School produced the diminutive TK4 single-seat racing aircraft in 1937. At the time of its first flight at Hatfield on 30 July 1937, TK4 E-4/G-AETK was the smallest aircraft built in Britain, with a 19ft 8in span and 15ft 6in length. During the 1937 King's Cup Air Race, the TK4 was flown at 230mph on its modest Gipsy Major power. The TK4 tragically crashed on 1 October 1937 killing de Havilland chief test pilot R.J. Waight, having only flown for a period of two months prior to this accident. The last TK Group design, the TK5 was reminiscent of a Rutan Varieze, complete with wing-tip fins, swept wings and a nose wheel. It was, however, a failure, refusing to become airborne when tested at Hatfield.

In 1998, the Comet flight test hangar and adjacent fire station and control tower at Hatfield were adopted for listing by English Heritage. When it was erected, the hangar was, with its

The last design of the de Havilland Technical School was the unsuccessful TK5. (BAE SYSTEMS plc via Ken Ellis)

This Wittman Tailwind is one of a small batch built as the AJEP Tailwind. (Author)

217ft span portal frames, 330ft length and 45ft height, the largest aluminium building in the world.

Hertford

AJEP Developments of The Lodge, Marden Hill Farm, near Hertford, marketed a modified Wittman Tailwind developed by A.J.E. Perkins in the mid 1970s. Modifications included a revised wing section, changes to the cockpit doors, a fin of increased sweep, engine cowling revisions and other modifications. The first demonstrator aircraft was registered G-AYDU.

Hitchin

J.R. Coates: The Spinney, Breachwood Green, Hitchin. The Coates SAII Swalesong, designed and built by Mr Coates, is a low-wing monoplane seating two side by side, with a tricycle undercarriage. The Swalesong G-AYDV first flew at Panshanger on 10 September 1973.

Leavesden/Watford

The **Watford Division of the de Havilland Aircraft Co. Ltd** was set up to provide additional manufacturing capacity for the Mosquito and Sea Mosquito. When the Leavesden factory was first established it was used for the production of Oxford components and assemblies, output including sixty fuselages and 147 wing sets for this type, prior to the switch to the Mosquito. 1,390 Mosquito were built at Leavesden, the marks built including the

This classic production line photograph showing Mosquito production at Leavesden in full flow with sixteen aircraft visible. (BAE SYSTEMS plc)

Mk. II, III, XIII, XVII, NF. XIII, NF. XIX, NF. 30, NF. 36, and TR. 33 (Sea Mosquito). A number of Mosquito aircraft were used for the development of the Sea Mosquito, the first deck landings taking place on 25 March 1944 on *HMS Indefatigable*. The first Leavesden production Sea Mosquito TW227 was first flown on 10 November 1945. The prototype Mosquito NF. 36, RK955, was also built at Leavesden, flying for the first time in May 1945. Much of the actual component manufacture was contracted out to the furniture industry.

Fairfield Aviation Ltd of St Albans Road, Watford, was set up in early 1942 and used a factory that had previously been used by the publishers, Odhams Press. Fairfield Aviation Ltd was a wholly owned subsidiary of **Redwing Aircraft Co. Ltd**. Test-flying was carried out at Elstree, under which further details may be found.

The **London Aircraft Production Group** was set up to provide dispersed production capacity for the Halifax. The production group comprised the following companies: **London Passenger Transport Board** (Chiswick: detail parts for the centre section and front fuselage; White City: engine cowlings, stores and spares; Aldenham (near Elstree): complete centre section and installation of front fuselage and engines; Leavesden: final assembly, test and delivery), **Chrysler Motors Ltd** (complete rear fuselage), **Duple Bodies & Motors Ltd** (front fuselage structure), **Express Motors and Body Works Ltd** (Inner wing), **Park Royal Coach Works Ltd** (outer wings and engine cowlings). Final assembly and test was conducted at Leavesden. Like many subcontract production centres, building up the production rate was a painful process. Only five aircraft were built in the first eighteen months according to one report, which also criticised the apparent desire of Handley Page Ltd to protect their design know-how. The first aircraft built was Halifax II BB189, this aircraft being accepted on 6 January 1942. Production comprised 450 Mk II and 260 Mk III for a total of 710 out of orders for 830 aircraft. The last aircraft to be delivered was PN460, which was proudly named *London Pride* at a ceremony at Leavesden on 16 April 1945.

Lettice Curtis reports in *The Forgotten Pilots* that London Aircraft Production Group aircraft featured green leather crew seats. These aircraft are also said to have been faster than those built by Handley Page Ltd at Cricklewood.

Right: *The London Aircraft Production Group assembly and flight-test activity at Leavesden was fed by a dispersed production system, including the construction of rear fuselages by Chrysler Motors Ltd.* (Handley Page Association)

Below: *This publicity photograph shows feverish activity on and around a Halifax Mk II in preparation for test-flying at Leavesden* (Handley Page Association)

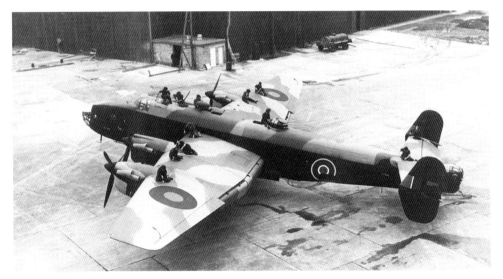

Jetstream Aircraft Ltd. This company was formed in September 1970 at Sywell (by Capt. Bill Bright of Terravia Trading, and Scottish Aviation Ltd), to complete the production of incomplete Handley Page Jetstream airframes. **Terravia Trading Services Ltd** acquired the rights to the Jetstream design in March 1970. After renaming as Jetstream Aircraft Ltd, the company moved to Leavesden. Subsequently all production rights were acquired by **Scottish Aviation Ltd** at Prestwick.

Panshanger airfield

The **Coates** SAII Swalesong G-AYDV, a low-wing, tricycle-undercarriage monoplane seating two side by side, first flew from Panshanger on 10 September 1973. See also Hitchin, above.

The **Gowland** Jenny Wren G-ASRF was an enclosed version of the Luton Minor, with a most ungainly cockpit enclosure. G-ASRF was built at Brookmans Park and first flown on 13 October 1966 at Panshanger.

The Gowland Jenny Wren was an inelegant cabin adaptation of the Luton Minor (via Author)

Radlett

Handley Page Ltd. This 154-acre airfield was purchased to replace the increasingly inadequate site at Cricklewood. Radlett was originally identified as a suitable site for an airfield by Handley Page's pilot Major Cordes, who had occasion to use it for a forced landing in bad weather in March 1928. Flight operations were moved to Radlett by June 1929, with the aerodrome and works being officially opened on 7 July 1930 by HRH Prince George.

In his speech at the opening, Mr Handley Page said that the company had been started twenty-one years previously in Barking, moving successively to Hendon, to Kingsbury and to Cricklewood. The present move was forced by the building value of the land at Cricklewood. The new aerodrome measured 1,700 by 700 yards, was fog free and was well drained, being sited on a layer of gravel. The aerodrome at Cricklewood was sold in February 1930 for £100,000, although the factory was retained.

Handley Page Ltd is rightly famous for its bomber designs, and Radlett was to continue the company's traditions in this regard. Cricklewood's First World War designs, the O/400 and V/1500, were succeeded at Radlett by the Heyford, Hampden, Halifax and Victor. Many of the most famous Handley Page types were first flown at Radlett, design being in the hands of G.R. Volkert. Mr Volkert worked with Handley Page on design tasks from 1919, becoming Chief Designer in 1923 and continuing in this post until 1945.

The main Radlett types included the following:

- The HP.42 transport for Imperial Airways. G-AAGX was first flown on 14 November 1930, having been built at Cricklewood and assembled at Radlett – see further comments below.
- HP.38 and HP.50 Heyford – 124 HP.50 were built for RAF, the HP.38 prototype J9130 being first flown at Radlett on 12 June 1930. Amazingly, the type persisted in RAF service in secondary roles (for example with the Air Observers Schools) at least until 1940.
- Hampden: the HP.52 prototype K4240 was first flown at Radlett on 21 June 1936. This was the precursor to the Hampden and Hereford, and led to a production prototype L4032 in May 1938. 502 Hampden were built by Handley Page Ltd, with a further 770 constructed by the English Electric Co. Ltd and 160 built in Canada.
- The Napier Dagger powered Hereford was a derivative of the Hampden and was first flown on 1 July 1937 (under Pegasus power). Further development was

undertaken in Belfast by Short & Harland Ltd, the prototype being flown on 6 October 1938 with Napier Daggers installed. 152 were built, all production being undertaken by Short & Harland in Belfast from May 1939.

- HP.54 Harrow – 100 Harrow bomber/transports were built, the prototype K6933 being first flown at Radlett on 10 October 1936.
- HP.57 Halifax – the most important Handley Page design of the Second World War. The prototype L7244 was first flown at Bicester on 25 October 1939. See additional comments below.
- The HP.75 Manx (H-0222), an experimental flying-wing aircraft powered by twin Gipsy Major engines, was first flown at Radlett on 25 June 1943.
- The Hastings transport was built at Radlett although the prototype TE580 was first flown from Wittering on 7 May 1946. Two prototypes were followed by 144 Hastings for the RAF, the type remaining in service from 1948 until 1968. Four additional Hastings C.3 served with the RNZAF, giving a production total of 150. At the end of their service lives, a small number of RAF machines were fitted with under-fuselage radar installations and used for V-bomber crew training.
- The Hermes airliner prototype G-AGSS was first flown on 3 December 1945, but the flight ended in a tragic fatal accident. A second prototype Hermes 2 G-AGUB was built, which flew on 2 September 1947. The first Hermes 4 G-AKFP flew at Radlett on 5 September 1948, introducing a nose-wheel undercarriage and a 13ft 4in fuselage stretch compared with the Hastings. Twenty-five Hermes 4 were ordered for BOAC. Two Theseus-powered Hermes 5 were built, the first G-ALEU flying on 23 August 1959. See additional comments below.

Above: *The staid and safe HP.42 appeared at the time of the move of Handley Page Ltd from Cricklewood to Radlett.* (via Author)

Left: *J9130 is the prototype Handley Page HP.38, which was subsequently developed as the HP.50 Heyford, 124 being built for use by the RAF.* (via J .S. Smith)

- Victor: Handley Page's magnificent crescent-winged V-bomber – see additional comments below.
- Herald: The Dart Herald was put into production at Radlett after initial development by Handley Page (Reading) at Woodley. See additional comments below.
- Jetstream: Prototype G-ATXH was first flown on 18 August 1967, see additional comments below.
- Handley Page Ltd also built seventy-five English Electric Canberra B. Mk 2 aircraft.

The HP.42 was outstandingly successful and safe, despite being almost eccentrically non-competitive with the likes of the Douglas DC-2, alongside which it was to see service. *Flight* commented wryly that 'the metal sides of the fuselage are corrugated which adds to rigidity, if not to appearance'. First flying in November 1930, the HP.42 fleet served Imperial Airways up to the outbreak of war. By September 1938, *Heracles* (G-AAXC) had completed 1H million miles of service and carried 95,000 passengers.

The Halifax bomber was designed from the outset with dispersed production in mind, with major sections sized to be transportable. The wing, for example, was constructed in five sections. Handley Page Ltd acted as technical advisors to the Halifax Production Group consisting of the English Electric Co. Ltd at Preston, London Aircraft Production Group at Leavesden, Rootes Securities Ltd at Speke, and the Fairey Aviation Co. Ltd at Stockport. There were, in total, some forty-one factories and dispersal units, 600 subcontractors, and 51,000 employees. Peak production across the Group was one aircraft every working hour.

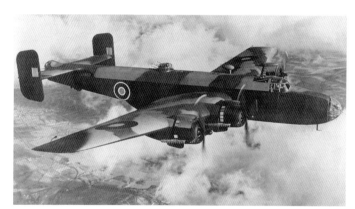

Halifax B.III LV857. More than 6,000 Halifax were built, about a quarter of these by Handley Page Ltd. The most important contractor was the English Electric Co. Ltd, who built more than 2,000 of the type. (Handley Page Association)

The second production Handley Page Hastings, TG500. The aircraft has been modified with external beams under the forward fuselage to allow the air-dropping of large externally carried loads. (BAE SYSTEMS plc)

G-AXUM is a Handley Page-built Jetstream 1, still in use as a flying classroom at Cranfield University. (Author)

WJ630 is an English Electric Canberra which was built by Handley Page Ltd as a B.2, being subsequently modified to become a T.17. (Author)

More than 6,000 Halifax were built in twenty-six versions. (One production total quoted is 6,135 (although the same source gives a breakdown of 1,564 by Handley Page Ltd including two prototypes; 2,145 by the English Electric Co. Ltd; 662 by the Fairey Aviation Co. Ltd; 710 by London Aircraft Production Group; and 1,070 by Rootes Securities Ltd – a total of 6,151); another source quotes a total of 6,177.) At its service peak, seventy-six RAF squadrons were Halifax-equipped.

From 1953 to 1963, the main product was the outstandingly successful and long serving Victor V-Bomber. From 1953 until at least 1957, Handley Page used this 'flagship' product in their advertising:

The Handley Page Four-jet Victor flies
   Fastest
     Farthest
       Highest
V for VICTOR. Surpassing the most stringent operational requirements, the four-jet crescent-winged Victor is Britain's premier bomber.

With its striking crescent wing and towering tailplane, the Victor served in bomber, strategic reconnaissance and flight-refuelling roles. Production consisted of two prototypes, fifty production B. Mk 1 (first flown 1 February 1956), and thirty-four B. Mk 2 (first flown on 20 February 1959). The type's service life included adaptation for the air-to-air tanker role, and for use as a strategic reconnaissance platform. Victor K. Mk 2 tanker conversions were carried out by Hawker Siddeley at Woodford after the collapse of Handley Page Ltd. The last aircraft was withdrawn from service on 15 October 1993.

Handley Page's civil ventures (Hermes (twenty-nine built), Herald, Jetstream) were less successful commercially. The Hermes was the first British pressurised aircraft to enter production, but its service life was limited by main spar fatigue life limits. As a result, the Hermes 4 saw service with BOAC only from 1950 to 1952.

The first Leonides-powered Herald made its first flight from Radlett on 25 August 1955. Radlett was used for Dart Herald production flying, fifty aircraft being built comprising two prototypes, four Srs 100, thirty-six Srs 200 and eight Srs 400. The Herald, despite its limited sales success, proved to be a robust aircraft in service, and the type was also noted for its well-harmonised controls. By the end of 1998, however, only one example remained in use, just over forty years after the first flight of the Dart Herald. This last example (G-BEYF) was retired in 1999. For further details, see Woodley, Berkshire.

Despite market enthusiasm for the Jetstream, with 165 ordered before the prototype's first flight, performance and production difficulties were to force Handley Page Ltd into voluntary liquidation on 8 August 1969. **Handley Page Aircraft Ltd** was set up to administer the company's affairs in receivership, but also failed in February 1970. The subsequent development of the Jetstream was carried out by Scottish Aviation Ltd and British Aerospace at Prestwick.

Today the airfield at Radlett has nearly disappeared, being no longer even marked as a disused airfield on the aeronautical chart. In fact, the layer of gravel, which (as Handley Page noted at the official opening of the airfield) provided the site with excellent drainage, is now being extracted leaving behind only a series of gravel pits.

The Mosquito prototype W4050 is preserved at Salisbury Hall with the Mosquito Aircraft Museum, part of the de Havilland Heritage Museum. (Author)

Camouflaged hangars and workshops contrast in this photograph with the leafy elegance of Salisbury Hall, birthplace of the Mosquito. (BAE SYSTEMS plc)

Rush Green
Farm Aviation Ltd of Rush Green, Langley, Hitchin, developed a single-seat agricultural conversion of the Chipmunk, and, in early 1971, built the ill-fated Owl Racer G-AYMS. G-APOS was the first of five Chipmunk conversions known as the Chipmunk 23, and was first flown on 6 June 1958.

St Albans
Kingsbury Works Ltd. 'Aeronautical Engineers and Manufacturers – Doping, woodwork, metal fittings of seaplanes and land machines.' Nothing else is known.

Salisbury Hall, London Colney
Salisbury Hall was used by **The de Havilland Aircraft Co. Ltd** for the construction of the prototype of one of the most successful aircraft of the Second World War, the de Havilland DH98 Mosquito. The yellow prototype E.0234/W4050 is preserved here with other de Havilland machines at the Mosquito Aircraft Museum. The first prototype was constructed at Salisbury Hall, and then dismantled and taken to Hatfield for its first flight on 25 November 1940. Four additional Mosquito prototypes were constructed at Salisbury Hall, three of these being flown directly from the adjacent fields, rather than being taken by road to Hatfield. Total Mosquito production was 7,781 aircraft, and no fewer than thirty-eight versions saw service.

Kent

Deal
Kent Aircraft Services Ltd at Kingsdown (formerly RNAS Walmer) assembled seven Avro 504K in 1930 and 1931 from parts purchased from the Aircraft Disposal Company. Their registrations were G-AAUJ, G-AAUK, G-AAUL, G-AAWC, G-AAWD, G-ABJF and G-ABOL.

In 1930 the company was advertising 'Avro 504K spares – mainplanes, cowlings, undercarriages, skids, tanks, etc. Private aerodrome and hangar. Storage for 60 machines. Kent Aircraft Services, 7 Radnor Chambers, Folkestone, and Bekesbourne Aerodrome near Canterbury.'

Gillingham (Kent)

The **Mitchell Brothers** hydro-aeroplane (a convincing-looking 37ft span biplane with twin floats) was built in 1914 and tested on the Medway. Powered by a 100hp Mors engine, it unfortunately overturned during taxiing trials.

Gravesend

Gravesend Airfield was constructed in 1932 at Thong Lane as 'Gravesend–London Airport East', officially opening on 26 August 1932. After service as an RAF Fighter Command airfield during the Second World War, the site was progressively covered by a large housing estate constructed from the late 1950s.

CLW Aviation Co. Ltd (whose name was derived from the initials of its founders' surnames, being Messrs S. Wilding Cole, A. Levell and F.S. Welman) was formed on 12 January 1935, becoming **CLW Aviation (1936) Ltd** on 30 April 1936. The company built one aircraft, the CLW Curlew, G-ADYU, which was constructed at Bexleyheath and first flew at Gravesend in September 1936, and was scrapped in 1948. The Curlew was a most attractive all-metal two-seat open-cockpit low-wing monoplane. The crew were seated in tandem in a slim full-monocoque fuselage, and the aircraft had a well-proportioned tapered monospar wing of original structural design and high torsional stiffness. Power was provided by a 90hp Pobjoy Niagara III engine. When shown publicly on 20 September 1936, the type had only flown for a single hour, the first flight being on 3 September. Despite its attractive appearance, the Curlew did not enter production and only the single prototype was built.

Essex Aero Ltd, who advertised as 'designers and constructors in Magnesium Alloy' were not manufacturers as such, but are famous for the preparation of racing and record-breaking aircraft – in particular, Alex Henshaw's Mew Gull and A.E. Clouston's DH88 Comet. The company was founded by Jack Cross, initially at Stapleford Tawney – this explaining the name 'Essex Aero', despite its main operating base being in Kent. Jack Cross had been Chief Engineer of Hillman Airways before founding Essex Aero Ltd in 1935.

Essex Aero contemplated entry into the light aircraft market with a two-seat project known as the Essex Aero Sprite, intended to be powered by a Nuffield horizontally opposed engine. A model of the project featured a low-wing monoplane configuration with side-by-side seating under a cockpit canopy resembling that of the Provost. The aircraft also had a retractable undercarriage and butterfly tail.

Essex Aero worked on self-sealing fuel tanks during the war, subsequently constructing the fuselage fuel tanks for the Supermarine E.10/44, and the fuel tanks for the Miles Merchantman. Essex Aero went into liquidation in 1956.

The Percival Aircraft Co. Ltd was registered in 1933, and established their works at Gravesend in 1934, the company name being changed to **Percival Aircraft Ltd** in the August

Only one example of the attractive CLW Curlew was built. (Peter Green collection via Ken Ellis)

Jean Batten's famous long-distance record-breaking Gull 6, G-ADPR Jean was a product of Percival's Gravesend factory. (Author)

of that year. Twenty-two Percival Gull, a number of Mew Gull aircraft and the prototype Vega Gull were built at Gravesend, the company moving to a new site at Luton in October 1936.

The prototype Gull, G-ABUR was built by the British Aircraft Company at Maidstone, following which initial production of the type was undertaken by Parnall at Yate. After the construction of twenty-four aircraft at Yate, production was transferred to Gravesend. The change of production location coincided with the introduction of the Gull Six, with a 200hp Gipsy Six engine replacing the 130hp Gipsy Major of the Parnall-built aircraft. One relatively little-known Gull aircraft built at Gravesend was the special Gull Six with two open cockpits in tandem, which was built for the Maharajah of Jodhpur. The Gull was a popular touring aircraft and the type was advertised in glowing terms, thus:

> *A LUXURY AIRCRAFT The Percival Gull has introduced this year a new standard of merit to aviation. It is the fastest and shapeliest three-seater ever produced. The Gull in fact is the last word in flying luxury for it combines speed and beauty of line with comfort and safe flying qualities as they have never been combined in one aircraft before. Own a Percival Gull and you own the finest light aeroplane in the world today.*

The first Mew Gull G-ACND flew at Gravesend in March 1934, the type being specifically designed for racing and long distance touring. The most famous of the Mew Gull aircraft is G-AEXF, which was raced by Alex Henshaw and still survives today (albeit after multiple rebuilds and much bad luck). In racing trim the aircraft achieved a speed of 247mph and excelled at long-distance record breaking. In an extraordinary flight in 1938, Henshaw smashed the record for a flight from London to Cape Town and back. The round trip was

*Alex Henshaw's Mew Gull was built at Gravesend by Percival Aircraft Ltd, and prepared for racing by Essex Aero Ltd.
(Author and James Goggin)*

completed in only 4 days and 10 hours. The outbound leg covered the 6,377 miles in 30 hours 28 minutes' flying time, with an elapsed time of only 39 hours 23 minutes. The return was almost equally fast, with 30 hours 51 minutes' flying in 39 hours 36 minutes' elapsed time.

The Vega Gull differed from the Gull in having a four-seat configuration and increased wing span. The prototype G-AEAB was flown at Gravesend in November 1935. Both the Gull and Vega Gull achieved notable successes in racing and long-distance flights, the Vega Gull prototype winning the King's Cup Air Race in 1936. Jean Batten used Gull Six G-ADPR for many of her long-distance flights. Production of the Vega Gull amounted to ninety aircraft and was undertaken in the new Percival factory at Luton.

The **Perman** Parasol G-ADZX was first flown at Gravesend by A.E. Clouston on 23 May 1936, and it (and the later Broughton-Blayney Brawney) are referred to, in Mr Clouston's autobiography, as the Clouston Midget. The aircraft was later (October 1936) referred to as the Perman Grasshopper.

Short Brothers (Rochester & Bedford) Ltd. The Short Scion G-ACJI made its first flight at Gravesend, on 18 August 1933.

Isle of Grain

Port Victoria. Aircraft manufacture on the Isle of Grain had its origins in the Royal Naval Aeroplane Repair Depot, which set up an experimental section in late 1915, later named the Marine Experimental Aircraft Depot. The types produced are summarised below:

Type	Comments
PV1	An improved Sopwith Baby with high lift aerofoil sections.
PV2	Small sesquiplane with no wire bracing, intended as an anti-Zeppelin fighter and flown in June 1916.
PV2bis	Modified PV2, flown in March 1917, Serial N1.
PV4	N8, an unsuccessful pusher design.
PV5	Sesquiplane developed from the PV2bis and flown on 25 July 1917, N53 and N54 (PV5A).
PV7	An attractive 18ft span biplane, N539, flown on 22 June 1917 and designed for ship-based operation.

Type	Comments
PV8	Eastchurch Kitten, N540, flown 7 September 1917.
PV9	Biplane seaplane fighter, N55, flown during December 1917.

The PV7 and PV8 were built with an eye to possible use against airships. The name Eastchurch Kitten for the PV8 reflects the fact that its construction was begun at Eastchurch, and completed at Port Victoria. The last aircraft to be built here were seven Grain Griffin reconnaissance aircraft, N100 – N106, built in 1918.

George Parnall & Co. Ltd. The Parnall Puffin N136 was first flown from the Isle of Grain on 19 November 1920. Only three were built.

The Fairey Aviation Co. Ltd. The Fairey F.127, serial N9, was a tractor biplane seaplane powered by a 200hp Rolls-Royce Falcon I, and designed to Specification N.2(a). N9 was first flown at the Isle of Grain on 5 July 1917 and was a precursor to the extremely successful Fairey III series. The Fairey F.128 N10 (which was retrospectively designated as the prototype Fairey III) was first flown from the Isle of Grain on 14 September 1917. The F.128 was also designed against specification N.2(a), and benefited from an increase of power provided by a 260hp Maori III engine. The Fairey III was initially tested on floats, being designated Fairey IIIA when modified for land use.

The Fairey N.4 flying boats (Atalanta and Titania) were tested at the Isle of Grain Marine Experimental Aircraft Depot. The first aircraft, N.4 Atalanta N119, was flown on 4 July 1923; the N.4 Titania N129 following on 24 July 1925. The N.4 programme involved production of major assemblies at sites dispersed around the UK, including activity at Bradford, West Yorkshire; Preston, Lancashire; Hayes, Greater London; and Hamble, Gosport and Southampton Water in Hampshire.

Isle of Sheppey – Shellbeach, Leysdown and Eastchurch

The Isle of Sheppey, site of the first Short Brothers' factory, and the Aero Club flying fields, contains some of Britain's most significant aviation heritage locations. A number of pioneer

Mussel Manor at Shellbeach has associations with the Short brothers, the Wright brothers, C.S. Rolls and J.T.C. Moore-Brabazon. (Author)

The Hon. C. S. Rolls making a cross-country flight from Shellbeach to Eastchurch in December 1909 using the first Short-Wright biplane. (Bombardier Aerospace, Belfast)

constructors flew at Shellbeach and Eastchurch, and the Short Brothers set up the world's first aircraft factory here. The entry below provides a chronology of Short's operations on Sheppey, followed by an alphabetical listing of other pioneer flying at Shellbeach and Eastchurch.

The **Short Brothers** were active at Leysdown and nearby Shellbeach, and subsequently at Eastchurch. The company telegraphic address was 'Flight, Eastchurch'.

Leysdown and Shellbeach

The initial flying on the Isle of Sheppey was at Mussel Marshes, next to Mussel Manor (alternatively spelt as Muswell Manor), with a factory at neighbouring Leysdown. The Short brothers – Horace, Eustace and Oswald – were the first aircraft manufacturers in the world, having set up their factory in 1909 to build aircraft on a series production basis. **Short Brothers** was registered as a company in November 1908 with capital of £600.

The Short brothers were active in balloon manufacture at Battersea, and came to know Griffith Brewer, who was a keen balloonist and also held the British rights to the Wright patents. Eustace and Oswald Short had connections with the Aero Club and, as a result of Eustace seeing the Wright machine flying in France in 1908, decided that they would construct heavier-than-air aircraft as well as balloons.

The Short Brothers were contracted, in February 1909, to construct six Wright biplanes under licence, which were sold to members of the Aero Club. The purchasers were C.S. Rolls (Aero Club Certificate No. 2), F.K. McClean, Maurice Egerton, Cecil Grace (Aero Club Certificate No. 4) and Alec Ogilvie – all important pioneers. The drawings that enabled these machines to be constructed were largely developed by Horace Short, who sketched the details of the Wright machine during its French tour of late 1908/early 1909.

The connection with the Wright brothers was a feature of the company's early advertising: 'Aeroplane and Balloon Manufacturers. Sole Manufacturers and Agents in Great Britain & Ireland for Messrs. Wilbur & Orville Wright. Early Deliveries for Wright Machines can be given, fitted with both wheels and skids.'

Before these Wright machines were available, Short built a Wright glider for C.S. Rolls, the machine being constructed at Battersea and flown from a rise near Leysdown. The Short brothers set up their factory at Leysdown, and lived in Mussel Manor, which had been purchased for the use of the Aero Club by F.K. McClean (later Lieut. Col. Sir Francis K. McClean, AFC).

The Wright brothers visited the Leysdown factory on 4 May 1909 and they were photographed outside Mussel Manor in a famous group, which also included Oswald, Horace and Eustace Short, F.K. McClean, Griffith Brewer, Frank Butler, J.T.C. Moore Brabazon and C.S. Rolls.

A major advantage of Shellbeach (Leysdown) as a flying ground was the large area clear of obstructions. C.G. Grey wrote: 'there is a clear 7 miles run to Queensborough, practically without a tree or a house in the way, and with good landing ground everywhere.' On the other hand, the dykes at Shellbeach rendered the ground unsuitable for wheeled machines.

By August 1909, eighty employees were working for the Short Brothers factory. Alongside the Short-Wright biplanes, Short Brothers began to manufacture their own designs. The Short No. 1 was built for F.K. McClean, but was unsuccessful. The Short No2, which was built for J.T.C. Moore Brabazon, was used on 30 October 1909 to win the £1000 *Daily Mail* prize for the first Briton to make a circular flight of one mile using an all-British aeroplane. J.T.C. Moore Brabazon (Aero Club Certificate No. 1) later became Lord Brabazon of Tara, and was the Minister of Aircraft Production in 1941-42.

The buildings erected at Leysdown (and later moved to Eastchurch) were adapted from a standard design used for buildings such as church halls. F.K. McClean had a bungalow built to the same design.

Eastchurch

In late 1909, a new flying field of 400 acres was found below Stamford Hill at Eastchurch, and the decision was taken to move both the Aero Club activities and the Short Brothers factory to this site. Horace and Eustace Short discovered the site of the flying ground at Eastchurch as a result of a cross-country survey of Sheppey using their 7hp Panhard car, which was considered to be particularly good at crossing dykes and ditches.

The field was purchased by F.K. McClean, and leased back to the Royal Aero Club for one shilling a year (the Aero Club had become the Royal Aero Club on 15 February 1910). Eastchurch was a large field with a pond in the middle, sloping towards a dyke that bordered the marshes. By spring 1910, the move had been completed with nearly all the sheds at Leysdown being pulled down and relocated to Eastchurch.

Eastchurch was used for much of the early flying training and aircraft construction for the fledgling Royal Naval Air Service (RNAS). This connection arose in part because the Royal Aero Club offered free instruction to naval officers from February 1911, the first officer to qualify being Lieut. C.R. Samson on 24 April 1911.

After construction of the Wright machines, Shorts produced a series of successful designs based upon the Farman/Sommer Boxkite configuration. During this period, Short's designs were known by their construction numbers (e.g. S.27, S.38). These aircraft were built for both private use and for use by the RNAS, to whom Shorts were a major supplier before and during the First World War. The main Short 'Boxkite configuration' designs were as follows:

Designation	Comments
S.27 Type	A series of machines built for private owners and subsequently used for training of RNAS pilots. The purchasers were F.K. McClean (S.26), Cecil Grace (S.27, S.29), J.T.C. Moore Brabazon (S.28). S.28 was modified to become the *Eastchurch Gun Machine*, RNAS serial 66, first flying in this form on 24 September 1913. S.34 was built as a

After flying as the 'Triple Twin' (with two Gnome engines and three propellers), the Short S.39 was converted to a more conventional configuration. (A.J. Rae)

Designation	Comments
	replacement for S.29, after Cecil Grace had been lost at sea while flying this machine on 22 December 1910. S.26, S.28 and S.34 were used for the training of RNAS officers.
Improved S.27	S.35 featured a covered fuselage nacelle and was built for Maurice Egerton. It flew on 9 March 1911 and was known as the 'improved type 27'. A further example was S.38, which was flown on 24 May 1911. After further development this became the S.38 type, see below.
S.32 Type	S.32, 33, 43 and 44. The S.32 was a further variant with side-by-side seating and dual controls built for F.K. McClean and flown for the first first time on 29 July 1911. S.33 was flown on floats at Harty Ferry from May 1912, being based in a hangar next to the Harty Ferry Inn. S.33 was flown along the Thames and through Tower Bridge on 10 August 1912. S.32 was later modified to have S.38 features including a nacelle and greatly increased span for an expedition by McClean to the Nile. It proved too slow and was rebuilt in a more standard S.38 configuration.
S.38 Type	S.38 was rebuilt with an enclosed nacelle, extended wing span and new controls. In this form it became the prototype of the S.38 type and set a British endurance record of 4 hr 58½ min on 19 August 1911. This was the aircraft flown from HMS *Africa* on 10 January 1912, and from HMS *Hibernia* while steaming at sea on 9 May 1912. The S.38 was very successful, and nine additional aircraft were built by Shorts, twelve by Pemberton-Billing (Supermarine Aviation Works), and twenty-four by White & Thompson/Norman Thompson Flight Co. Three more received serials 145, 152 and 190, although their origin is uncertain.
Nile Seaplane	The S.80 and S.81 were new designs for the Nile expedition, featuring a double Gnome two-row rotary engine of 160hp and 67ft wingspan. The S.80 was first flown on 2 October 1913.

A total of sixty-one of these Farman-style biplanes were built by Short, almost challenging the success of the Bristol Boxkite.

The Short M2 monoplane (basically very similar to a Blériot) was flown on 24 February 1912, but did little flying.

In parallel with their Farman-inspired designs, Shorts carried out a number of developments with tractor biplanes and twin engine machines. The twin engine types are summarised below:

Designation	Comments
S.39 Triple Twin	First flown on 18 September 1911, this design featured a Farman-style layout with a central nacelle mounting two independent Gnome engines, at the front and rear of the nacelle. The rear engine drove a pusher propeller, while the front used chains to drive two tractor propellers mounted at the wing leading edge at mid-span. S.35 was later modified to Triple Twin configuration by Maurice Egerton.

Designation	Comments
Tandem Twin	First flown on 29 October 1911, this was S.27 (Cecil Grace's machine) converted to a simple push-pull arrangement reminiscent of the Cessna Super Skymaster.
Triple Tractor	First flown on 24 July 1912, the S.47 featured two nose-mounted Gnome engines, the forward engine driving a tractor propeller. The second engine used chains to drive two tractor propellers mounted mid-way between the wings at mid-span. This two-seat side-by-side design was known as the Triple Tractor, but could just as well have been called the Triple-Twin-Tractor or the Tractor-Triple-Twin!

After these activities, Shorts' main line of development switched from Farman-style designs to tractor biplanes and, in particular, seaplanes. The first tractor biplane S.36 was built for F.K. McClean and was first flown on 10 January 1912. Two similar machines (S.41 and S.45) were ordered for the Admiralty, S.41 flying on 2 April 1912. The Admiralty machines were successfully flown in both landplane and seaplane form. Three further S.45 derived tractor biplanes were built for use by the CFS at Upavon with service serials 413, 423 and 424.

From this point Shorts grew from strength to strength, particularly with a rapidly evolving series of naval seaplanes (particularly the Short 184, 310, 827, and 830), followed after the First World War by a switch to flying boats. With the increasing emphasis on seaplanes, the decision was made to establish a factory on the banks of the Medway at Rochester. The works at Rochester were constructed between October 1913 and January 1914, work being progressively transferred away from Eastchurch. Rochester subsequently became the company's headquarters, and the further development of the Shorts range of designs is presented under that heading.

C.R. Fairey moved from the Dunne Syndicate to join the Short brothers in 1912, soon becoming their Chief Engineer. Fairey decided to leave Shorts and set up his own company when Shorts decided to move to Rochester in 1914.

The Shorts Admiralty Type 830 was built at both Eastchurch and Rochester. This is an Eastchurch-built example, seen during a road move. (Terry Treadwell & Alan Wood)

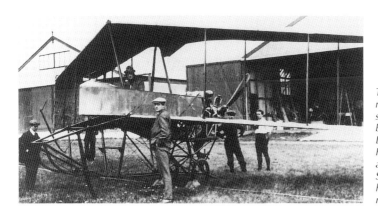

The Dunne D.8 was the most successful of the series of swept, tailless biplanes designed by J.W. Dunne and tested at Farnborough, Blair Atholl and Eastchurch. C.R (later Sir Richard) Fairey is seen here standing by the wing root. (J.W.R. Taylor)

Blair Atholl Aeroplane Syndicate Ltd/Dunne. Lt J.W. Dunne experimented with the design of tailless inherently stable aircraft configurations from 1905 until 1913. His initial work was officially funded and carried out at the H.M. Balloon Factory at Farnborough. Testing was conducted away from the gaze of press and public at Glen Tilt and Blair Atholl in Scotland. Official funding was discontinued in 1909 and Dunne left the Balloon Factory, setting up the Blair Atholl Aeroplane Syndicate Ltd and continuing his flight experiments on the Isle of Sheppey.

The first Dunne type to be tested on the Isle of Sheppey was the D.5, which was built by Shorts and flown at Eastchurch. The D.5 flew extremely successfully, including hands-off straight and level flight. The D.5 is described as flying with a peculiar steady train-like motion. In August 1911 the Dunne monoplane was flying at Eastchurch, it being reported that its 'flights prove beyond doubt that his machines must be reckoned among the most practical of the day'. Dunne himself lived at Parsonage Farm, near Eastchurch.

In 1911 C.R. (later Sir Richard) Fairey joined the Blair Atholl Aeroplane Syndicate and sometimes flew from Eastchurch. The D.7, D.8 and D.10 were also built there, with Fairey in charge of their construction. The D.8 was sent to France for demonstrations in 1913, and spectators at Deauville were treated to the spectacle of the pilot leaving the cockpit in flight and walking out along the lower wings – a possibly unmatched demonstration of hands off stability and confidence in the machine. The D.8 was Dunne's most successful machine.

The **Dunne-Huntington** triplane was an extraordinary machine with three wing surfaces and no vertical fins (although interplane fins were later added). The machine was built in 1910, and it was reported to be flying easily at Eastchurch in March 1913.

The **Jezzi Brothers** built two successful biplanes at Bromley, Kent in 1910 and 1912, which were flown at Eastchurch. The first machine resembled a Wright Baby and flew in mid-1910, and was continuously modified to improve performance. The second machine was a small tractor biplane with wings of unequal span, and with a large gap between the wings in which the fuselage was suspended. Later the lower plane was extended to create a two-bay biplane configuration. This diminutive aircraft was powered by a 35hp JAP engine and had a wing span of 27ft 7in. First flown in spring 1912, the second machine was built in a workshop in Mr Jezzi's private house at Bromley.

Mr Jezzi was a true enthusiast and camped out at the weekends in his aeroplane shed at Eastchurch in order to get the maximum amount of flying in. To increase his creature

This memorial in Eastchurch celebrates the aeronautical pioneers of the Isle of Sheppey. (Author)

comforts, the shed was equipped with a coke stove and a table. Visitors noted that newspaper was used as a tablecloth and the large enamel mugs of tea provided were most welcome when visiting in winter. Both Jezzi machines were good flyers, it being reported regularly in *Flight* throughout 1911 and 1912 that 'the Jezzi biplane was out for trials at Eastchurch'. Also: 'the machine displays high speed and extreme steadiness'. Despite its low power, the second machine would readily fly with pilot and passenger.

Stamford Hill, to the rear of Eastchurch aerodrome, was used for glider trials in September 1913.

The role of the Isle of Sheppey in Britain's aviation heritage is recorded in the words of a memorial in Eastchurch Village:

> THIS MEMORIAL COMMEMORATES THE FIRST HOME OF BRITISH AVIATION 1909
> *Near this spot at Leysdown (Mussel Manor) and Eastchurch (Stonepitts Farm), flights and experiments were made by members of the Aero Club (later Royal) of Great Britain. Also the establishment of the first aircraft factory in Great Britain by Short Brothers 1909. And the formation of the first Royal Naval Air Service station 1911.*
> AVIATORS: *J.T.C. Moore Brabazon, The Hon. Charles S. Rolls, Frank K. McClean, Prof. A.K. Huntington, The Hon. Maurice Egerton, T.O.M. Sopwith, Alec Ogilvie, Percy Grace, G.P.L. Jezzi, James L. Travers, and others.*
> DESIGNERS AND CONSTRUCTORS: *Horace Short, Eustace Short, Oswald Short and the craftsmen of Sheppey.*
> ROYAL NAVAL AIR SERVICE: *Lt. Cdr. C.R. Samson, Lieut. A.M. Longmore, Lieut. R. Gregory, Capt. E.L. Gerrard and 12 RN technical ratings.*

The Eastchurch flying ground is now part of the prison to the south of Eastchurch. The original flying sheds are among the buildings in use on the prison farm. In 1997, these buildings were under the threat of being demolished. The then owners of Mussel Manor were trying to persuade the local council that the buildings should be dismantled and moved back to Shellbeach to commemorate the site's role in the establishment of the British aircraft industry.

Joyce Green

Vickers Ltd set up a private airfield at Joyce Green, the facilities being described as a large wooden shed next to the Long Reach Tavern, with the River Darent forming the Western boundary. Joyce Green was used for all experimental testing of early Vickers aircraft. The last aircraft to make its first flight at Joyce Green was the prototype Vickers Vimy Commercial K-107 (later G-EAAV) on 13 April 1919. The last aircraft to be built at Joyce Green was the Vickers Vellore G-AASW, which was flown at Brooklands in 1930. Joyce Green was used during the First World War as an air-raid defence airfield for London, closing in December 1919.

Vickers Ltd adopted the procedure of carrying out first flights and initial tests at Joyce Green, before moving the aircraft to Brooklands for further development flying. The earliest designs were the series of Vickers No. 1-8 monoplanes, which were initially derived from the French REP design and proved both popular and successful. The Vickers No. 2-5 monoplanes were used at the Vickers Flying School at Brooklands. As each of these monoplanes was produced, there was an evolution in design away from the original modified REP design. Monoplane No. 6 featured side-by-side 'sociable' seating, and was entered into the 1912 Military Trials

Above: *The Vickers F.B.26A Vampire II B1485 was test flown at Joyce Green.* (Terry Treadwell & Alan Wood)

Right: *The moustachioed pilot posing in front of its bulbous nose at Joyce Green lends scale to the almost surreally inflated fuselage of the Vimy Commercial prototype. This aircraft later received the registration K-107, becoming G-EAAV in due course.* (BAE SYSTEMS plc via Ken Ellis)

at Larkhill. Unfortunately, engine trouble prevented it from showing its true potential at the Trials. The last of the early Vickers monoplanes, No. 8, also featured side-by-side seating.

Significant first flights made at Joyce Green included the F.B.5 Gunbus in late 1914, and the Vimy B9952 on 30 November 1917.

Lympne

Although not at the time a manufacturing site, Lympne had considerable importance in the 1920s as the site of the 1923 motor glider competition, and of the 1924 and 1926 light aircraft competitions. The contestants for these competitions are discussed below, followed by a listing of other types flown from Lympne.

The Lympne competitions are significant not least because of the involvement of the country's major manufacturers in exploring the capabilities required of a practical light aeroplane.

The 1923 motor glider competition generated entries from **The English Electric Co.** (Wren), **A.V. Roe & Co. Ltd** (Avro 558/560), **Gloucestershire Aircraft Co. Ltd** (Gannet), **The de Havilland Aircraft Co. Ltd**, **George Parnall & Co. Ltd** (Pixie), **Vickers Ltd** (Viget), **Handley Page Ltd**, and **Handasyde Aircraft Co**. Other entrants included the **RAE Aero Club**, **Gnosspelius** Gull, and the **ANEC** monoplane. The Gnosspelius Gull G-EBGN first flew at Lympne on 26 May 1923. Remarkable performances were turned in:

- The Wren and Pixie both achieved a fuel economy of 87.5mpg.
- The ANEC monoplane achieved good speed and climbed to an altitude of 14,400ft.
- The Avro 558 biplane was flown to an altitude of 13,850ft.
- The Avro 560 monoplane flown by Hinkler flew a cumulative distance of more than 1,000 miles during the trials at 63.3mpg.

Unfortunately, no practical product was to emerge.

The 1924 two-seat competition attracted a similar cross-section of the industry, including the following: **The Bristol Aeroplane Co. Ltd** (Brownie, three entries with a choice of wing designs), **William Beardmore & Co. Ltd** (Wee Bee), **Westland Aircraft Works** (Woodpigeon and Widgeon Mk.1), **Short Brothers (Rochester & Bedford) Ltd**, **The Supermarine Aviation Works Ltd** (Sparrow), **Blackburn Aeroplane & Motor Co. Ltd**, **ANEC**, **A.V. Roe & Co. Ltd** (Avis), **Vickers Ltd** (Vagabond), and **H.G. Hawker Engineering Co. Ltd** (Cygnet). Amateur interest was limited to the **Cranwell Light Aero Club** CLA.2 to the design of the talented Nick Comper. The 1924 competition was dominated by engine reliability, and the winner was the Beardmore Wee Bee G-EBJJ, designed by W.S. Shackleton, the designer of the ANEC machine that had performed so well in 1923. An honourable mention should also be made of the CLA.2, which flew 762.5 miles during the competition, this taking a stately 18 hours.

The 1926 competition saw a move towards the inclusion of more practical machines such as the Moth and Avian, albeit with the Genet engine (as the competition rules excluded the ultimately much more successful Cirrus engine due to its weight). Many of the competitors from the 1924 competition entered again, including the Blackburn Bluebird, Bristol Brownie, Hawker Cygnet, Supermarine Sparrow, and new designs such as the Cranwell CLA.3/4, the RAE Aero Club Scirocco and Hurricane and the ANEC Missel Thrush. This event was won by the Hawker Cygnet, which represented something of a *tour de force* of efficient lightweight design.

It is a striking fact that, like the 1912 military trials, these competitions were won by aircraft that ultimately proved unsuccessful, whereas more practical designs that were less optimised to the constraints of the competition proved to be the real winners. Thus the Bluebird, Moth, Avian and Widgeon all eventually became successful production machines. The failure of the competition winners to enter production should not be allowed to detract from the important part played by Lympne and the *Daily Mail* in the history of British aircraft construction.

The **Currie** Wot single-seat light biplane was first flown at Lympne in November 1937. The prototype G-AFCG was built at the Cinque Ports Flying Club by students from the Chelsea College of Aeronautics, to the design of J.R. Currie. A separate company was formed at Lympne (**Cinque Ports Aviation Ltd**) to carry out this work. Two aircraft, G-AFCG and G-AFDS, were built before the Second World War, but were both destroyed in 1940 when their hangar was bombed. Both aircraft made use of the same Aeronca E113C engine, perhaps reflecting the limited finances available to the club. The Hampshire Aero Club subsequently revived the type at Eastleigh, and new plans were drawn up and issued by **Phoenix Aircraft Ltd**. The type is an approved design of the Popular Flying Association and continues to be popular with amateur constructors. The **Isaacs** Fury was also derived from the Currie Wot design. See also Denham and Eastleigh, Hants (*British Built Aircraft: Volume 2*).

Short Brothers (Rochester & Bedford) Ltd used Lympne for the flight-testing of their landplane designs from spring 1926 until mid-1929. Types first flown at Lympne included the Shorts-built Gnosspelius Gull, and the Short Satellite, Chamois and Gurnard (in its landplane configuration). The Gurnard was a competitor to the Hawker Osprey, the two prototypes bearing the serials N228 and N229. The first aircraft to fly was the Kestrel powered seaplane N229 (on 16 April 1929 from the River Medway), followed by the Jupiter-powered landplane N228 from Lympne on 8 May 1929.

Maidstone

The **British Aircraft Company Ltd** (BAC) was formed by C.H. Lowe-Wylde in 1930 in a disused brewery in Lower Stone St, Maidstone. The company initially built a series of

Currie Wot G-APNT was made famous as Airymouse *by the Westland test pilot Harald Penrose in his lyrical stories of west country flying.* (Author)

gliders, the BAC I-IX, of which more than thirty were built. The Planette powered glider was essentially a BAC VII with a pylon mounted 600cc Douglas Sprite engine driving a pusher propeller. The Planette entered production in late 1932, four Planettes being demonstrated at Hanworth in December 1932. The type was developed with an improved fairing for the engine pylon, in which form it was known as the Drone. After Lowe-Wylde's death in May 1933, the design was taken over by **Robert Kronfeld**, and production moved to Hanworth, the aircraft being restyled the Kronfeld Drone, Super Drone and Drone de Luxe. Thirty-three Kronfeld Drone were built before the Kronfeld company closed in 1937.

The prototype **Percival** Gull G-ABUR was built in the British Aircraft Company Ltd workshops at Maidstone in 1932.

The airfield at Maidstone eventually became RAF West Malling.

Penshurst (near Royal Tonbridge Wells)

Air Travel Ltd converted three Avro 504K – G-ABVH, G-ABVY, G-ACCX – to Armstrong Siddeley Mongoose IIIA engines in 1932-33. Operations were later moved to Gatwick, where the company continued to operate a successful business based on conversions, overhaul and refurbishment of the Avro 504.

Rochester (River Medway and Rochester Airfield)

The entry for Rochester deals first with a chronological review of the activities of Short Brothers, followed by an alphabetical listing of other types/manufacturers that made use of Rochester as a production or test centre.

Short Brothers (Rochester & Bedford) Ltd. The three Short brothers (Horace, Eustace, and Oswald) began aircraft manufacture in Great Britain when they established a factory at Leysdown on the Isle of Sheppey to manufacture Wright biplanes under licence. The Royal Naval Air Service also began its operations on the Isle of Sheppey, with Shorts becoming one of its most important suppliers.

The most important First World War product of Short Brothers (Rochester & Bedford) Ltd was the Short Admiralty Type 184 floatplane. 926 were built, the type being extensively contracted to other firms. (Bombardier Aerospace Belfast)

Sheppey is, however, somewhat remote and Shorts were reported in September 1913 as taking an important site on the Medway near Rochester Bridge due to the increasing inconvenience of their Sheppey works. The Medway seaplane and flying boat works were progressively established during 1914, opening one week before the outbreak of the First World War. In March 1914, two shops had been erected which were 60ft wide and 240ft long, with slipways directly to the river.

The company's most important products during the First World War were its series of folding wing seaplanes (typified by the Short 184), which were widely subcontracted. This rapidly evolving series of tractor seaplane biplanes began with designs built at Eastchurch, the first notable type being known as the 'improved S.41'. The first of these (bearing RNAS serial number 20) flew on 23 April 1913. Three were built, the last (RNAS 42) using steel tube in its construction and including a number of other refinements. A series of 160hp two- and three-bay folding seaplanes were developed from this aircraft, nine aircraft being built as RNAS 81, 82, 89, 90, 119-122 and 186.

The next production design was the Admiralty Type 74, a 100hp non-folding seaplane with three-bay wings. Seven were built; the first, RNAS 74, flew on 4 January 1914 (the RNAS had begun to use the serial number that it allocated to an early machine of a given type as a generic identifier for all machines of the same type).

After building a further four 80/100hp non-folding seaplanes, two Salmson-powered two-bay designs were built: S.87/RNAS 135 of 135hp and S.88/RNAS 136 of 200hp. The production version of S.87 became the 'improved Type 74', or Type 827, or Type 830, dependent on engine installed, whereas the production version of S.88 became the Admiralty Type 166. Shorts built six Type 166, with a further twenty being contracted to the Westland Aircraft Works of Petters Ltd.

Eight 'Improved Type 74' with the 100hp Gnome engine were built as RNAS 811-818, these being the first aircraft to be built at Rochester. These were followed by eighteen Type 830, which were generally similar except for their use of the 135hp Salmson. Twelve of these aircraft were constructed at Eastchurch. In 1916 a further ten aircraft were built for training use. These aircraft (RNAS 9781-9790) were essentially Short 830, albeit with minor engine differences.

The Short 827 was more successful. This type was powered by the 150hp Salmson, and was widely subcontracted. A total of 108 were built, production being split between Shorts (thirty-six), Brush Electrical (twenty), Parnall & Sons (twenty), Sunbeam Motor Co. Ltd (twenty), and Fairey Aviation (twelve).

After all this development, Shorts and the Admiralty finally arrived at the Short Admiralty Type 184, the most important seaplane of the First World War. The Short 184 was a three-bay 225hp folding tractor seaplane, which was used for bomber, reconnaissance and torpedo duties. A total of 926 were built, production being split between Shorts (107 including prototypes); The Brush Electrical Engineering Co. Ltd (190); Mann, Egerton & Co. Ltd (twenty-two, ten as the 184B or Mann, Egerton Type B); The Phoenix Dynamo Manufacturing Co. Ltd (sixty-two); Robey & Co. Ltd (256); Frederick Sage & Co. Ltd (seventy-two); S.E. Saunders Ltd (eighty); The Supermarine Aviation Works Ltd (fifteen); Westland Aircraft Works (twelve); and J. Samuel White & Co. Ltd (110).

A rare landplane design followed, this being the Short Bomber. Initially derived from the Short 184, the Bomber featured a substantial increase in wing span to 84ft, and an 8ft 6in

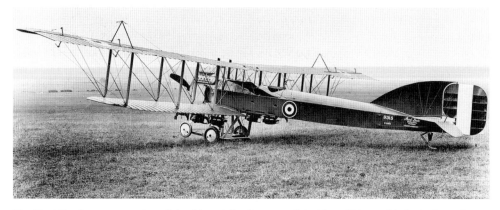

The Short Bomber was an enlarged, land-based development of the Short 184, notable for its large size as a single-engine machine. (Bombardier Aerospace Belfast)

increase in fuselage length. Including prototypes, eighty-four were built, production being split between Shorts (thirty-five); Mann, Egerton & Co. Ltd (twenty); the Sunbeam Motor Car Co. Ltd (fifteen); the Phoenix Dynamo Manufacturing Co. Ltd (six); and Parnall & Sons Ltd (six).

The last important production type of the First World War was the Short 310 biplane – a 320hp Cossack powered torpedo seaplane following on from the 225hp Short 184. Two prototypes were flown during the summer of 1916, followed by a production variant the Short 310-A4, also known as the Short 320. A total of 128 Short 310/320 were built, fifty of these being built by The Sunbeam Motor Co. Ltd.

In addition to production of their own designs for naval use, Short Brothers also undertook contract production of 100 AIRCO DH9 at Rochester, together with the Felixstowe F.3 and F.5 flying boats. Flying boat production consisted of thirty-five F.3 and twenty-five F.5 aircraft and resulted in considerable expansion of the works. Hulls were manufactured in a boatyard on the opposite bank of the Medway at Strood and were then towed to the main works to allow assembly to be completed. Additional F.3 aircraft were reconditioned for export customers and twelve F.5 from a cancelled RAF order were exported to Japan. Twenty-four Felixstowe F.5 returned to Rochester for major overhaul in 1925. Shorts also received contracts for the repair and modification of a total of eighty-four DH9A, some of these being assembled from unused airframes taken from store. The Shorts construction numbers of the machines involved were S649–S670, S679–S692, S706–S709, S732–S735 and S737–S743. Although this gives an apparent total of fifty-one aircraft, three machines (S656, S657 and S664) were processed twice, each receiving a new construction number in the process. (DH9A information provided by Alan Faupel, RAeS Medway Branch.)

The company was an early pioneer of duralumin stressed skin construction with the private venture 'Silver Streak', leading to the 1921 advertising slogan: 'All metal aeroplanes and seaplanes'. The Air Ministry regarded the all-metal construction of the Silver Streak with extreme suspicion and the type did not progress beyond the prototype stage.

Short Brothers were to become Britain's premier manufacturer of flying boats. Short's famous designer was Sir Arthur Gouge who worked for the company from 1915 to 1943 and was responsible for all designs from 1926 to 1943, including the Singapore, Calcutta, Kent, Valetta, Sarafand, C Class, Golden Hind, Sunderland, Stirling and Shetland, before moving to continue his career with Saunders-Roe Ltd.

Equally long serving was test pilot John Lankester Parker, who instructed for the Hall School of Flying from 1914, moving to the Lakes Flying Co. in 1915. From 1916 until 1918, he carried out freelance testing for the Prodger-Isaac Aviation Co., as well as flying for Short Brothers (Rochester & Bedford) Ltd, a role in which he continued until 1945. Lankester Parker carried out many first flights of new types from the Medway, as summarised in the following table:

Type	Serial or Registration	Date	Comments
Silver Streak	G-EARQ	20 August 1920	Pioneer of stressed skin construction. Later allocated serial J6854.
N.3 Cromarty	N120	19 April 1921	Shorts' first flying boat. An enlarged development of the Felixstowe F.5, powered by two Rolls-Royce Condor engines.
Satellite	G-EBJU	16 September 1924	Two-seat mid-wing monoplane first flown at Lympne, and featuring an all-metal fuselage and wooden wing.
Cockle	G-EBKA	7 November 1924	Diminutive all-metal single-seat flying boat intended for private use. Flown on 7 November 1924. The type was severely underpowered.
Felixstowe F.5	N177	5 January 1925	Metal hull.
Mussel	G-EBMJ	6 April 1926	Named after Mussel Manor, see Isle of Sheppey. The Mussel was a single-engine low-wing monoplane seaplane. The type was later flown as a landplane, and with various float configurations.
Singapore I	N179/ G-EBUP	17 August 1926	Used by Sir Alan Cobham to complete a 25,000-mile survey flight around Africa in 1929.
Calcutta	G-EBVG	14 February 1928	Nine built, used by Imperial Airways for Mediterranean and Nile operations.
Gurnard	N229	16 April 1929	Competitor to the Hawker Osprey, see also Lympne.
S.7 Mussel II	G-AAFZ	17 May 1929	An improved version of the Mussel, featuring an all-metal wing structure. Used like its predecessor for float development work.
Singapore II	N246	27 March 1930	Four Rolls-Royce XII engines arranged in tandem pairs.
Rangoon	S1433	24 September 1930	Military derivative of the Calcutta, six built.
S.11 Valetta	G-AAJY	21 May 1930	For Sir Alan Cobham.
S.17 Kent	G-ABFA	24 February 1931	Three built, with two landplane versions S17L *Scylla* and *Syrinx*. *Scylla* flown at Rochester Airport 26 March 1934.
Sarafand	S1589	30 June 1932	Six-engine flying boat.

Type	Serial or Registration	Date	Comments
'Knuckle-duster'	K3574	30 November 1933	Designed to R.24/31. Flying boat with high-cantilever gull wing with two Goshawk VIII engines, one each on each 'knuckle' of the wing. One only.
Singapore III	K3592	15 June 1934	Thirty-seven built for the RAF, nineteen still being in service at the start of the Second World War.
S.23 Empire Flying Boat	G-ADHL	3 July 1936	*Canopus*. See comments below on Short 'Empire' series flying boats.
S.21 'Maia'	G-ADHK	27 July 1937	Short-Mayo composite – lower.
S.20 Mercury	G-ADHJ	5 September 1937	Short-Mayo composite – upper.
Sunderland	K4774	16 October 1937	Shorts' most important military flying boat, see additional comments below.
S.30	G-AFCT	28 September 1938	*Champion*, nine built.
S.26	G-AFCI	21 July 1939	*Golden Hind*.
S.33	G-AFPZ	April 1940	*Clifton*, two built.
Seaford	MZ269	30 August 1944	Originally Sunderland IV.

Right: *Ahead of its time, the all-metal Silver Streak was a pioneer of stressed skin construction, a design approach that was not to be accepted as the norm in the UK for another fifteen years.* (Bombardier Aerospace Belfast)

Below: *The Short Rangoon was a military derivative of the three-engine Short Calcutta. Only six were built, S1433 being the first of these.* (Bombardier Aerospace Belfast)

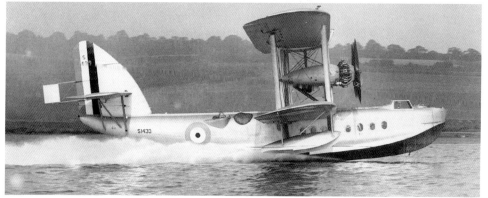

The Sarafand was an imposing six-engine biplane flying boat of no less than 120ft wing span. Only the single prototype was built. (Bombardier Aerospace, Belfast)

The unique Mercury and Maia combination flew (separately) in 1937, the first separation of the combination being achieved in February 1938. Although successful in allowing great range to be achieved by Mercury, this proved to be an evolutionary dead-end. (Bombardier Aerospace, Belfast)

Type	Serial or Registration	Date	Comments
Shetland	DX166	14 December 1944	Second aircraft G-AGVD flown on 17 September 1947.
Sandringham I	ML788/ G-AGKX	28 November 1945	Converted Sunderland III.

The fifteen years after the First World War saw hard times for Short Brothers. As might be inferred from the above table, many types were constructed, but production contracts were few and far between. The total number of aircraft of their own design constructed by Shorts in this period (including types additional to the table above) was forty-seven aircraft of some twenty-three different types.

Although labour was cheap by modern standards, the costs of design, tooling, construction and testing of each type had to be borne and it is difficult to understand how Shorts survived this difficult period. In fact, like many contemporary firms in the industry, Shorts diversified, building water craft (motor boats, lifeboats and electric canoes), and bus bodies, which were used by local corporation fleets all over England.

Improvements were on the way, however. Not included in the above list is the Short Scion, a twin-engine five/six passenger transport. John Lankester Parker flew the first Scion G-ACJI from Gravesend Airport on 18 August 1933. A total of sixteen Scion I and II were built by Shorts, with a further six by Pobjoy Airmotors and Aircraft Ltd. The Scion II G-ACUZ was first flown on 13 February 1935. When combined with the princely total of thirty-seven Singapore III constructed for the RAF, these two types represented more than the total of the remaining Shorts designs that had been flown since the end of the First World War.

The land airfield at Rochester was opened in 1934 and was initially used by Shorts for flight-testing, and subsequently for aircraft manufacture. The first Shorts design to fly at Rochester Airport was the S.17L Scylla G-ACJJ on 26 March 1934. The twin-engine Scion was built at Rochester airfield by Shorts, and later by Pobjoy Airmotors and Aircraft Ltd. A four-engine derivative, the S.22 Scion Senior, was less successful, only six being built. The first Scion Senior VT-AGU was flown in seaplane configuration from the Medway on 22 October 1935. The penultimate Scion Senior L9786 was used at Felixstowe and Helensburgh for experimental flying boat hull trials.

Shorts' flying boat development moved into the modern era with the development of the Short Empire series, which ultimately led to the production of the Sunderland. The Empire (or C-Class) flying boat was Imperial Airways' main long-distance aircraft in the immediate pre-war years. These flying boats were used on the routes to South Africa, India and Australia, fully justifying the title of Empire flying boat. The class represented a transition in technology to stressed skin monocoque construction combined with cantilever monoplane configuration, high-lift flaps and variable-pitch propellers. Thirty-one S.23 'C-Class' were built (including three for QANTAS), followed by nine S.30 of increased weight and power, and two S.33, all being referred to as Empire flying boats.

Alongside its Empire flying boat construction, Shorts built and flew the *Mercury* and *Maia*, two aircraft which together constituted the pick-a-back Short-Mayo composite mail carrier. The S.20 *Mercury* G-ADHJ was a four engine seaplane which was carried on the top of the S.21 *Maia* G-ADHK, a purpose-built flying boat based upon the design of the S.23 'C-Class'. The first separation of the combined ensemble was achieved on 6 February 1938. The project demonstrated that it was based upon sound principles with a flight by *Mercury* non-stop from Foynes to Montreal on 21/22 July 1938. This was followed by an FAI seaplane distance record of 5,997.5 miles from Dundee to the Orange River in South Africa.

Interspersed with the development of the Empire series, Shorts flew two other 'boats', these being the S.26 Golden Hind and the Sunderland. The Golden Hind was much larger than the 'C-Class', and had a wingspan more than 20ft greater than that of the Sunderland. Only three were built.

The Short S.31, a small-scale test aircraft for the Stirling bomber, first flew at Rochester Airport on 19 September 1938 under Class B markings as M4. First of the four-engined 'heavies', the Stirling was built in large numbers at Rochester, Belfast, Birmingham (Austin Motors), and Swindon/South Marston. More than twenty factories were involved, with a peak production rate of some eighty aircraft per month. 2,383 Stirling were built (other figures can also be found), mainly as bombers (two prototypes, 724 Mk I, three Mk II converted from Mk I, 1,037 Mk III). These were followed by some 460 Mk IV glider tugs and 160 Mk V transports.

The Stirling got off to an ignominious start when the prototype, L7600, was badly damaged in a landing accident at the end of its first flight on 14 May 1939. The Stirling production line at Rochester was bombed in August 1940 causing at least six aircraft to be

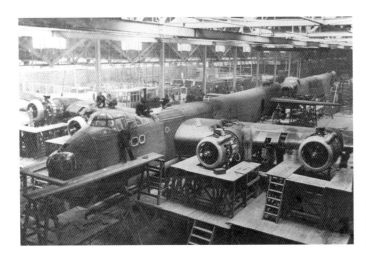

This photograph shows the extensive staging required to allow access during final assembly of the Stirling.

The Sunderland is famous for its long and successful service with RAF Coastal Command on anti-submarine and convoy escort duties. This photograph shows fuselage construction under way at Rochester.

destroyed in the factory. The decision was then taken to move to dispersed production, this being in effect from 1940 until 1942 when production was resumed at Rochester.

The Short Sunderland played a major role in anti-submarine warfare and convoy protection throughout the Second World War. A total of 749 were built at Rochester, Belfast (133), Windermere (thirty-five) and Dumbarton (240). Rochester Sunderland production comprised 331 aircraft made up of the prototype, seventy-four Mk I, twenty-three Mk II, 186 Mk III and forty-seven Mk V (Source *British Aircraft at War*, Gordon Swanborough) – other totals can be found elsewhere. Note that the total of 749 includes the two Sunderland IV and eight Seaford.

The Sunderland, Hythe, Sandringham and Solent were to provide BOAC and Aquila Airways with the backbone of their long distance fleets in the immediate post-war years, until succumbing to the superior economics of such types as the Constellation, Stratocruiser and DC-6. Nevertheless, the Sunderland had a long and meritorious military career; its RAF service lasting from mid-1938 until 20 May 1959, and the very last military aircraft being retired from service in New Zealand in March 1967.

The Hythe was a modification of the BOAC-operated Sunderland III with a more refined passenger interior. The Sandringham featured the smoother nose contours of the S.26 'G-Class', and a twenty-four-seat passenger interior. With the exception of the first aircraft, the

Sandringham was powered by 1,200hp Twin Wasp engines, replacing the Pegasus of the Sunderland/Hythe. The first Sandringham I ML788/G-AGKX was converted at Rochester, this aircraft being launched for the first time on 28 November 1945. Production included nine 'Plymouth class' Sandringham 5, and three 'Bermuda class' Sandringham 7 for BOAC, with others for export customers in Uruguay, Argentina, Norway and New Zealand.

The Solent was the civil equivalent of the Seaford and was characterised by its tall fin with sweeping dorsal extension. Twelve Solent 2 were ordered for BOAC and built at Rochester, six Solent 3 were converted from RAF Seaford aircraft, and four Solent 4 were built in Belfast. The first Solent G-AHIL *Salisbury* flew on 11 November 1946.

On 15 September 1947, the second Short Shetland prototype G-AGVD was launched at Rochester, this being referred to at the time as the last flying boat launch from Rochester prior to the transfer to Belfast. Some seven months later, however, in April 1948, *The Aeroplane* published a photograph entitled: 'END OF AN ERA – Launching the last Short Solent, and the last aircraft to be built at Rochester.' This aircraft, G-AHIY, was actually the last Solent 2 for BOAC, and was launched on 8 April 1948. Further Solent 3 and Solent 4 aircraft were constructed at Belfast.

Two Short Shetland were built, DX166 and G-AGVD, the type being a collaborative effort between Shorts and Saunders-Roe. The main Shetland flight test activity was undertaken at Kingsnorth.

After the Second World War, Shorts found it difficult to sell flying boats in the face of increasing competition from conventional transport aircraft supplied from the USA. An air of the rearguard action crept into their advertising, as illustrated by the following examples from early 1947: First a quote from *The Times* concerning flying boats – 'the British public likes them. They are roomy and clean and do not have to employ airfields which are hot and dusty in summer, and cold and muddy in winter.' Also: 'To my mind, the most important factors in air travel are real comfort and restfulness, and time-tables designed for convenience rather than speed. That is why I travel by flying boat when I possibly can.' Passengers find 'it's fun to fly by flying boat'.

The Government, through the Minister of Aircraft Production, took control of **Short Brothers (Rochester & Bedford) Ltd** in March 1943, Oswald Short having resigned from the chairmanship of the company in January. Sir Arthur Gouge left the company on 23 March as it passed into Government control; Gouge subsequently joined Saunders-Roe Ltd with a number of other staff from Shorts. In 1947, the Harland & Wolff shareholding in **Short & Harland Ltd** was bought out by the Government and the company name was changed to **Short Brothers & Harland Ltd** in November 1947. The operations at Rochester, for both landplane and flying boat manufacture, were then progressively transferred to Belfast.

The penultimate landplane prototype to be built by Shorts and flown from the airfield at Rochester was the first Short Sturgeon RK787, which was flown on 7 June 1946. Four of the five Sturgeon TT.3 conversions (from TT.2) were also carried out at Rochester. The final Shorts design to be built and flown at Rochester was the sole Short Nimbus low-wing gull-wing glider BGA470, which was first flown on 18 January 1947.

The **Batchelor** Monoplane was built at Rochester in 1910 and featured wings and tail that resembled those of a Blériot, but with the pilot sitting underneath the centre section in the manner of a Demoiselle.

Short Brothers constructed the **Gnosspelius** Gull to the design of Major O.T. Gnosspelius, head of Short's experimental department, for the 1923 Lympne motor glider competition. Two were built, one of which subsequently flew with the Newcastle Aero Club at Cramlington. The Gull was constructed entirely from wood, the fuselage being of notably clean monocoque construction. A single engine mounted in the centre fuselage drove twin pusher propellers mounted behind the wing trailing edge. The wing itself was shoulder-mounted with pronounced taper achieved by the swept-back leading edge of the outer wing sections. The first Gull, G-EBGN, was flown at Lympne on 26 May 1923.

Kent Alloys Ltd of Temple Manor Works, Rochester was set up by Short Brothers (Rochester & Bedford) Ltd in March 1939. The company provided castings and other components for the Mosquito, Stirling and Lancaster.

Percival Aircraft Ltd. The Proctor 6 floatplane X1/CF-EHF for the Hudson Bay Co. was tested from the Medway in June 1946.

Pobjoy Airmotors & Aircraft Ltd designed and built the Pobjoy Pirate which was powered by a 90hp Pobjoy Niagara III and bore some resemblance to a radial engined Leopard Moth. The aircraft was registered G-ADEY, but not painted as such. Sadly, it proved to be very unsuccessful, and was only flown on three occasions. Its first flight, piloted by John Lankester Parker of Short Brothers, was on 25 June 1935, and the design was effectively abandoned by mid-July. Harold Boultbee, who had previously been responsible for the Civilian Coupé, designed the Pirate.

Pobjoy undertook licensed production of the Short Scion II, building six of the type from 1936. Short Brothers acquired a major shareholding in Pobjoy Airmotors and Aircraft during 1938, effectively absorbing them into Short Brothers (Rochester and Bedford) Ltd.

Portsmouth Aviation Ltd was allocated space in the Short factory at Rochester to establish a production line for the Aerocar. These plans did not, however come to fruition.

Sevenoaks

Prince Serge **de Bolotoff** built an attractive biplane in the grounds of Combe Bank House at Sundridge. The aircraft was illustrated in the 1919 edition of *Jane's All the World's Aircraft*, but little else is known of it. The machine was registered G-EAKC, although photographs show it marked as 'SDEB14'. De Bolotoff & Co. had a shed at Brooklands in May 1913, in which they were constructing a large tandem triplane. This was not successful. Prince de Bolotoff's address in 1913 was Reigate Priory, Reigate.

Worsell Monoplane. Ord-Hume's meticulous research has uncovered the story of this parasol monoplane constructed from the remains of the Boulton & Paul P.9 G-EAWS, by Mr Tom Worsell. Unfortunately, the builder attempted to fly his creation using the limited power available from a 10hp Singer car engine. A Mr Anckhorn witnessed a single attempted flight, at the end of which the aircraft ran into a ditch and overturned.

Surrey

Addlestone

Louis Blériot Aeronautics, and its successors including **The Air Navigation & Engineering Co. Ltd (ANEC)**, had works at Addlestone and made use of Brooklands for test flying. This company was founded by Blériot as the **Blériot & SPAD Manufacturing Co.** Blériot & SPAD constructed 100 Avro 504A, orders for a further fifty being cancelled. In late September 1915, *Flight* reported that Blériot were building Avro machines at Brooklands.

The Blériot & SPAD concern (possibly in the guise of the Air Navigation Co., see below) also built 100 SPAD S.VII, and more than 300 SE5A. Serial numbers were allocated to 560 SE5A from Blériot & SPAD Manufacturing Co., with the number actually delivered being variously quoted as between 330 and 360 aircraft. The main source of this discrepancy seems to be a batch of 200 aircraft from serial B1 onward. In some references these aircraft are credited to Martinsyde, although Bruce Robertson allocates them to the **Air Navigation Co. Ltd**. If this attribution were correct, a figure closer to 560 would seem appropriate.

The company announced a change of name to **Air & Navigation Co.** in May 1917, but this appears not to have been implemented. A further announcement indicated that **L. Blériot Aeronautics** would be known as **The Air Navigation Co. Ltd,** from 1 January 1918. To further confuse the chronology, the Air Navigation Co. Ltd was actually registered as early as November 1916, with the considerable capital of £240,000, 'acquiring the business of L. Blériot Aeronautics' – it seems to have elected to continue trading under the L. Blériot name. Another clearly linked firm, **Blériot Manufacturing Aircraft Company** paid just over 15s in the pound in liquidation in January 1919.

The Air Navigation Co. Ltd was contracted to build the Sopwith TF2 Salamander 'trench fighter', reportedly delivering 107 aircraft from an order for 150, the first being F7801. Other sources, notably *Sopwith – The Man and His Aircraft*, state that this contract was cancelled. In

The Handasyde H.2 monoplane was built by the Air Navigation & Engineering Co. Ltd (ANEC) at Addlestone and flown at Brooklands. (Brooklands Museum Trust)

August 1918, it was announced that as from 5 August 1919, the **Air Navigation Co. Ltd** would change its style to **The Air Navigation & Engineering Co. Ltd.** (ANEC).

ANEC built the Handasyde glider, which took part in the Itford Hill trials, the machine having been designed by a famous triumvirate – Handasyde, Raynham and Camm of the Handasyde Aircraft Co. (see Woking). ANEC also constructed the Handasyde monoplane for the 1923 motor glider competition and the unsuccessful Handasyde H.2 monoplane, which flew at Brooklands on 9 December 1922. For details of these types, see Woking.

ANEC designed and built their own successful series of ultralights for the 1923, 1924 and 1926 motor glider and light aircraft competitions. The ANEC I and II motor gliders were designed by W.S. Shackleton, who subsequently moved to William Beardmore & Co. Ltd at Dalmuir. ANEC I G-EBHR was first flown on 21 August 1923 at Brooklands. The two-seat ANEC II, G-EBJO, was quite long lived, flying from 1924 until 1937, and was restored to flying condition in 2004 by the Shuttleworth Trust at Old Warden. The ANEC IV Missel Thrush G-EBPI was a particularly graceful I-strutted biplane, designed for the 1926 Light Aeroplane Competition. Like the Hawker Cygnet, it featured unusually high aspect ratio wings for a biplane, with a large gap to minimise biplane interference.

In 1926 ANEC constructed three ANEC III biplanes for use in Australia. The ANEC III was a large single-engine biplane of unequal span powered by a Rolls-Royce Eagle. The pilot sat in an open cockpit ahead of the upper wing centre section, and a passenger cabin filled the gap between the upper and lower wings. The first aircraft was flown at Brooklands on 23 March 1926 and took Australian marks as G-AUEZ.

In Australia two of the aircraft were re-engined with the 485hp Jaguar radial, and were renamed Larkin Lascowl. The third aircraft VH-UGF *Love Bird* was used in May 1930 for a 10,000-mile survey flight from Canberra to the interior of Australia including Alice Springs and Ayers Rock, where this aircraft was the first to make a landing.

The Alula-winged **Martinsyde** Semiquaver G-EAPX was assembled in the Blériot works at Addlestone, before being subjected to flight-testing at Northolt in 1921. The Blériot & SPAD/Air Navigation Co. Ltd/ANEC buildings at Addlestone were later used as a Plessey factory.

The Alula-winged Martinsyde Semiquaver G-EAPX was assembled in the Blériot works at Addlestone, before being subjected to flight-testing at Northolt in 1921. (Ken Ellis collection)

Lang Propeller Ltd – probably the largest First World War propeller supplier – supplied huge numbers of propellers from their Riverside Works. **Lang, Garnett & Co.** were already established propeller manufacturers at Riverside Works by 1912, advertising as the largest works devoted to propeller manufacture in the country. To give some idea of the scale of their activity, they delivered 15,000 propellers in 1918.

A November 1917 advertisement read: 'Lang Propellers – British Manufacture throughout; have been used by all the leading aviators with unqualified success during the last three years; standard propellers kept in stock, special types can be delivered in a few days.' C.G. Grey, the editor of *The Aeroplane*, paid a compliment to the firm when in 1936 he wrote: 'Mr A. Dashwood Lang, a Brooklands pioneer of 1910 made the name of the Lang Propeller as famous before and during the 1914-18 War as, in another line, Guinness or Bass.'

The **Aeronautical Corporation of Great Britain Ltd** (Aeronca) purchased Lang Propeller Ltd in 1936. The Lang Riverside Works were burnt down in 1942.

Brooklands and Weybridge

Although Farnborough and Eastchurch can respectively claim to be the birthplace of British aviation, and of British aircraft manufacture, there can be little doubt that Brooklands was the cradle for the developing child. So many pioneers and companies have been active at Brooklands that a purely alphabetical presentation has been adopted. The reader should note, however, the Sopwith/Hawker and Vickers-Armstrongs/British Aircraft Corporation linkages, which are reflected in this entry for Brooklands.

The motor racing circuit at Brooklands, with its famous banking, was constructed over a period of nine months in 1907. Brooklands was just as instrumental in the development of British motor racing as it was in pioneer flying, flight instruction and aircraft construction.

ABC Motors Ltd of Walton on Thames built the single ABC Robin G-AAID, which was flown at Brooklands from June 1929 until it was scrapped in 1932. The Robin was a very small high-wing single-seat cabin monoplane with folding wings designed around the ABC Scorpion II engine. The designer was by Tony Fletcher (previously of Martinsyde, London & Provincial, Whitehead, and Central Aircraft) who had earlier been responsible for the Central Aircraft Centaur. *The Aeroplane* unkindly suggested that the black-painted fuselage

Hawker Hurricane Mk.XII G-HURR at Farnborough. This aircraft was rebuilt by Autokraft Ltd at Brooklands. (Author)

looked 'like a railway sleeper'. This view was not universally held, however, with Ord-Hume describing the Robin as 'delightful'. The Robin had a fuselage length of only 17ft 7in and a span of 25ft 4in.

Aero Construction Co. – see Billing.

ANEC – The Air Navigation and Engineering Co. Ltd: This company, which had its origins in the **Blériot & SPAD Manufacturing Co.**, built a number of light aircraft at Addlestone which were tested at Brooklands. The first flight of the ANEC I motor glider G-EBHR was made at Brooklands on 21 August 1923. The first ANEC III (later G-AUEZ) was flown at Brooklands on 23 March 1926. For further information concerning the company and its activities, refer to the entry for Addlestone.

The pioneer pilot **H.J.D. Astley** flew from Brooklands, gaining his Royal Aero Club Certificate (No. 48) on a Sommer biplane. His first aircraft was the Astley monoplane, which was built in Willesden in 1909. The first machine was used as the basis of a further monoplane (Astley No. 2), which, while it was tested at Brooklands for a period from late 1910, was also unsuccessful. Astley was an Old Etonian and was the first Old Boy to land his aeroplane on the Eton playing fields. This pilot was closely associated with the **Universal Aviation** *Birdling* monoplane, of 1911, which was visually very similar to the Blériot. In June 1911, Astley attempted to fly the *Birdling* at the first flying meeting in Wales, but hit a wall when trying to take off from a recreation ground. In September 1911 he was flying the *Big Bat*, a two-seat Blériot (also flown by Gibbs and Gilmour) at Brooklands. Later, Astley flew REP and Blériot monoplanes, carrying out many cross-country flights, before being killed at Belfast on 12 September 1912.

Autokraft Ltd carried out the rebuild of Hawker Hurricane Mk XII BE417/G-HURR at Brooklands. After its rebuild, the aircraft was first flown at Blackbushe on 14 January 1996. The company was also working on the restoration of two Hawker Tempest II: MW763 and MW401. Autokraft subsequently entered receivership, with the two ex-Indian Air Force Tempest II aircraft being sold.

A.V. Roe moved his Roe I Biplane to Brooklands in September 1907 after its completion at his brother's house in Putney. Early flight-testing in 1907 was unsuccessful, but on 8 June 1908 Roe made initial hops of 75-150 feet (although these were not recognised by the Royal Aero Club). Roe had been given orders to quit Brooklands in May 1908, but was allowed to stay after he moved his shed and restricted his experimental activities. He was, however, given his final marching orders later in 1908, and had to return to his brother's stables at Putney to construct a new machine, the Roe I triplane, which was tested at Lea Marshes.

A.V. Roe was subsequently invited back to Brooklands to continue testing from 1 March 1910, initially flying the Roe I triplane and the Roe II triplane *Mercury*. By this time his aircraft were being constructed at Manchester (in the Bullseye Braces Factory at Brownsfield Mills, owned by his brother, H.V. Roe). On his return to Brooklands, Roe was somewhat ambitiously advertising: 'Aeroplanes from £450, 5-mile flight guaranteed'. A.V. Roe set up a flying school, which was subsequently moved to Shoreham as Brooklands rapidly became crowded. The first Roe III triplane flew at Brooklands on 24 June 1910, made a flight of eleven minutes on 4 July and was making flights of up to twenty-five minutes by 9 July 1910. Four Roe III were built and the first was still in use eleven months after its first flight. The Roe IV, last of the early Roe triplane designs, was operated at Brooklands for about eleven months from September 1910, being employed by the Avro Flying School.

The A.V. Roe Type D, which was essentially a biplane version of the Roe IV, was flown at Brooklands on 1 April 1911. The Type D was a significant step forward; six were built, and three of them remained in use at the Avro School (Brighton) Ltd as late as May 1914. A.V. Roe built a biplane to the order of J.R. Duigan in early 1912 that is significant in its adoption

Above: *An imposing mounted guard surrounds this Avro 500.* (BAE SYSTEMS plc)

Left: *Of startling appearance for its day, with a streamlined fuselage and enclosed cabin, the Type F had a brief flying career and can only be regarded as being ahead of its time.* (Brooklands Museum Trust)

of a rectangular fuselage section, and the characteristic central skid undercarriage, which became almost a company trademark on the Avro 504. By April 1912 the aircraft was flying successfully, its best flight being of one hour at 400–600ft altitude on 30 April 1912. The aircraft was subsequently rebuilt as a seaplane and flown by the Lakes Flying School at Windermere from June 1912.

The A.V. Roe Military Biplane (Type E) first flew at Brooklands on 3 March 1912 (also reported as 14 March 1912). This type was regarded by many (including A.V. Roe) as establishing the supremacy of the 'conventional' tractor biplane configuration. The Type E prototype joined the school fleet at Shoreham. A production version of the Type E with the Gnome engine (first flown at Brooklands on 8 May 1912) was the first Avro type to receive a government order, as the Avro 500. A total of twenty-one Avro 500 were built, and, for its day, the type must be regarded as a serious production machine.

Alongside the development of the Avro 500, A.V. Roe was also experimenting with the monoplane, the result being the advanced-looking Avro Type F, which featured a streamlined aerofoil shaped fuselage, and a totally enclosed cabin. The Avro F first flew on 1 May 1912 but was very little flown before being damaged on 25 May, and again in an accident on 13 September 1912, after which it was not flown again.

The hugely successful Avro 504 first flew at Brooklands in 1913 (the dates given vary, but 18 September 1913 is widely quoted) and was an instant success, particularly once ailerons had replaced the wing warping initially used. The Avro 504 captured a British altitude record of 14,420ft on 10 February 1914. The Avro 504 was an outstanding machine which was produced in large numbers and saw many years of service for military training and, in the inter-war years, civilian joy-riding. The Avro 504 brought large-scale production to the Manchester factories of A.V. Roe & Co. Ltd (the manufacturing centre for the company throughout its history).

C. Howard Pixton, Wilfred Parke, Ronald Kemp and Fred Raynham carried out much of the early test-flying for A.V. Roe. Kemp and Raynham later collaborated in setting up an air survey company – Kemp's Air Surveys Ltd. The author well remembers that the descendant of this company, Kemp's Aerial Surveys Ltd, was one of the last commercial users of the Avro Anson, operating five aircraft out of Thruxton until the company entered liquidation in 1972.

The **Eardley Billing** biplane of 1911, also known as the *Oozeley Bird* (sometimes also *Ouseley Bird*), was built from parts of a discarded Voisin. Mr Billing was associated with the Lane Flying School. Mr N.S. Percival was reported to be flying this machine regularly at Brooklands in mid-1911, and the machine was sometimes also referred to as the **Percival** biplane, particularly after its rebuild in late 1911. Thus, in March 1912, the **Aero Construction Co.**, Brooklands were offering instruction on the Percival biplane, which was described as the 'safest, easiest and cheapest machine for learners'. In January 1913, this company gave up trading, offering for sale one Caudron and one Percival tractor biplane.

Blackburn. Mr Robert Blackburn conducted most of his early flying and subsequent aircraft manufacture at Filey, Leeds and Brough in Yorkshire. The Blackburn Flying School operated at Hendon in 1912–13, but flying also took place at Brooklands during 1911. The Type II Mercury monoplane No. 1 crashed at Brooklands on 22 July 1911 and the Type III Mercury monoplane No. 3 was flown for the first time at Brooklands on 25 December 1911.

Also known as the 'Oozeley Bird', this machine was made up from Voisin parts in 1911. It was later rebuilt to become the Percival biplane. (Brooklands Museum Trust)

This dramatic photograph shows the TSR.2 production line at Weybridge. This is one of a number of images in this work that could have been entitled 'what might have been?' (Brooklands Museum Trust)

De Bolotoff & Co. had a shed at Brooklands in May 1913, in which they were constructing a large tandem triplane. This was not successful (see also Sevenoaks, Kent).

British Aircraft Corporation (BAC): Brooklands was the home of the BAC Weybridge Division from February 1960, this becoming the Commercial Aircraft Division from June 1971. This organisation was essentially the successor to Vickers-Armstrongs (Aircraft) Ltd, following its incorporation into BAC. Under BAC, the Weybridge factory was used for the manufacture of the TSR.2 prototypes. Major structural assemblies of the BAC One-Eleven were manufactured at Weybridge for final assembly at Hurn. A similar role was played in the manufacture of Concorde components for final assembly at Filton.

This group was itself incorporated into **British Aerospace** in 1977, transferring to the manufacture of Hawk fuselages, components and assemblies for Airbus wings and other aerostructures work in the 1970s and 1980s. Although the main Weybridge aircraft construction activity has ceased, the company remains present at this historic site in the form of **British Aerospace (now BAE SYSTEMS) Regional Aircraft** Spares and Logistics Centre, 16 Vickers Drive, Brooklands Business Park, Weybridge.

The **British & Colonial Aeroplane Co. Ltd** operated its London Headquarters and Flying School from Hangar 17 at Brooklands. Opened in 1910, this school was, with its partner establishment at Larkhill, undoubtedly the most successful of the pre-war flying schools. In 1911, the Bristol schools taught fifty-six pilots to fly, virtually half the total for the whole United Kingdom. In 1912, the two schools trained a total of ninety-eight pilots, the highest achieved by any other school being just twenty. In 1913 this figure was increased to 117. Up to the outbreak of the First World War, the Bristol schools had trained 309 pilots of a total of 664. Many of the school's students were subsequently to become well known in aviation circles, their influence reaching out through both manufacturers and service aviation for many decades. The machines used were the Bristol Boxkite, and the series of Bristol monoplanes. Further details of these aircraft are given under Filton and Larkhill in Volume 2 of *British Built Aircraft* (South West & Central Southern England).

Brooklands Aviation Ltd was founded at Brooklands in 1928 by Captain Duncan Davis for aircraft repair and overhaul. During the Second World War, the company repaired substantial numbers of Vickers aircraft, particularly at their second facility at Sywell, near Northampton. During the post-war years, the Brooklands-based part of the company (address Beech Hollow, Vale Road, Oatlands Park, Weybridge), was mainly engaged in light-aircraft hire and charter. Significant repair, overhaul and modification activity continued at Sywell, including, for example, Mosquito target tug conversions and support work on the Vickers Varsity.

In August 1913, the **Champel** Biplane was at Brooklands. Its United Kingdom agents were Messrs Ducrocq and Lawford.

The **Collyer-Lang** monoplane was flying at Brooklands in late 1910. The type was a high-wing monoplane with a pusher propeller rotating between twin tail booms, which had virtually no vertical fin surfaces. Its performance was erratic, and the type was nicknamed 'The Hellhound'!

The **Coventry Ordnance Works**. After the Warwick Wright company was taken over by Coventry Ordnance Works, that company used the Wright shed (No. 32) at Brooklands to erect their entry for the 1912 Military Trials. Initial test-flying was carried out by T.O.M. Sopwith and F.P. Raynham. The type was flying from April 1912, and showed great lifting capacity; Sopwith flew it with two additional passengers seated on the lower wing, either side of the fuselage. Not apparent in all photographs is the unusual tail, with twin fins and rudders on either side of the fuselage, in line with the longerons of the untapered rear fuselage. Some

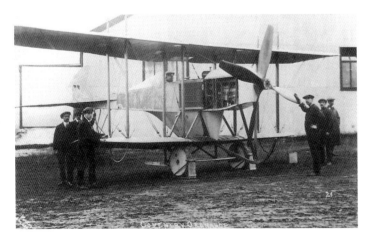

The Coventry Ordnance Works biplane No. 11 at the 1912 Military Trials. This, the second machine for the trials, is distinguished by its liquid-cooled engine and single fin and rudder. (Treadwell/Wood)

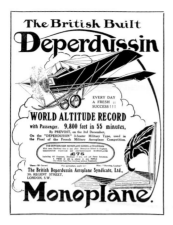

idea of the characteristics of early aircraft engines can be gleaned from the oil capacity of twenty-two gallons in proportion to fifty gallons of fuel.

The **Deperdussin British Aviation School** was formed in July 1911 and, in March 1912, was advertising: 'Our Brooklands School is the safest and best organised monoplane school in England.' In the same month, it also advertised 'thorough instruction in flying by competent staff; special terms to Army and Navy officers'.'This firm was an offshoot of **The British Deperdussin Aeroplane Syndicate** and **The British Deperdussin Co. Ltd**.

The **DFW German Aircraft Works** was set up in 1914, an announcement made in May 1914 stating: 'Flying at Brooklands aerodrome, Offices Streatham Hill, Works under construction to start manufacture at Richmond from July 1914.' The company occupied hangar No. 18 at Brooklands. The DFW company negotiated a production licence with Beardmore, who also built its Austro-Daimler engine. The first example in Britain, imported by E. Cecil Kny, first flew at Brooklands in December 1913. The outbreak of the First World War brought these plans to an abrupt end.

DW Aircraft Co.: The racing pilot Dudley Watt was responsible for two aircraft designs, the DW1 and DW2. One of his racing mounts was the Sopwith Scooter, a parasol monoplane based on a Sopwith Camel fuselage. The Scooter K135/G-EACZ was first flown in June 1918, and was being raced by Dudley Watt in the summer of 1926.

The Dudley Watt DW1 G-EBOG was an SE5A purchased from ADC Ltd and modified at Brooklands for racing purposes. The chief change was to the engine, with a 300hp Hispano-Suiza replacing the normal 200hp Wolseley Viper. As late as May 1930, the company was advertising its SE5A interests as follows: 'DW Aircraft Co., Brooklands Aerodrome, have for sale several SE5A reasonable figure, new condition with C of A. Storage, overhauls, reconditioning, lowest terms.'

The single DW2 G-AAWK was a two-seat biplane powered by a Cirrus III, designed by K.N. Pearson (who also designed the Glenny & Henderson Gadfly and the Pickering Pearson KP2). G-AAWK was first flown at Brooklands in mid-May 1930. The DW2 featured a 38ft span and the generous wing area of 350sq. ft. As a result, the wing loading was only 4.25lb/sq. ft and the aircraft had a very low stalling speed. See also Ford, West Sussex.

The Flanders F.4 was flown in mid-1912. Four were purchased by the RFC but their use was curtailed by the banning of monoplane flying by that service. (Brooklands Museum Trust)

L. Howard Flanders Ltd, of Hangar 33, Brooklands, was registered in February 1912. In March 1912, the company was advertising: 'FLANDERS SCHOOL. – Tuition on Monoplane with dual control.' R.L. Howard Flanders built a series of clean tapered wing monoplanes, which were tested at Brooklands. The first design to be flown was the Flanders F.2, which first flew on 8 August 1911 (also reported as 31 July 1911). This aircraft was modified as a two-seater in October 1911 to become the Flanders F.3. This type continued to fly for several months before crashing fatally on 15 May 1912.

Flight-testing was taken over by F.P. Raynham following the death of Mr Flanders' friend and test pilot Mr E.V.B. Fisher in the Flanders F.3. The next design was the Flanders F.4 monoplane, which was flown for the first time at Brooklands on 7 July 1912. The Flanders F.4 was produced for the RFC who purchased four examples. Although it was extremely successful, use of the type was curtailed by the banning of monoplane flying in the RFC in 1912.

The F.4 was followed by a successful biplane, the Flanders B.2, which was a tandem two-seater with 43ft wing span. The B.2 was initially flown with a 45hp ABC engine at Brooklands on 22 December 1912, eventually succeeding in lifting three occupants on its limited power. Power was progressively increased by the installation of an engine of 60hp and then 70hp. The aircraft flew well, and was purchased by the Admiralty (serial number 918) and used by the RNAS at the start of the First World War. The B.2 had a deep front fuselage, upswept to the propeller (like an Aeronca or an REP), an Avro style 'comma' rudder, semi-circular tailplane and triangular elevators. Like a number of other successful designs of the time, the upper wing area was more than twice that of the lower, which had reduced span and chord. A low wing loading (about 2.5lb/sq. ft) contributed to its strong flying performance.

Handley Page Ltd effectively absorbed the Flanders Company in late 1912. From June 1912, Handley Page were advertising themselves as 'sole selling agents for the L. Howard Flanders monoplane'. The Flanders shed (No. 53) was opposite that occupied by Walton & Edwards (see below).

The **Fritz** monoplane, to the design of Fritz Goetze, was built by Messrs **H. & D.J. Oyler & Co.**, London W1, and was photographed at Brooklands in August 1911, the photograph being published in *Flight* magazine. The type featured a Demoiselle configuration with the pilot seated below the wing. Power was provided by a 40hp ENV. It is not known if the machine was successful – certainly it does not feature in later reports of flying at Brooklands.

THE COVENTRY ORDNANCE WORKS, LIMITED,
COVENTRY.

MONOPLANES AND BIPLANES

Specially designed for **NAVAL** and **MILITARY SERVICE**.

Manager, Aeroplane Department :—**HOWARD T. WRIGHT**.

The **Gaskell-Blackburn** biplane was, in part, an assemblage of components from other designs, although reports differ as to its precise origins. The type was a conventional two-bay tractor biplane whose general appearance was reminiscent of the Avro Type E. *British Aircraft Before The Great War* reports that its first flight was made on 2 April 1914, the outbreak of the First World War bringing an end to its trials.

Glenny & Henderson Ltd, Pritchards Yard, Station Rd, West Byfleet. (The company is also listed at York Road, Byfleet, in the catalogue to the 1929 Olympia Exhibition, and the 1929 Schneider Trophy issue of *Flight*.) The Gadfly prototype (G-AAEY) was a single-seat low-wing monoplane powered by an ABC Scorpion. The type first flew in April 1929, and set an altitude record for its class of 9,915ft (3,021m) on 16 May 1929. Designed by K.N. Pearson, three aircraft were built at Byfleet, the Tarrant workshop being used for component manufacture. The last example was fitted with a Salmson radial.

1929 advertising ran: 'The "Gadfly" Scorpion holds the World's Height Record for single-seater light aeroplanes – 3,021 metres, 4th category (under 200 kg). Price with ordinary ailerons £360, price fitted with Pearson rotary ailerons £370.' The Pearson rotary ailerons referred to in this advertisement were first tested on an Avro 548, G-EBAJ. A.P. Glenny provided financial backing to the company, while Henderson was Lt-Col. G.L.P. Henderson of the Henderson School of Flying (see below). Sadly, Lt-Col. Henderson was killed on 21 July 1930 while flying in Junkers F.13 G-AAZK.

Gordon England. E.C. Gordon England flew as a freelance test pilot, testing many different types of aircraft at Larkhill, Brooklands, Shoreham and Cowes including designs built by Weiss, Bristol, Blériot, Cedric Lee, Hanriot, Farman, Wight, Short, Radley-England and A.V. Roe. Mr Gordon England also collaborated with James Radley in the Radley-England Waterplane, tested at Huntingdon and at Shoreham. Mr Gordon England designed the Bristol biplane entries for the 1912 Military Trials and was the general manager of Sage & Co. (at Peterborough) from 1916 to 1919. After a period concentrating on motor car body design, he became the managing director of General Aircraft Ltd, acting in this capacity until 1942.

Hammond. Mr E.V. Hammond built a number of aircraft to his own design, which were tested at Brooklands. This activity began in 1910 and the configurations tested included a biplane (1910), a triplane of generally boxkite configuration (February 1911) and a tractor monoplane of mid-1913. The triplane had twin tractor propellers, belt-driven at mid-span, and was probably the most practical of the designs. None of these designs is thought to have been successful.

The **Handley Page Ltd** flying school operated at Brooklands, before moving to Hendon.

Hanriot (England) Ltd, Brooklands Aerodrome (managed by Ducrocq) advertised that 'Hanriot monoplanes are now being built in England'. The first order placed with **Hewlett & Blondeau** in April 1912 was for a Hanriot monoplane to be supplied to Hanriot (England) Ltd.

Hawker (including **H.G. Hawker Engineering Co. Ltd**, and **Hawker Aircraft Ltd**). Harry Hawker, the test pilot for T.O.M. Sopwith, learned to fly at Brooklands, gaining Aero

Club certificate number 297 on 17 September 1912 flying a Farman biplane of the Sopwith School. Hawker then became one of the principal test pilots for the Sopwith Aviation Co. Ltd, continuing in this role throughout the First World War. He made a major contribution to the success of Sopwith's famous line of fighter aircraft and also contributed to the company's reputation with a series of spectacular record-breaking flights in their early aircraft.

After the establishment of H.G. Hawker Engineering Co. Ltd, which was registered on 15 November 1920 as a successor to the **Sopwith Aviation & Engineering Co. Ltd**, the company followed the practice of its forbear in that the majority of its aircraft were built at Kingston, and test-flown at Brooklands. Some of the Hawker first flights made at Brooklands are summarised below in chronological order:

Type	Serial	Date	Comments
Duiker	J6918	July 1923	Parasol monoplane. Single example only.
Woodcock	J6987	1923	Woodcock I, production Woodcock II flown early 1924. Sixty-four built by Hawker, together with fifteen of the similar Danecock, twelve of which were constructed by the Royal Danish Navy Dockyard factory at Copenhagen.
Heron	J6989	early 1925	Essentially a metal-structure Woodcock with Jupiter VI.
Danecock	No 151	15 December 1925	Fifteen built, twelve in Denmark.
Horsley	J7511	1925	Medium day bomber also used for engine trials. 138, all built by Hawker, see additional comments below.
Hornbill	J7782	June 1926	One aircraft only.
Hawfinch	J8776	March 1927	To F.9/26, losing to Bulldog.
Hart	J9052	June 1928	Two-seat day bomber, extensively developed, see below. Also used as engine test bed. 1,042 built, of which Hawker constructed 246. The Hart was also built under contract by Sir W.G. Armstrong Whitworth Aircraft Ltd (456), Gloster Aircraft Co. Ltd (seventy-two) and Vickers (Aviation) Ltd (226), together with forty-two aircraft under licence at Trollhäten, Sweden.
F.20/27	J9123	August 1928	Fury I progenitor. Powered by Jupiter VII and later Mercury VI.
Tomtit	J9772 (later)	November 1928	Trainer for the RAF and civil use – prototype, five civil machines, twenty-four RAF aircraft, two aircraft for the RCAF, and four aircraft for the RNZAF – total thirty-six aircraft. These figures are given by F.K. Mason in *Hawker Aircraft since 1920*, but he also cites a production total of forty-five.
Hornet	J9682	April 1929	Effectively prototype Fury I with Rolls-Royce F.XIS. Advertised in May 1930 as 'The fighter which has set a new standard'.

Type	Serial	Date	Comments
Fury I	K1926	25 March 1931	Single-seat fighter. First production with Kestrel IIS. 146 fighter aircraft which, although bearing a clear family resemblance to the Hart and its derivatives, is distinguished by its single-seat configuration.
Nimrod	S1577	14 October 1931	Naval single-seat fighter similar to Fury in concept. Eighty-seven built.
Audax	K1438 (prototype)	February 1931	Two-seat army co-operation aircraft. 718 built, 265 by Hawker, plus A.V. Roe & Co. Ltd (244), Bristol Aeroplane Co.Ltd (141), Gloster Aircraft Co. Ltd (twenty-five) and Westland Aircraft Ltd (forty-three).
	K1995 (first production)	29 December 1931	
Osprey	S1677	from 1931	Two-seat folding-wing naval version of Hart to O.22/26. Hart prototype J9052 used for development (from 1930). 144 built, 136 by Hawker, and eight at Trollhäten, Sweden.
Hart Trainer	K1996	20 April 1932	

Left: *Hawker Tomtit G-ABAX being displayed at Brooklands by P.W.S. Bullman for publicity purposes. This aircraft is one of three owned by Wolseley Motors Ltd and fitted with Wolseley A.R. 9 engines for the 1935 King's Cup air race. (via* J.S. Smith)

Below: *S1581/G-BWWK is a recently restored Nimrod naval fighter, seen here flying from its Duxford base.* (James Goggin)

Type	Serial	Date	Comments
Demon	K2842	10 February 1933	First production. Two-seat fighter derived from Hart. 298 built, 192 by Hawker, the remainder by Boulton Paul Aircraft Ltd, fifty-nine at Norwich, and forty-seven at Wolverhampton.
Hart (Sweden)	1301	6 January 1934	Pegasus 1M2. Four built by Hawker, followed by forty-two under licence in Sweden.
Hardy	K3013	7 September 1934	Hart derivative for tropical policing work.
Hartbees	803	28 June 1935	Audax development for SAAF; four were built by Hawker, and a further sixty-five by Roberts Heights Artillery and Aircraft Depot, Zwartkop, Pretoria.
Hind	K2915	12 September 1934	Interim day bomber to replace Hart. First production aircraft K4636 flew exactly one year later. 592 built, all by Hawker.
Hurricane	K5083 (prototype)	6 November 1935	The most numerous fighter aircraft used during Battle of Britain. A total of 14,553 were built,

Left: *The Hart Trainer prototype K1996 at Brooklands. This aircraft made its first flight on 20 April 1932.* (BAE SYSTEMS plc)

Below: *K4636 is the first production Hawker Hind. General Aircraft Ltd at Hanworth subsequently converted this aircraft to become a Hind Trainer.* (BAE SYSTEMS plc)

Hurricane production proceeds apace at Brooklands. (Ken Ellis Collection)

Type	Serial	Date	Comments
	L1547 (production)	12 October 1937	10,030 by Hawker, together with UK production by Austin Motor Co. Ltd (300), Avions Fairey (two), and Gloster Aircraft Co. Ltd (2,750). The Canadian Car and Foundry Corporation built 1,451 in Canada. The Hurricane was the most successful aircraft in the Battle of Britain in terms of enemy aircraft destroyed. Other production totals can also be found.
Fury II	K7263	3 December 1936	First production. 118 built, forty-three by Hawker and seventy-five by General Aircraft Ltd.
Hector	K3719	14 February 1936	Audax replacement. 179, one only by Hawker, and the remainder by Westland Aircraft Ltd.
Henley	K5115	10 March 1937	202, all but two built by Gloster Aircraft Co. Ltd for use as target tugs. The prototype was used as a test bed for the Vulture engine.
Hotspur	K8309	14 June 1938	Defiant competitor, one only, used by RAE for trials.

Horsley engine test activity involved many engine types, chief among these being the Armstrong Siddeley Leopard, Junkers Jumo, Rolls-Royce Condor, Eagle, Buzzard, H.10 and P.V.12 (Merlin), and the Napier Lion.

The Hart was an outstanding design, produced in many variants. Developments included the Demon, Audax, Osprey, Nimrod, Hind, Hardy, Hector and Fury. From 1931 onward, Hart (and Hart variant) production was extensively contracted out – halving its price in the process, much to Hawker's anguish. Including all their variants, the Hart and Fury accounted for a total production run of nearly 3,300 aircraft. The Hart was also extensively used for engine testing, examples being host to various versions of the Napier Dagger, Bristol Perseus, Mercury, Pegasus and Jupiter, and the Rolls-Royce PV12 and Merlin.

The fantastically elegant Hornet and Fury are, for many, the epitome of the fighter biplane. Renown for their excellent handling, they also had an exceptional climb rate. The Fury II could climb to 15,000ft in 5 min 49 sec, with a climb rate at the top of the climb of 1,910ft/min. This remarkable performance was only marginally inferior to that of the first production models of the Spitfire. The Fury was exported with a variety of engine types to Yugoslavia, Norway, Persia, Portugal and Spain. This trend was also followed by the Audax, exported with various engine types to Persia, Iraq and Canada.

The Hind was highly successful, being third only to the Hart and Audax in production numbers, a total of 592 being built. Export successes for the Hind included sales to Switzerland (one), Portugal (four), Yugoslavia (three), Persia (thirty-five), Afghanistan (twenty, twelve of which were transferred from RAF), Latvia (three), and Ireland (six).

Hurricane production was initially established at Kingston with flight-test at Brooklands, and parallel production lines were set up at Langley from 1939; at Gloster Aircraft Company at Hucclecote also from 1939; with Austin Motors in Birmingham from 1940; and in Canada. Production at Brooklands continued until August 1942.

Henderson School of Flying. The Henderson HSF.1 G-EBVF was built specifically for joy-riding in 1928. The type is stated by A.J. Jackson to have been 'built in a shed near Byfleet Station', the company address being Pritchards Yard, Station Road, West Byfleet (which was also used by Glenny & Henderson Ltd, see above). The HSF.1 was a six seat low wing aircraft with twin tailbooms, a 160hp Beardmore pusher engine and 51ft wing span. The aircraft was first flown at Brooklands on 27 April 1929. It was apparently popular with the joy-riding public, although a modern passenger might have found the large (not to say bath-like) open cockpit a trifle insecure. A glasshouse-like cockpit enclosure was swiftly fitted, but the type had only a brief career before being scrapped in 1930.

The Henderson School of Flying built up an SE5A G-EBTK from spare parts purchased from the Aircraft Disposal Company Ltd. Six Avro 548 were also constructed from spares. The company used a fleet totalling nine Avro 548, some of these aircraft passing to the Henderson School's successor, the Brooklands School of Flying.

The **Hewlett & Blondeau** flying school was advertising in July 1911 that 'Exhibition and passenger flights can be arranged anywhere in England'. The school used Farman-type biplanes of their own manufacture, and three additional machines were built for the Vickers School. Mrs Hilda Hewlett, wife of the novelist Maurice Hewlett, was the first female pilot to obtain a Royal Aero Club Certificate (No. 122, in August 1911, flying a Henri Farman), and is said (in *The Aeroplane*, October 1917) to have founded the first flying school at Brooklands. In November 1911, Mrs Hewlett was teaching her son Francis to fly, he successfully passing his certificate on 9 November 1911. T.O.M. Sopwith had his first flight in a powered aeroplane in a Farman of the Hewlett & Blondeau School. Hewlett & Blondeau manufactured aircraft before and during the First World War, with premises in Battersea, later moving to Leagrave near Luton.

In December 1912, Hewlett and Blondeau were constructing three Hanriot monoplanes at Battersea under contract to Hanriot. In February 1913, the company was advertising 'Aeroplanes of any description from customers' designs'. Ten different types of aircraft were built at Battersea, the company building the Dyott 1913 monoplane, and later the BE2A,

BE2C and other types. During 1914 the company moved to a new factory at Leagrave near Luton, Bedfordshire to expand production capacity. In April 1914, the company **Hewlett & Blondeau Ltd** was formed to carry on the business.

Holle Varioplane: The Holle Varioplane of 1917 was one of a number of experimental aircraft built to test the bird-like Alula/Holle wing form. Related companies include **The Varioplane Co. Ltd** and **The Commercial Aeroplane Wing Syndicate Ltd**. Operations were conducted at Brooklands, Sherburn-in-Elmet, Northolt and Addlestone and the companies had offices in the City of London.

Humber Ltd of Coventry built a number of monoplanes and one biplane between 1910 and 1912. Flying took place at Brooklands, with the company occupying two sheds from early 1910. The first monoplane was tested in France from January 1910 and was essentially a Blériot variant powered by an engine of Humber design. This machine was flown briefly at Brooklands in mid-1910.

The second machine also resembled a Blériot with a modified undercarriage and was flying at Brooklands in May 1910. *British Aircraft Before The Great War* describes two unsuccessful machines (one monoplane and one biplane) before the construction of a biplane of conventional (Farman/Sommer) design, which was flown at Brooklands in October 1910. This machine was also active in May 1911, completing a 1½ hour flight on 7 May 1911. The Humber monoplane was reported to be flying at Brooklands in July 1911. In October of the same year it was being flown by the Pashley brothers. Humber Ltd withdrew from aircraft construction in August 1912.

Humphreys monoplane. Jack Humphreys tested a series of monoplane designs in 1909-1910 at Wivenhoe, Essex and at Colchester without success. His monoplane No. 3 was, however, brought to Brooklands in 1911 and flown successfully. During early taxiing trials on 30 September 1911, the machine became airborne unintentionally at half throttle, despite nose down control being applied. An undignified landing resulted, the engine being switched off, and the undercarriage was damaged. The aircraft flew again on 12 December 1911, again climbing strongly at half throttle. With so much power and lift available, the modified machine proved capable of flying with three persons on board without needing full throttle. In January 1912, the aircraft was flying with revised tail surfaces. Testing continued until the aircraft was destroyed in a ground accident in May 1912.

The **Lane** monoplane of 1910 was essentially a Blériot with a biplane tail, the machine being powered by a NEC (New Engine Co.) four-cylinder, supercharged, two-stroke engine. Cecil Pashley was reported to be flying Lane's monoplane at Brooklands in August 1911. Mr Charles Lane also constructed a glider, a Boxkite biplane and a two-seat monoplane. This led to the formation of **Lane's British Aeroplanes Ltd**, with offices in Central London.

R.F. Macfie (see also Fambridge, Essex) flew the Boxkite-like Empress biplane briefly at Portholme on 12–13 May 1910. He moved to Brooklands, where the aircraft was flying again from 18 June. James Radley took it to the Dunstall Park meeting at the end of the same month. Much modification ensued and by late 1910 the aircraft was flying strongly. In summer 1911, it was reported as still in use at Brooklands. In 1912, it was sold to Herbert Spencer, who rebuilt it as the **Spencer-Stirling** biplane.

Mr Macfie's next type was a tractor biplane intended for the 1911 Circuit of Britain, and known in consequence as the Circuit biplane. This type was flown in July 1911, but does not seem to have been particularly successful.

Martin & Handasyde Ltd/Martinsyde Ltd, had works at Brooklands, and a head office at Woking. The collaboration of G.H. Handasyde and H.P. Martin in the aircraft construction business began in 1908. Initially located at Trinity Works, Camberwell, Martin & Handasyde came to Brooklands in 1909 and were the first concern to occupy permanent quarters there.

Their first successful design was the Martin & Handasyde No. 3 monoplane of May 1910. This machine was clearly influenced by the Antoinette monoplane, which it closely resembled. During the period up to 1914, Martin & Handasyde favoured the monoplane, their designs being characterised by a slim triangular-section fuselage, with cooling radiators mounted on the fuselage sides below the mid-set wing. The power levels of the later machines were quite high (up to 120hp), bestowing very respectable performance. In July 1911 the Martin & Handasyde No. 4B *Dragonfly* was reported to be flying well at Brooklands. In November, the Martin & Handasyde (No. 5) was being flown by T.O.M. Sopwith and was reported as flying excellently and being very fast. This aircraft was flown for the first time on 13 November 1911.

Another of the successful series of Martin & Handasyde monoplanes was the No. 5, which was first flown on 13 November 1911. These aircraft were clean powerful and workmanlike, attributes shared by many of the Martinsyde designs that were to follow. (Brooklands Museum Trust)

Typical of the work contracted to many manufacturers, this is one of fourteen Royal Aircraft Factory BE2C built by Martinsyde Ltd. (Brooklands Museum Trust)

The Martinsyde F.4 was a powerful and fast single-seat fighter powered by a 300hp Hispano-Suiza engine. (Brooklands Museum Trust)

By 1913, the company was advertising: 'The finest monoplane is the Martinsyde. Martin & Handasyde, Brooklands' and 'The "Martinsyde" 120hp two-seater military type monoplane. Fuel for six hours' flight at 85mph. Messrs. Martin & Handasyde, Brooklands Aviation Ground, Weybridge Surrey. Contractors to the War Office.' In 1914, the copy read: 'The Martinsyde – Martin & Handasyde, Brooklands – for the highest quality material, best class workmanship, ease in flying, comfort for passenger, aerodynamic efficiency, sound engineering, intelligent construction.' By March 1915, nine hangars were occupied, covering an area of 35,000 sq. ft.

The use of the two designers' names run together as Martinsyde became the adopted style of the company when it changed its name on 24 March 1915 to **Martinsyde Ltd**. The company built some fourteen BE2C and at least 258 SE5A (from orders for 400 aircraft of this type). Martinsyde were, however, to become famous for their own designs, which were typically clean, powerful biplanes. The first design to attain large-scale production was the Martinsyde S.1, sixty-eight of which were built. Next came the G.100 (and G.102) Elephant. 271 G.100/G.102 were built, the first (serial 4735) flying from Brooklands in August 1915. This type was designed by A.A. (Tony) Fletcher, later of the Central Aircraft Co.

Single examples of the Martinsyde F.1 and F.2 were followed by some six Martinsyde F.3 before the company produced its most famous product, the fast and powerful Martinsyde F.4 Buzzard. This aircraft, powered by a 300hp Hispano-Suiza engine, is said to have been the highest-performance aircraft of the war. It achieved 142mph at sea level, and 134mph at 15,000ft. It could also climb to 20,000ft in less than 20 minutes. A large number of F.4 Buzzards were ordered, Martinsyde delivering some 327 aircraft from orders for more than 600. Sixteen Martinsyde F.4 and three F.6 were allocated British civil registrations. A scaled-down development of the F.4, the 300hp Semiquaver G-EAPX, set a speed record of 161.45mph in March 1920 and won the 1920 Aerial Derby. After the First World War, the company featured the F.4 in its advertising thus: 'Designers of the famous F.4. First from London to Lisbon and from Madrid to Lisbon. Fastest London to Paris.' (The Martinsyde F.4 set a London to Paris speed record of 75 minutes.)

After the First World War, the company produced a new design, the Martinsyde Type A, which made use of F.4 parts. Eight examples of this clean two-bay biplane were built in two

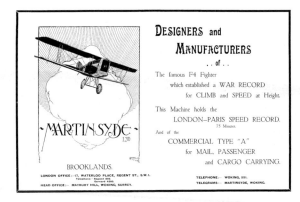 

variants. Other types were also produced in small numbers and like a number of others, the company tried its hand at building motorcycles (the V-twin Martinsyde-Newman). The company suffered a financial collapse due to the imposition of excess profits duty, going into receivership on 2 November 1920. In December 1920, action was taken to wind up the company against the petition of Brighton Motor Coach Works. This was, however, withdrawn following the promise of payment of the debt and the cost of the petition. The company's assets, including airframes in storage, were acquired by **Handley Page Ltd** in April 1923 and transferred to the **Aircraft Disposal Co.** (ADC) at Croydon.

G.H. Handasyde left Martinsyde Ltd in 1920, setting up the **Handasyde Aviation Co.** at Woking, which see for further details.

Neale's Aeroplane Works, Baker St, Weybridge. J.V. Neale built several early types from 1909 ranging from Blériot-style monoplanes to a Boxkite-style biplane. F.P. Raynham, later of Handasyde, flew the Neale 6, which resembled a Blériot with a biplane elevator, the rudder being formed as a longitudinal extension of the rear fuselage. The Neale 7 is described by R. Dallas Brett as 'being an interesting machine with twin rudders between the wing tips designed expressly to avoid infringing the Wright patents'. The Neale 7 was first flown in early August 1910.

Nieuport: Maurice Ducrocq was 'General Agent for the British Empire for Nieuport monoplanes' from 1911. M. Ducrocq was also the UK agent for Viale engines, managed Hanriot (England) Ltd and had the distinction of teaching John Alcock to fly. Alcock was later to be the first to fly the Atlantic non-stop, with Arthur Whitten-Brown.

The **Parsons** biplane was a two-seat design of 1913. The aircraft was designed and built by P.M. Muller and test flown at Brooklands by John Alcock. The machine was a three bay biplane, the extended upper wing tip trailing edges being flexible to improve lateral stability. Initially fitted with a 40hp Aster car engine, it was re-engined with a 70hp Gnome, and proved to fly well. In June 1913, with the original engine, it was flying at heights of up to 2,000ft. At this stage, the 'Parsons pendulum paddle wheel stabiliser' was yet to be fitted. By August, it was being re-engined, but even with its original engine was said to 'climb like a rocket'. The Parsons biplane was advertised for sale (Shed 6, Brooklands) in September 1913.

This Walrus aircraft was photographed at the Weybridge works of Saunders-Roe Ltd, and is one of some 150 of the type to be built there. (Brooklands Museum Trust)

The **Pashley Brothers/Sommer biplane** was a French Farman-type design, used by the Pashley brothers for training. The Sommer biplane was flown by a number of pilots including (during the summer of 1911) C. Pashley and Mr Percival. The Pashley brothers moved to Shoreham in May 1913, where their business thrived.

Perry-Beadle & Co. had works in Twickenham and built a small tractor biplane (the T.1) that was flown at Beaulieu in 1913. This machine was developed into the T.2, which was flown at Brooklands from June 1914. This aircraft was taken into RNAS service with serial number 1322. An unsuccessful flying boat design, the B.3, with a notably clean plywood hull was tested at Windermere in 1915.

The **Radley-Moorhouse** monoplane was a Blériot development, which was flying at Brooklands in May 1912. After initial experiments at Portholme, Huntingdon, this machine was also raced at Hendon. Radley and Moorhouse also experimented with a seaplane design, the Waterplane, at both Huntingdon and Shoreham, West Sussex.

Saunders-Roe Ltd had a factory at Weybridge during the Second World War. This was used for production of the Supermarine Walrus, the last example to be built being HD936, which was delivered at the end of 1943. About 150 Walrus aircraft are reported to have been built at this factory, which also manufactured other components for assembly at Cowes, including wings and floats, and hulls for both the Walrus and the Sea Otter.

Walrus aircraft were flown from Chertsey Mead, between Weybridge and Addlestone, an area of open ground about ¾ mile from the factory. Brooklands was not used, because the factory did not adjoin the airfield, and the few early production aircraft that were flown at Brooklands were found to be prone to damage while en route to Brooklands by road.

Having completed production of the Walrus, the factory was transferred by the Ministry of Aircraft Production to the control of **The Fairey Aviation Co. Ltd**, after which production consisted of Firefly fuselages, wings and tailplanes and the repair and salvage of Swordfish and Barracuda components.

The **Skinner** monoplane was built by **Mulliners Coachworks Ltd** at Vardens Road, Clapham Junction, and was flown at Brooklands in August 1911. The machine was clearly Antoinette-inspired.

The **Sopwith Aviation Co.** (and its successors – **The Sopwith Aviation Co. Ltd** and **The Sopwith Aviation & Engineering Co. Ltd**). T.O.M. Sopwith announced the setting up of a flying school at Brooklands on 1 February 1912, sharing the instruction with F.P. Raynham. After the 1912 Military Trials, T.O.M. Sopwith decided to start aircraft manufacture assisted by Fred Sigrist, his yacht engineer. After initially working at Brooklands, Sopwith moved his Sopwith Aviation Co. works to Kingston upon Thames and set up the arrangements (which were later to be continued by Hawker) whereby aircraft were constructed at Kingston and test-flown at Brooklands. The Sopwith sheds were located at the west end of Brooklands, and were later described in an article by R. Dallas Brett as 'a row of dilapidated wooden hangars backing on to the Byfleet banking'.

One of the main Sopwith test pilots was the Australian Harry Hawker who was to make an unsuccessful attempt to fly the Atlantic in May 1919, and was destined to give his name to the company. Hawker was a brilliant pilot and contributed to the success of Sopwith's designs, before taking over the Company's assets on its voluntary liquidation in 1920. Hawker had experience of designing and building engines and motorcycles in Australia and was initially taken on as a mechanic, before learning to fly at the Sopwith Flying School. Hawker succeeded in flying solo only four days after starting his course of instruction, and gained his certificate on 17 September 1912. He subsequently flew many Sopwith prototypes on their first flights.

The Sopwith Three-Seater biplane was outstandingly successful, and set a number of British altitude records during the summer of 1913. (Brooklands Museum Trust)

Of the company's early machines, the Sopwith-Wright was a modified Burgess-Wright Baby that featured a small protective nacelle for the pilot, modified controls and a 35hp Green engine (later replaced by a 40hp ABC engine). This machine was first flown on 2 May 1912 and was used by H.G. Hawker to win the 1912 British Empire Michelin Trophy with a non-stop flight of 8 hours 23 minutes on 24 October 1912. This remarkable flight was made within seven weeks of Mr Hawker making his first solo flight.

The first Sopwith/Sigrist machine was a hybrid tractor biplane with the wings from a Burgess-Wright, the engine from a Blériot, and a fuselage of their own design. Accurately, if unimaginatively, called *The Hybrid*, it was first flown on 4 July 1912 and sold to The Admiralty on 21 October 1912, receiving serial number 27.

On 31 May 1913 Hawker captured the British altitude record with 11,450ft using a Sopwith Three-Seater tractor biplane. A new record was set on 21 June 1913 of 12,900ft with one passenger, and 10,600ft with two passengers. The same pilot and machine achieved 8,400ft with three passengers on 27 July 1913.

One of the most significant of Sopwith's designs appeared in November 1913, when the Tabloid was first flown at Brooklands. It was, in effect, the forerunner of Sopwith's wartime single-seat fighters. A diminutive tractor biplane, the Tabloid could climb at 1,200ft/min and fly at 92mph. Sopwith gained great publicity when the closely related Sopwith Schneider won the 1914 Schneider Trophy race for Britain at Monaco in April 1914.

Another significant Sopwith design was the Bat Boat, the first successful British flying boat. The Bat Boat was the first truly practical amphibian, as demonstrated by its success in winning the Mortimer Singer Prize. This was achieved by performing twelve alternate land and sea landings in 3hr 25min, out of an allotted maximum of 5hr.

Sopwith created many outstanding designs, both as a pioneer, and for military use in the First World War. Many notable Sopwith machines were flown at Brooklands including the influential Sopwith Three Seater, the Tabloid, 1½ Strutter (December 1915), Pup (February 1916), Triplane (30 May 1916), Camel (December 1916), Snipe (B9962, March 1917), and Dolphin (May 1917). Details of the main types are tabulated below.

Type	**First Flight**	**Comments**
Three Seater	7 February 1913	Eleven built, used for setting height records in May, June and July 1913.
Bat Boat	1913	Hull constructed by S.E. Saunders Ltd. Three initial aircraft, the third winning the Mortimer-Singer Prize on 8 July 1913. Followed by a number of more powerful machines along the same lines.
Tractor Seaplane	Mid-1913	Three built. Two-seat tractor biplane seaplane. Serial numbers 58, 59, 60.
Tabloid	November 1913	Small single-seat tractor biplane. Outstanding performance included 1,200ft/min climb rate and 92mph maximum speed. Total production numbers not clear. Figures between twenty-nine and fifty are variously quoted.
Schneider	1914	Modified Tabloid used for 1914 Schneider Contest at Monaco, April 1914. Subsequently adopted for production, about 136 production aircraft built. Developed into Sopwith Baby

Howard Pixton won the 1914 Schneider Trophy competition in Monaco flying this Sopwith Schneider floatplane. (BAE SYSTEMS plc)

Type	First Flight	Comments
Type 807 naval seaplane	Autumn 1914	At least twelve aircraft built, the type being a folding wing seaplane developed from the 1914 Circuit of Britain entry. Serials 807-810, 919-926.
Gunbus	October 1914	Large two-seat three-bay pusher biplane of 50ft span. Six were built by Sopwith, and a further thirty by Robey & Co. Ltd as the Sopwith Admiralty Type 806. At least thirteen of these were delivered as spares.
Type D.5	Late 1914	Twenty-four built for RNAS, serials 1051 to 1074. Known as the 'Spinning Jenny'.
Admiralty Type 860	Late 1914	A large two-seat seaplane similar to the Short 184, of which eighteen are believed to have been built with serials 851-860, 927-932, 935, 938.
Baby	September 1915	Light bomber based on Schneider. 286 built, split between Sopwith (100) and Blackburn. Developed into Fairey Hamble Baby.
1H Strutter	December 1915	5,466 built, at least 1,513 in UK (other figures for UK production can be found), 246 of these being built by Sopwith. Initially flown as Sopwith A1 or Admiralty type 9400. Prototype serial 3686.
Pup	Spring 1916	A total of six Sopwith Pup prototypes and 1,770 production aircraft is normally quoted, although some sources give 1,847 aircraft. Of these, Sopwith built only ninety-seven. First flown in early February 1916 as Admiralty Type 9901, prototype serial 3691.
Triplane	28 May 1916	This type served with distinction with the RNAS. Perhaps among the most famous were the aircraft of B Flight 10 Sqn

Type	First Flight	Comments
		RNAS – the Black Flight of *Black Maria*, *Black Death*, *Black Roger*, *Black Prince* and *Black Sheep*. Some 152 were built, the prototype N500 being flown in early June 1916. Sopwith built 103 aircraft from this total.
Camel	22 December 1916 (cleared for flight)	Wide variations can been found in total production numbers. A figure of 5,747 (F.1 and 2F.1 Camel) is given in the Sopwith biography *Pure Luck*, but a figure of 5,490 is documented by J.M. Bruce. Francis Mason in *The British Fighter Since 1912* states 5,695 plus a total of 230 2F.1 (grand total 5,925), of which at least 100 were cancelled. Total orders for 5,497 Camel, plus 250 2F1 are also cited by Bruce Robertson, this figure being consistent with that given in *Pure Luck*. J.M. Bruce states that 1,325 Camel were built in 1917, and 4,165 in 1918. Sopwith built only around 10 per cent of the total (503 Camel and fifty Ships Camel), with Boulton & Paul Ltd and Ruston, Proctor & Co. Ltd the major sub-contractors. The prototype 2F.1 with 150hp Bentley rotary was N5. This variant was mainly used for naval service and first flew in March 1917.
T1 Cuckoo	mid-1917	233 built, prototype N74 built by Sopwith. Production carried out by Blackburn Aeroplane & Motor Co. Ltd (162 aircraft, including thirty of a batch of fifty aircraft ordered from Pegler & Co., Doncaster); Fairfield Shipbuilding & Engineering Co. (fifty from an order for 100); and Pegler & Co. (twenty). Blackburn-built aircraft manufactured at Sherburn-in-Elmet.
Dolphin	May 1917	Production numbers for the Sopwith 5F.1 Dolphin range from 1,532 to 2,074, dependent upon source. Robertson's *Sopwith – The Man and His Aircraft* indicates the following production: 1,043+ built by Sopwith, with Darracq Motor Engineering contributing 300 from orders for 400; and Hooper & Co. 216 from orders for 350 (a grand total of 1,559 aircraft). *British Military Aircraft Serials* by the same author indicates a slightly higher figure (e.g. 331 from Darracq).
Snipe	November 1917	The Snipe production prototype B9962 followed a number of experimental Camel derivatives fitted with BR1 and BR2 rotary engines. Large production orders followed, with delivery totals quoted as low as 1,100, and as high as 2,178 (including six prototypes). Robertson's *British Military Aircraft Serials* indicates a Sopwith total of 544, plus thirty-four Dragonfly-powered Sopwith Dragon within an overall total of 2,038. Robertson's *Sopwith – The Man and His Aircraft* indicates total production as 2,103, 560 by Sopwith.
3F.2 Hippo	13 September 1917	Two only, X11 and X18, competitor to Bristol F.2B. Also reported as X10 and X11, with X18 being cancelled.
Salamander	27 April 1918	The TF.2 Salamander was heavily armoured for trench strafing. The prototype E5429 was first flown on 27 April 1918.

Type	First Flight	Comments
		Sopwith built some 163 from orders for 500. The Salamander was very much affected by the mass cancellation of orders which occurred after the Armistice, leaving considerable uncertainty over actual production numbers (production totals of 175, 183+, 210, 292 and 419 can be found).

In addition to the above, the company built a number of aircraft that did not proceed to production. This rich variety of unfamiliar types includes the Bee, Buffalo, Bulldog, Grasshopper, Rhino, Scooter, Snail, Snapper, Snark and Swallow.

After the First World War, Sopwith attempted to replace its lost aircraft contracts with manufacture of ABC motorcycles, advertising in January 1920: 'The outstanding excellence of the Sopwith war and peace aeroplanes characterises another of its productions: the ABC motorcycle – *The best of its kind*.' The company was renamed **The Sopwith Aviation & Engineering Co. Ltd** in May 1919 but only manufactured fifteen aircraft in the two years between the Armistice and September 1920.

Ultimately there came a financial crisis, and Sopwith entered voluntary liquidation, on 11 September 1920, eventually paying off all its creditors. The **H.G. Hawker Engineering Co. Ltd** was registered on 15 November 1920 with capital of £20,000. Formed after the Sopwith Aviation & Engineering Co. Ltd went into voluntary liquidation, Hawker Engineering took over all Sopwith patent rights, and the support business for the Sopwith aircraft then in RAF service.

Spencer and **Spencer-Stirling**
Spencer-Stirling biplane. This was a typical Boxkite type built by Herbert Spencer of 40 Sackville Street, London; it was flying at Brooklands in November 1910 and again in the summer of 1911. This machine used the engine from the Spencer-Stirling monoplane, which was built by C.G. Spencer and Sons in 1910.

Spencer went on to produce a similar Boxkite machine based on parts of the Macfie Empress. This machine was first flown at Brooklands on 31 March 1912. Spencer also produced a machine known as the 'Spencer Farman', which was very similar to the Farman F.20. This machine was used by the RNAS with serial number 200. In March 1912, *Flight* carried an advertisement for 'HERBERT SPENCER FLYING SCHOOL, Brooklands Aerodrome. – Tuition and practical constructional work from £40. Passenger flights from £2 2s.'

Star monoplane. After testing at Dunstall Park, Wolverhampton, the Star Engineering Co. monoplane was re-engined and tested at Brooklands in December 1910 and January 1911.

W.G. Tarrant. The Tarrant company was a woodworking concern that had considerable experience of sub-contract aircraft construction. The company had works at Byfleet and were contracted to build the tragically unsuccessful Tarrant Tabor. The Tabor was tested at Farnborough on 26 May 1919, but tipped onto its nose on take-off, killing its two pilots. Further details are provided in Volume 2 of this series (*British Built Aircraft - South West & Central Southern England*) under the entry for Farnborough, Hants.

The Sopwith Dragon was a version of the Snipe, fitted with an ABC Dragonfly fixed radial engine, rather than the Bentley rotary engine of the Snipe. (Brooklands Museum Trust)

The Buffalo was one of a number of Sopwith designs that failed to enter production. The Buffalo was intended for low-level contact patrol work and was armoured against small arms fire. (Brooklands Museum Trust)

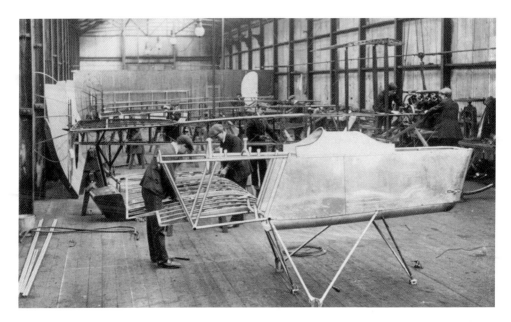

The Vickers Aviation Department was set up at Erith in 1911, where the Vickers E.F.B.1 (Experimental Fighting Biplane) fuselage is seen under construction before being displayed at Olympia in February 1913. (Brooklands Museum Trust)

The **Universal Aviation** 'Birdling' monoplane of 1911 was used with great success by H.J.D. Astley and then by F.K. McClean. Contemporary photographs show that this machine was a close copy of the Blériot monoplane. Cecil Pashley was also reported in September 1911 to be flying the Universal Aviation Sommer from Brooklands.

Vickers Ltd (and successor companies)

Pioneers

Vickers, Sons and Maxim Ltd set up an aviation department at Erith in 1911, the design office being in Vickers House, Broadway, London. Experimental flying was initially at Joyce Green, Kent with Brooklands used for further development testing, becoming a factory in its own right during the First World War.

The Vickers School at Brooklands used the company's early monoplanes, together with three Farman-style Boxkite biplanes, originally supplied by **Hewlett & Blondeau**. Having suffered the inevitable modifications consequent upon school use, the Boxkite biplanes were eventually regarded as Vickers machines. Famous students included W. Sefton Brancker, Hugh Dowding, R.K. Pierson (Vickers designer), J. Lankester Parker (Short Brothers' famous test pilot), and Noel Pemberton Billing (founder of Supermarine). Pemberton Billing – ever a self-publicist – took his test for the Royal Aero Club Certificate following a single day of private instruction on his own Farman in September 1913, as a result of a bet with Frederick Handley Page. His instructor was Robert Barnwell of the Vickers School (acting in a private capacity). The Vickers flying school trained seventy-seven pupils from 1912 to 1914, second only to the Bristol school.

Vickers Ltd entered aircraft production with a series of monoplanes derived from the French REP design. These were initially tested at Joyce Green in Kent before being moved to Brooklands for further development and school use. (Brooklands Museum Trust)

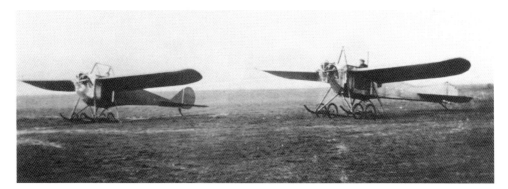

The Vickers No.3 and No.5 monoplanes were built and test flown at Joyce Green before joining the Vickers School at Brooklands. (Brooklands Museum Trust)

The Vickers No.6 monoplane was unsuccessful in the 1912 Military Trials and was rebuilt as the No 8, last of the initial series of Vickers' monoplanes. (Brooklands Museum Trust)

In July 1911 the Vickers (REP) machine was reported by *Flight* to have flown at Long Reach, Dartford (i.e. Joyce Green), and 'is now at Brooklands for further tests'; it was reported during the next month to be flying well. Details of the early Vickers monoplanes are given under the entry for Joyce Green, Kent. Joyce Green remained in use for experimental flight testing throughout the First World War, the last aircraft to make its first flight there being the Vickers Vimy Commercial on 13 April 1919. The design offices moved to Crayford from August 1914, and Vickers' Weybridge Works were established during 1915 on the eastern edge of Brooklands airfield in the former Itala car works. The design office moved back to London in 1916 (to Imperial Court, Knightsbridge), and thence to its final home at Weybridge. Aircraft were constructed at Erith, Crayford and Weybridge, with a further experimental works at Bexleyheath.

First World War Production

After initial design experience with REP-derived monoplanes, Vickers moved on to develop a number of pusher biplane designs, which progressively evolved, via the Experimental Fighting Biplane (EFB) series, into the F.B.5 and F.B.9 Gunbus. The name Gunbus reflected the fitting of a machine gun in an unobstructed position in the nose of the fuselage nacelle.

F.B.5 production included four for the RNAS and 241 for the RFC. Other production comprised a total of ninety-nine F.B.5 and F.B.9 built in France by Darracq, and twelve F.B.5 built in Denmark. Fifty F.B.9 were built at Weybridge, and an additional forty-five at Crayford. Tractor biplanes were not ignored, and Vickers built a series of Scout designs, of which the best known was the F.B.19 series, sixty-five of which were ordered in two versions. More successful in terms of numbers built, but paradoxically less well known, was the F.B.14. This was an underpowered two-bay biplane, some 100 being built at Weybridge. Many of these were delivered directly to store and not flown.

These fighter designs were followed by a move to the twin-engined bomber, which resulted in the Vimy. Appearing in late 1917, large numbers of Vimy were ordered, with many contracts being cancelled after the Armistice. Vickers built 147 at Bexleyheath, Crayford and Weybridge, and contracts were placed with a number of other suppliers including Clayton & Shuttleworth Ltd, Kingsbury Aviation Co., Metropolitan Wagon Co., Morgan & Co., The Royal Aircraft Factory and Westland Aircraft Works (branch of Petters Ltd). In the confusion of cancelled orders, the total eventually delivered is uncertain but appears to have been in excess of 230.

There can be little doubt that the Vimy would have had an important part to play had the First World War continued beyond 1918. After the war, the type revealed its capability in long distance record-breaking flights, including the famous transatlantic flight of John Alcock and Arthur Whitten-Brown, and the Ross Smith and Keith Smith flight to Australia. Its potential as a military type is clearly demonstrated by its subsequent developments which included the following types: Vimy Commercial (forty-four), Vernon (fifty-five), Virginia (126), Victoria (ninety-seven) and Valentia (twenty-eight) – aircraft which sustained the company through what were, for many others, the lean post-war years.

During the First World War, Vickers also built significant numbers of aircraft under contract, as summarised below:

- Royal Aircraft Factory BE2C – 103 machines, seventy-five at Weybridge (the first aircraft to be built there).
- Royal Aircraft Factory BE8/8A – comprising six BE8 and twenty-one BE8A.
- Royal Aircraft Factory FE8 – fifty aircraft, built at Weybridge.
- Royal Aircraft Factory SE5A – 1,650 built at Weybridge, additional aircraft at Crayford, and 431 by Wolseley Motors, a Vickers subsidiary. This was the main product of the Vickers factory at Brooklands during the First World War.
- Sopwith 1½ Strutter – 150 aircraft, built at Crayford.

In the four years ending 1919, Vickers built three large and six small airships, 3,500 aeroplanes, 167 flying boats and (Wolseley) 4,165 engines. Vickers' great designer was R.K. Pierson, who served the company as chief designer from 1914 until late 1945, designing the Vimy, Viking I, Wellington and VC1 Viking, among other notable types. The company's famous test pilot was Joseph 'Mutt' Summers, who served as chief test pilot from 1929 until 1951. Another long-serving famous name associated with Vickers-Armstrongs (and the Viscount, in particular) was George (later Sir George) Edwards who joined the company in 1935, becoming Chief Designer in 1945 and then General Manager, Chief Engineer, and ultimately the Chairman of the British Aircraft Corporation.

Collapse and Rebirth between the Wars

The Vickers Viking I amphibian G-EAOV first flew in October 1919 at Brooklands; thirty-one were built, the majority being Viking IV, of which twenty-three were exported. A non-flying replica of a Viking IV was built at Fairey Marine, Hamble, for use in the film *The People that Time Forgot*. This replica has been restored for the Brooklands Museum to represent G-EBED.

May 1922 saw the first flight of the 'over-inflated' Vickers Vulcan. The prototype was G-EBBL and a total of nine were built. The three operated for Instone Airlines were unflatteringly known as 'Flying Pigs'. At the opposite end of the aeronautical spectrum was the diminutive Vickers Viget for the 1923 Lympne trial, which first flew at Brooklands in mid-1923.

Products of the inter-war years included the alliteratively named Vernon, Victoria, Virginia, Valentia, Vildebeest and Vincent. The prototype Victoria J6860 first flew at Brooklands on 22 August 1922. The prototype Virginia J6856 first flew at Brooklands on 24 November 1922.

Less well known are the series of single engine military biplanes designed by Vickers in the 1920s. These made little impact on the home market, but did achieve some export success. This family of aircraft included the Vixen, Venture, Valparaiso, Valiant, Vivid, Vendace, and Vespa. Although not themselves purchased for RAF operations, this family laid the foundation for the Vildebeest and Vincent, which were to see extensive RAF service in the 1930s. Production of these aircraft is summarised below:

Vixen	Two prototypes (G-EBEC flown February 1923 and G-EBIP) plus eighteen production aircraft for Chile.
Venture	Six aircraft for RAF trials. Prototype J7277 first flown on 3 June 1924.
Valparaiso	Total of fifteen exported to Portugal, with additional thirteen manufactured locally. One aircraft to Chile.
Valiant	Single prototype G-EBVM exported to Chile.
Vivid	One only G-EBPY, modification of Vixen G-EBIP.
Vendace	Prototype N208 flown in March 1926. Five additional machines, three of which were exported to Bolivia.
Vespa	Prototype (Mk I) G-EBLD to Spec. 30/24 flown in September 1924. This machine was successively modified to become Mk II, Mk VI G-ABIL and Mk VII K3588. Six Mk III exported to Bolivia and eight (four each, Mk IV, Mk V) to the Irish Air Corps. The Vespa VI was flown from Filton to a height record of 43,976ft on 16 September 1932.

In addition to the above, Bolivia also ordered six Vickers Type 143 single-seat fighters in 1929. The Vildebeest was advertised as 'A torpedo-carrying bomber for coast defence, or day bombing. Metal construction with fabric coverings. Designed and constructed to the order of the British Air Ministry by Vickers (Aviation) Ltd.' The prototype Vildebeest N230 was first flown at Brooklands in April 1928; 209 were built, including twenty-six exported to Spain. The prototype Vincent S1714 was a modified Vildebeest; 197 Vincent were built, a number of these being Vildebeest conversions. A private-venture fighter prototype, the Vickers Type 279 Venom, was designed and built to meet Specification F.5/34, flying for the first time on 17 June 1936. This was a low-wing monoplane powered by a 625hp Bristol Aquila AE3S radial engine, with eight Browning 0.303 machine guns. Vickers also held contracts between the wars to build the Armstrong-Whitworth Siskin (fifty-two), Hawker Hart (162) and Hart Trainer (114). The first Vickers-built Hart was K2424. Sixty-five Siskin were also refurbished at Weybridge.

Above: *The twin engine Vellox biplane G-ABKY was flown for the first time at Brooklands on 22 January 1934. Although it saw brief service with Imperial Airways as a freighter, only one example was built.* (Brooklands Museum Trust)

Right: *The Vickers Vivid G-EBPY was one of a family of single-engine biplanes built by Vickers in the 1920s and early 1930s. The pilot is Mr John Rae.* (Andrew Rae)

Vickers Ltd (Aviation Dept) became (in July or August 1928) **Vickers (Aviation) Ltd**, and then (in October 1938) **Vickers-Armstrongs Ltd**. The 1928 change in designation to Vickers (Aviation) Ltd was associated with a merger of the heavy engineering (i.e. non-aviation) interests of Vickers Ltd, and Sir W.G. Armstrong Whitworth Ltd to form Vickers-Armstrongs Ltd. (Sir W.G. Armstrong Whitworth Aircraft Ltd was not affected by this merger, having previously passed into the control of John Siddeley in December 1926.) Vickers-Armstrongs Ltd was the parent company for Vickers (Aviation) Ltd, and also of the Supermarine Aviation Works (Vickers) Ltd, which was acquired in November 1928.

An example of contemporary styling from November 1930 advertising is (i) 'The Supermarine Aviation Works Ltd, proprietors: Vickers (Aviation) Ltd'; and (ii) 'Vickers (Aviation) Ltd, Vickers House, Broadway, Westminster'. In September 1935 the Supermarine concern was using the style 'The Supermarine Aviation Works (Vickers) Ltd, Southampton'.

The 1938 reorganisation saw Vickers-Armstrongs Ltd take direct control of these two subsidiaries. After this date the company was generally known only as Vickers-Armstrongs Ltd, the subsidiaries being respectively distinguished as 'Vickers-Armstrongs Ltd (Aircraft Section) (Weybridge Works)' or 'Vickers-Armstrongs Ltd (Aircraft Section) (Supermarine Works)'.

To complete this saga of nomenclature, one should also note that in December 1954, the aircraft business was again reorganised to form **Vickers-Armstrongs (Aircraft) Ltd**, with subsidiary interests trading as the Supermarine Division and Weybridge Division. It is not surprising that a confusing array of names and titles is to be found in various reference sources.

As its aviation interests grew, the company concentrated its activities at Weybridge, and created further facilities nearby for experimental work (at Foxwarren, Cobham) and flight-testing (at Wisley). The company also made use of their own hangar at Farnborough (where the Vickers Windsor and the Vickers Type 432 made their first flights). Additional production capacity was created with Second World War shadow factories at Chester and Blackpool. After the Second World War, an additional factory at Hurn was used for Varsity, Viscount and (later) BAC One-Eleven production – see Volume 2 of *British Built Aircraft* for details.

Second World War Mass Production

The lead-up to the Second World War saw the Wellesley and Wellington added to the list of Vickers-Armstrongs products, followed by the B.1/35 Warwick. The Wellesley was first flown at Brooklands as the private venture G.4/31 on 19 June 1935; 177 were built.

The B.9/32 prototype (later named Wellington) K4049 first flew from Brooklands on 15 June 1936, the first of a total 11,461 to be built, 2,514 of which were constructed at Weybridge. The other production sites for the Wellington were Blackpool (total 3,406) and Chester (total 5,540). A large number of local firms and organisations also participated in dispersed Wellington production, including **Permastic Ltd**, **The Press at Coomblands Ltd** and **Weybridge Automobiles Ltd**, with the **New Haw Club** and the **Rendezvous Dance Hall** being used as stores. A number of Wellington aircraft were used as engine test beds, including Z8570/G, W5389/G and W5518/G, all with rear fuselage-mounted Whittle W2 turbojets. The Wellington V prototype R3298 was first flown at Brooklands during September 1940. Wellington T. Mk X LN715 was fitted with Dart turboprop engines in support of Viscount development. The Warwick prototype K8178 was first flown at

This photograph provides a perfect illustration of Barnes Wallis' geodetic structural design for the Wellington. The type was to prove extremely robust and battle damage tolerant in service. (BAE SYSTEMS plc via Ken Ellis)

The Warwick was larger than the Wellington, but slow development and the arrival of successful four-engine bombers resulted in relatively modest production by comparison with the Wellington. (Brooklands Museum Trust)

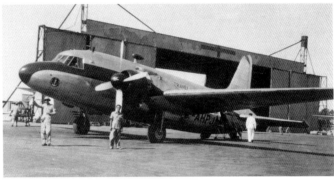

Vickers Viking of Hunting Air Travel photographed at Baringden in 1948. (A.J. Rae)

Brooklands on 13 August 1939 with (to its detriment) Vulture engines. A total of 861 Vickers Warwick were constructed, all at Weybridge.

All these aircraft used the robust and damage-tolerant geodetic construction invented by the structural designer Barnes Wallis, which effectively became a Vickers trademark. The name geodetic arises from the designer creating load paths along geodesics – a geodesic being the shortest path between two points on a curved surface. For the non-technical, the resultant structure has all the appearance of a product from a basket-weaving evening class. Barnes Wallis is rightly famous for many other engineering contributions ranging from the structure of the airship R.100 to the dam-busting 'bouncing bomb' and his innovative concept for the swing-wing 'Swallow' design.

The wartime shadow factory at Chester constructed 235 Lancaster bombers in addition to the 5,540 Wellington noted above. The total production from Vickers-Armstrongs-controlled shadow factories included 11,988 Spitfire, 8,946 Wellington and 569 Lancaster aircraft.

Post-war

Immediate post-war production included the twin-engine VC1 Viking airliner, and the related Valetta and Varsity. The Viking prototype was flown from Wisley on 22 June 1945, the first production machine following on 23 March 1946. 160 Viking were built, the VC designation standing for Vickers Commercial. The Valetta, the military version of the Viking, was first flown (VL249) at Brooklands on 30 June 1947. 252 were built, the last Valetta being delivered on 29 September 1952. The Valetta remained in RAF service until mid-1969 when

VX573 was retired from service in Germany. The final member of this family was the tricycle-undercarriage Varsity navigation and bomb-aiming trainer. 163 were built, seventeen at Weybridge, and the remainder at Hurn. The last airworthy Varsity WL679 joined the Cosford Aerospace Museum on 27 July 1992.

The Viking was used by a variety of operators at home and abroad, as indicated in the following advertisement published in April 1948:

Viking – Designed and built for the World's Airlines. Britain's first post-war airliner, the Viking is still the safest, most economical twin-engined passenger airliner and is outstandingly popular because of its comfort and smooth flying. Vikings are operated by British European Airways, Indian National Airways, Central African Airways, Danish Airlines, Air India Ltd, South African Airways, Iraqi Airways, Suidair International Airways, FAMA Argentine, Airwork Ltd, Hunting Air Travel and British South American Airways.

Vickers' outstanding commercial design after the war was the Viscount; 445 Viscount were built with production split between Weybridge (166) and Hurn (279). Vickers also produced the Valiant, Britain's first 'V Bomber'. Although the Valiant prototypes flew from Wisley, production took place at Brooklands, with the first production machine WP199 flying in December 1953. A total of three prototypes and 104 production Valiant aircraft were built. The last Valiant to leave the production line flew out of Brooklands to Wisley on 27 August 1957.

The Vanguard G-AOYW first flew at Brooklands on 20 January 1959 (this flight being a short hop to Wisley for continued testing). The type was unsuccessful on the world stage due

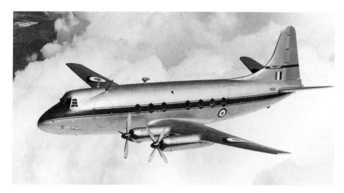

The prototype Viscount 630 seen carrying RAF serial VX211. Both port engines are shut down with propellers feathered. (Ken Ellis collection)

The Vanguard was developed against a specification that reflected the requirements of BEA. This, together with the development of economically successful short-haul jets, proved to be the type's undoing and only forty-four were built. (via Author)

The impressive VC10 prototype takes shape at Weybridge. This photograph is dated 4 February 1962, less than six months before its first flight. (BAE SYSTEMS plc via Ken Ellis)

to the rapid growth of the short-haul jet market, combined with a specification that was over-constrained by the requirements of BEA. Only forty-four were built, production consisting of the prototype, six Vanguard 951 (first flown 22 April 1959) and fourteen Vanguard 953 (first flown 1 May 1961) for BEA, and twenty-three Vanguard 952 (first flown 21 May 1960) for Trans-Canada Airlines. Aviation Traders Ltd subsequently converted nine aircraft to Merchantman freighters.

The last flight of a Vanguard was the delivery of Merchantman G-APEP to Brooklands on 17 October 1996, to join other Vickers types (including Wellington, Viking, Viscount, and VC10) in the superb Brooklands Museum. The Wellington displayed is N2980, famously recovered from the depths of Loch Ness in September 1985.

Rationalisation

The last Vickers-built design to make its first flight from Brooklands was the VC10 G-ARTA, on 29 June 1962, by which time Vickers formed part of the **British Aircraft Corporation (BAC)**. The VC10 was, perhaps, too closely constrained by its BOAC specification and, despite consistent popularity with its passengers, saw service only from 1964 to 1975. Including prototypes, thirty-seven VC10 and twenty-seven Super VC10 were built. The Super VC10 (G-ASGA first flown on 7 May 1964) continued in service for a while longer, and the type continues in transport and tanker service with the RAF.

From the base of its First World War production, the Vickers Company established itself as one of Britain's greatest aircraft manufacturers. One of Vickers' most impressive achievements was its ability to create successful designs in every phase of its existence. Thus, the early monoplanes were followed by the Gunbus and the Vimy, the interwar years saw the Virginia, Vincent, Vildebeest and Wellesley, while the Second World War produced Vickers' greatest design, the Wellington bomber. The post-war Viscount, Valiant and VC10 all broke new ground, with the Viscount becoming one of Britain's best loved and most successful commercial aircraft.

Walton & Edwards Aeroplane Co. Ltd. The Walton Edwards *Colossoplane* of 1911 was a tractor biplane with the wings mounted well forward and separated by an unusually large gap. The engine and seats were mounted in a nacelle between the wings, which could be adjusted fore and aft to control the centre of gravity. Three triangular fin surfaces were provided, one at the tail, and one on each side between the tail booms. The machine was powered by a 100hp Clerget and is reported regularly as flying at Brooklands from mid-1911, although *British Aircraft Before the Great War* gives the first flight date as 25 September 1911. In October it put in some good straight flights six feet off the ground. The machine was also referred to as the Walton & Edwards *Elephantoplane*!

Messrs Gordon Watney & Co. Ltd, Aeronautical and General Engineers, of South Lodge Motor Factory, Weybridge (Telegrams: Mercedes, Weybridge). Known for their Mercedes cars, this company specialised in aircraft engine repair, being 'a recognised hospital for Le Rhône, Clerget, Gnomes, Beardmores and RAF motors'. The company advertised as 'Contractors to His Majesty's War Office' and repaired as many as 2,000 engines per year during the First World War. Gordon Watney is famous for his race at Brooklands in May 1911, pitting his 60hp Mercedes against an Antoinette flown by Hubert Latham.

José Weiss monoplanes. These aircraft featured an elegant naturalistic wing shape developed by Weiss in an attempt to achieve the flight characteristics of birds. A thick wing centre section flowed into a swept wing tapered in both planform and thickness and incorporating considerable wash-out towards the tips. Weiss moved to Brooklands after testing his early designs at Fambridge, Essex, at Amberley, Sussex, and at Littlehampton. Flown by E.C. Gordon England, the No. 2 monoplane flew some respectable straights in June 1910, but crashed in the sewage farm on 22 December of that year.

Howard Wright. A number of Avis and related Howard Wright monoplanes were flying during 1910 at Brooklands. One of these, flown by the Hon. Alan Boyle, was successful in a flight of more than five miles at a height of 40ft. Mr Boyle gained his Aero Club Certificate (number 13) flying the Avis in June 1910. Several monoplanes were built, T.O.M. Sopwith purchasing one (his first aircraft) and flying it for the first time on 22 October 1910.

José Weiss experimented at a number of locations before moving to Brooklands. His naturalistic wing-form influenced the design of the early Handley-Page monoplanes. (Brooklands Museum Trust)

This well-known photograph shows T.O.M. Sopwith seated at the controls of his second aircraft, a biplane purchased from Howard Wright. (BAE SYSTEMS plc)

In November 1910 T.O.M. Sopwith purchased a 60hp Howard Wright biplane (which was of conventional Farman 'Boxkite' configuration), gaining his Aero Club Certificate at Brooklands on this machine on 21 November 1910. Sopwith subsequently used this machine for a number of notable flights. These included gaining the Michelin Cup for a flight of 3hr 12min on 24 November 1910 and winning the Baron de Forest prize for the longest non-stop flight (169 miles) from any point in England to the Continent, with a flight from Eastchurch to Thirimont, Belgium on 18 December 1910. Sopwith subsequently toured with this machine in the USA. In May 1912, the Grahame-White school at Hendon was using a Howard Wright biplane for tuition and in all some nine aircraft of this type were built.

The above listing gives some idea of how important Brooklands was to the pioneer industry before the First World War. An arbitrarily selected snapshot of the types being flown at Brooklands in October 1912 provides a further indication of the breadth of activity here. Among others, we find the Sopwith 70hp biplane, Flanders monoplane, Martin-Handasyde monoplane, Howard Wright biplane (flown by T.O.M. Sopwith), Vickers monoplane, Sommer biplane, ABC-engined Burgess-Wright flown by Harry Hawker, ABC-engined Avro, Bristol school monoplanes and biplanes, Howard Spencer biplane, Hanriot monoplane....

During the First World War an aircraft acceptance park was established at Brooklands (No. 10 AAP), accepting aircraft directly from the local factories. During the Second World War, Hawker Aircraft Ltd used Brooklands for Hurricane production until 1942, sharing the site with Vickers-Armstrongs Ltd. The Ministry of Aircraft Production subsequently requisitioned Brooklands for use by Vickers-Armstrongs Ltd, the Vickers factory lying between the racetrack and the Weybridge to Byfleet road. A bridge over the River Wey was used to move aircraft from the factory to the airfield. The airfield and racetrack were sold to Vickers-Armstrongs Ltd on 7 January 1946.

Camberley

Airmaster Helicopters Ltd (office address c/o Bering Ltd, Doman Rd, Camberley) built the Airmaster H2-B1 G-AYNS in an attempt to create a practical two-seat light helicopter for private ownership. This was a market later to be fulfilled by the Robinson R22. For further details, see Redhill, Surrey.

Roy Procter of Greenball, Crawley Ridge, Camberley, was a partner in the design of the Mitchell-Procter Kittiwake, and from November 1968 traded as **Procter Aircraft Associates Ltd**. This company initiated the design of the Procter (later Nash) Petrel, with construction sub-contracted to Miles Aviation & Transport (R&D) Ltd, and then to Southborough Engineering Ltd of West Byfleet. See also Farnham, Surrey.

Cobham

Vickers-Armstrong Ltd set up an experimental works at Foxwarren, Cobham. These works were used for the construction of two prototypes of the pressurised Wellington V; the experimental pressurised Vickers 432 DZ217; and airframe assemblies for the prototypes of the Viscount and the Valiant. The Wellington V prototype R3298 was first flown at Brooklands during September 1940. The Vickers 432 was first flown from Farnborough on Christmas Eve 1942. The last prototype to be constructed at Foxwarren was the Valiant B.2 WJ954, which was assembled at Wisley, making its first flight there on 4 September 1953.

Cranleigh

Phoenix Aircraft Ltd of St James's Place, Cranleigh (and also of Wykeham, St Nicholas Avenue, Cranleigh) was founded in 1958 (by C.H. Latimer-Needham and Arthur Ord-Hume) taking over the design rights of Luton Aircraft Ltd. Later, Phoenix Aircraft also marketed Currie Wot plans following the post-war revival of the type. Other plans marketed included those for the Luton Minor and Major, and the Jodel D9 and D11. In 1971 Phoenix Aircraft (Developments and Holdings) Ltd was formed, but went into liquidation on 15 January 1972.

Dunsfold Airfield (south of Guildford)

Dunsfold was a Canadian wartime airfield, which was constructed over a period of nine months in 1942. Aircraft types that used this airfield operationally included the Mitchell, Typhoon, Mustang, Mosquito, Spitfire and Tempest. After the Second World War, Dunsfold was used as a destination airfield for returning prisoners of war, some 47,000 landing here.

From August 1946, Dunsfold was leased for use as the base of Skyways Ltd, operating civilian Lancaster and York aircraft among other types. During Skyways' operations at Dunsfold, the company published a series of advertisements based upon evocative Terence Cuneo sketches. One of the most attractive (from April 1948) was entitled 'Night Shift at Dunsfold – Skyways Maintenance Organisation at your service'. Others in this series were entitled, as if vying for the title of least romantic artwork of all time, 'The sheet metal shop at Dunsfold', and 'Hydraulics shop at Dunsfold'. In 1953, Skyways were operating twenty-four York and five Halifax aircraft.

Hawker Aircraft Ltd acquired the tenancy of Dunsfold in 1950, as Langley was unsuitable for jet aircraft operations, and was also overshadowed by Heathrow. The remainder of this entry presents the activities on the site conducted by Hawker Aircraft Ltd and its successor companies, Hawker Siddeley and British Aerospace, followed by a summary of other flight-test activity conducted at Dunsfold.

Dunsfold was used for the flight test of the initial thirty-five (Hawker-built) Sea Hawk aircraft – subsequent production being transferred to Sir W.G. Armstrong Whitworth Aircraft Ltd – followed by the Hawker Hunter. The first Hunter flew in July 1951 at Boscombe Down, with the first production aircraft WT555 flying from Dunsfold on 16 May 1953. WB202, a Sapphire-powered development aircraft, flew from Dunsfold in November 1952. The two-seat Hunter T.7 was developed as a private venture, the prototype XJ615 flying for the first time on 8 July 1955. A total of 1,985 Hunter aircraft were built (some sources say 1,972), including some 460 built overseas under licence. A number of ex-RAF aircraft were converted at Dunsfold for export, an early customer being Peru in 1956. Export customers for the Hunter (including refurbished aircraft) included Abu Dhabi, Belgium, Chile, Denmark, India, Iraq, Jordan, Kenya, Kuwait, Lebanon, Netherlands, Peru, Qatar, Rhodesia,

Above: *The development of jet aircraft, combined with the proximity of Langley to Heathrow Airport, was a major factor in the move of Hawker flight-test activity to Dunsfold. WF144 is the second production Sea Hawk.* (BAE SYSTEMS plc)

Below left: *Hawker's classic jet fighter, the clean and versatile Hunter, is seen here displaying at Kemble in 2001, celebrating the fiftieth anniversary of the type's first flight.* (Author)

Below right: (© BAE SYSTEMS plc)

Above: This photograph taken in November 1962 shows a number of surplus Royal Navy Sea Fury aircraft awaiting disposal at Dunsfold. (BAE SYSTEMS plc)

Left: Nine examples of the Kestrel were built for the Tripartite Trial Squadron, providing valuable operational input in their role as a stepping stone between the experimental P.1127 and the Harrier. (BAE SYSTEMS plc)

Saudi Arabia, Singapore, Sweden and Switzerland. RAF aircraft were also modified at Dunsfold to later variants, for example from F.6 to FGA.9 and GA.11.

In March 1958, the company was advertising vacancies for machinists, toolmakers, inspectors, pre-production staff and process and planning engineers, with the following strap-line: 'Hawker Hunter – THE WORLD'S MOST SUCCESSFUL AIRCRAFT. Big Export Orders – Many Good Jobs.'

From 1957 onward, a number of surplus Sea Fury aircraft from the Fleet Air Arm were refurbished at Dunsfold for export. Deliveries comprised a total of twenty-one to Burma, seventeen to Cuba and eight TT Mk. 20 for use in West Germany as target tugs.

At Dunsfold, Hawker pioneered British vertical take-off and landing developments in the form of the P.1127 and the Kestrel. The first tethered hover by the prototype Hawker P.1127 (XP831) was achieved at Dunsfold on 21 October 1960. The first free hover was on 19 November 1960, just less than one month later. This was to be followed by conventional take-off and landing on 13 March 1961 at RAE Bedford, and full transitions on 12 September 1961. The six P.1127 prototypes were followed by nine Kestrel FGA.1 for tripartite evaluation, the first being XS688, first flown on 7 March 1964. The tripartite squadron was operational from 15 October 1964 to 30 November 1965.

Under **Hawker Siddeley Aviation Ltd**, Dunsfold was mainly used as the flight test centre for the Harrier and Hawk. The first Harrier development aircraft XV276 flew on 31 August 1966, followed by the first production GR. Mk 1 aircraft (XV738) on 28 December 1967, and the type entered service on 1 April 1969.

Production of the Harrier series comprises: (RAF aircraft)

- six prototypes, and seventy-eight production GR. Mk 1.
- thirty-six new build GR. Mk 3.
- two development aircraft and forty-one GR. Mk 5 (Harrier II), nineteen G.R Mk 5A, and thirty-four GR. Mk 7.

The first United Kingdom Harrier II – GR. Mk 5 ZD318 – flew at Dunsfold on 30 April 1985, and GR. Mk 5 aircraft have now been brought up to GR. Mk 7 standard, this version being first flown on 29 November 1989. The latest service standard is the further improved GR.MK 9.

In addition, a number of two-seat trainer variants have been built, these aircraft being designated T.2 (fourteen built), T.4, T.6, T.8, and T.10 (trainer Harrier II, thirteen ordered). The prototype Harrier T.10 was first flown at Warton on 7 April 1994.

The first export aircraft were supplied to the US Marine Corps as the AV-8A. The 102 AV-8A were followed by more than 300 AV-8B, TAV-8B and Harrier II Plus aircraft in joint programmes with McDonnell Douglas (now Boeing). The Harrier II Plus was first flown in the United States on 22 September 1992. Additional exports of have been made to the navies of India (twenty-seven Sea Harrier Mk 51, plus two two-seat Harrier), Thailand (ex-Spanish AV-8S and TAV-8S), Spain (eleven AV-8S, twelve EAV-8B, one TEAV-8B and nine Harrier II Plus) and Italy (two TAV-8B and a number of ex-Marine Corps AV-8B, to be followed by sixteen Harrier II Plus). Two ex-RAF T.4 aircraft were transferred to India and fitted with modified cockpit displays for use as trainers for the Indian Navy Sea Harrier. These aircraft replace the two two-seat Harriers initially delivered, but subsequently lost in accidents; the replacement aircraft carry Indian serials IN655 and IN656. The first aircraft to fly after cockpit reconfiguration was IN656, this flight being made at INS Hansa on 14 May 2003.

The highly successful Hawker Siddeley HS.1182 Hawk trainer was first flown (XX154) at Dunsfold on 21 August 1974. A single-seat version of the Hawk, the Hawk 200, was built as

The Harrier T.10 prototype was first flown at Warton, but development flying was conducted at Dunsfold. (J.S. Smith)

ZA101/G-HAWK was retained by BAe as a demonstrator aircraft and was flown in many different colour schemes during its life. It is seen here in an early configuration with a short nose and without fin-mounted RWR. (BAE SYSTEMS plc)

a private venture, the first example XG200 flying at Dunsfold on 19 May 1986. Hawk production and development was transferred to Warton and Brough in 1989. A summary of the Hawk orderbook, totalling 823 aircraft and spanning the activities of Hawker Siddeley, British Aerospace and BAE SYSTEMS, is given below: In July 2002, BAE SYSTEMS announced that Bahrein was to become the latest customer for the type, the contract being signed on 29 January 2003.

Hawk T Mk 1	**(175)** made up of	**Hawk Srs 100**	**(119)** made up of
United Kingdom (RAF)	175 T Mk 1	Abu Dhabi	18 Mk 102
Hawk Srs 50	**(89)** made up of	Oman	4 Mk 103
Finland	50 Mk 51, 7 Mk 51A	Malaysia	10 Mk 108
Kenya	12 Mk 52	Indonesia	8 Mk 109
Indonesia	20 Mk 53	Canada	22 Mk 115
Hawk Srs 60	**(144)** made up of	South Africa	24 Mk 120
Zimbabwe	8 Mk 60, 5 Mk 60A	Australia	33 Mk 127
Dubai	9 Mk 61	**Hawk Srs 200**	**(62)** made up of
Abu Dhabi	16 Mk 63A, 4 Mk 63C	Oman	12 Mk 203
Kuwait	12 Mk 64	Malaysia	18 Mk 208
Saudi Arabia	30 Mk 65, 20 Mk 65A	Indonesia	32 Mk 209
Switzerland	20 Mk 66	**T-45 Goshawk**	**(234)** made up of
South Korea	20 Mk 67	United States Navy	234 (planned total)

On 30 July 2003, the UK Ministry of Defence announced that it would be ordering twenty Hawk Mk 128 aircraft from BAE SYSTEMS, with an option to order a further twenty-four aircraft. Entry into service is expected in 2008, and these aircraft will support the fast jet training requirement to provide RAF pilots for the Eurofighter Typhoon and F-35 JSF.

On 3 September 2003, BAE SYSTEMS announced that the Indian Government had selected the Hawk for service with the Indian Air Force as its Advanced Jet Trainer (AJT).

A total of sixty-six aircraft are included in the order, with the first twenty-four being manufactured at Brough, with flight testing to be conducted at Warton. The remaining forty-two aircraft will be manufactured in India by Hindustan Aeronautics Ltd.

British Aerospace/BAE SYSTEMS. As the Kingston site was run down, Harrier II fuselage production, assembly of United Kingdom aircraft, and Sea Harrier new build and conversions to FA.2 standard were transferred to Dunsfold. The first Sea Harrier XZ450 flew at Dunsfold on 20 August 1978. The first Sea Harrier FRS.2 development aircraft ZA195 flew on 19 September 1988. Sea Harrier production has comprised three development aircraft for the FRS.1 and two for the FRS.2; fifty-four production FRS.1 for the Royal Navy; twenty-seven Mk 51 for India; and eighteen new-build FA.2 for the Royal Navy, the remaining FRS.1 fleet also being converted to this standard. Sea Harrier development (and in-service training) was supported by three Hunter T.8M fitted with the Sea Harrier Blue Fox radar. Development of the FA.2 was supported by HS125 ZF130, fitted with a Blue Vixen radar, and used for radar development and integration trials.

As the only western military V/STOL combat aircraft to reach production status (so far), the Harrier has been an extraordinary success. In a programme that has been running for more than forty years, nearly 900 aircraft have been built. The development of the airframe has been accompanied by remarkable growth in the Pegasus engine, from a maximum thrust of 11,000lb for the Pegasus 2 of the P.1127 to the 23,800lb thrust of the Pegasus 11-61 used by the Harrier II Plus.

In addition to Harrier production work, Dunsfold was contracted to carry out the refurbishment and 2,000-hour major service on twelve Hawk Mk 64 aircraft of the Kuwait Air Force. The first refurbished aircraft was handed over in October 1998. Dunsfold also conducted extensive refurbishment of the Royal Navy Historic Flight Fairey Firefly WB271 and Sea Hawk WV856.

On 24 June 1999, BAe announced that with the completion of the Harrier production programme, it would be closing the Dunsfold site by the end of the year 2000. Thus passed the last of the Hawker Aircraft sites to remain in use, with BAE SYSTEMS concentrating military aircraft production at its sites in northern England, Brough, Samlesbury and Warton.

Indian Navy Sea Harrier Mk 51 IN601/G-9-478. (Author)

Gnat Trainer production test flying was carried out at Dunsfold after the absorption of Folland Aircraft Ltd into Hawker Siddeley Aviation Ltd. (BAE SYSTEMS plc)

A.V. Roe & Co. Ltd. The Avro 707 VX790 carried out some 100 hours of test-flying at Dunsfold in 1951.

Airwork Ltd used Dunsfold on a temporary basis in 1953 for a refurbishment contract covering RAF Supermarine Attackers and USAF F-86 Sabre aircraft.

Folland Aircraft Ltd: From 1961 Dunsfold was used for Folland Gnat production flight testing after the closure of Chilbolton, as Folland were absorbed into **Hawker Siddeley Aviation Ltd**. Gnat T.1 aircraft were built at Hamble and transported (with wings fitted) to Dunsfold by road for flight-testing. A Gloster Meteor was also used at Dunsfold for the development of the Gnat ejector seat.

Esher

The **Hawker Aircraft Ltd** design office was moved to Claremont House, Esher, during the Second World War.

Fairoaks

This airfield was originally known as Fair Oaks aerodrome. During the Second World War, **Airtraining (Fairoaks) Ltd** used it for the repair and modification of aircraft under the Civilian Repair Organisation scheme. This company was one of two subsidiaries of General Aircraft Ltd: Airtraining (Oxford) Ltd and Airtraining (Fairoaks) Ltd. During the Second World War, these companies, which operated pre-war flying schools, were responsible for the overhaul and reconditioning of over 1,200 RAF aircraft and the training of more than 6,000 RAF pilots. The main types handled were the Hurricane, Blenheim, Mustang and Beaufighter. The prototype **Garland Bianchi** Linnet G-APNS first flew at Fairoaks on 1 September 1958, having been constructed at White Waltham.

Phoenix Duet, G-AYTT, the sole example of this two-seat side-by-side development of the Luton Minor, was built by Alf Knowles and first flown at Fairoaks on 22 June 1973. The type was originally known as the Luton Minor III.

The angular two-seat Phoenix Duet reveals little in its appearance of its Luton Minor ancestry. (Author)

Farnham

Abbott-Baynes Sailplanes Ltd was formed in 1931 as a subsidiary of **E.D. Abbott Ltd**, coachbuilders, of Farnham/Wrecclesham. The attractive Scud glider was designed by L.E. Baynes, and built at Farnham. A total of twelve Scud 1 and one Scud 2 were built.

The Scud III Auxiliary powered glider was built to the order of Sir John Carden, and led to the formation of **Carden-Baynes Aircraft Ltd** at Heston. The Scud III Auxiliary was first flown at Woodley on 8 August 1935 and was later registered G-ALJR. Power was provided by a 249cc Villiers single-cylinder motorcycle engine driving a pusher propeller, the whole assembly being mounted on a folding pylon that allowed engine and propeller to be retracted for soaring flight.

E.D. Abbott/**Abbott-Baynes Aircraft Ltd** also built the strut braced Cantilever Pou version of the Flying Flea designed by L.E. Baynes, building a number of aircraft in 1936. Some of these were flown at Heston, including G-AEGD and G-AEJD. In mid-1935, the company was advertising: 'Carden-Baynes Auxiliaries – Scud Sailplanes – Pous. Parts and materials. Abbott-Baynes Aircraft (Branch of E.D. Abbott Ltd), Farnham, Surrey.'

Goddard & Sons of East St, Farnham, made propellers during the First World War.

Farnham has been the base for a number of companies seeking to exploit various developments of the Mitchell-Procter Kittiwake. These include **Procter Aircraft Associates Ltd** (a change of name from **Mitchell-Procter Aircraft Ltd** effective from November 1968) and **Nash Aircraft Ltd** (formed in 1980, reflecting the controlling interest of Mr A. Nash from 1978), all at the Trading Estate, Farnham. The first Nash Petrel G-AXSF, a two-seat derivative of the Kittiwake, flew on 8 November 1980.

Guildford

The RFD Co., Address: R.F. Dagnall, 17 Stoke Road, Guildford, is known today for safety equipment. The company advertised in 1930 that they were 'now in a position to accept orders for gliders and sailplanes of types approved by the BGA. Orders will be accepted in strict rotation.' Their first product was an improved Zögling, which was sold as the Dagling.

G-AXSF is the prototype Nash Petrel, a two-seat development of the Kittiwake, similar in concept to the Mitchell Kittiwake II. (Author)

The company also built a glider designed by C.H. Latimer-Needham, the Albatross. In 1934 the company became **The RFD Co. Ltd**, moving in 1936 to Godalming.

Hamsey Green, Surrey

In 1936, Mr Richard Taylor built a high-wing cantilever monoplane of his own design at Hamsey Green, registered G-AEPX. Regrettably, on what is widely thought to have been its first flight, on 7 January 1937, the aircraft suffered a structural failure of its wing, resulting in a fatal accident. As is clear from material published by Ord-Hume, the wing structural design was irrevocably flawed from the outset.

Kingswood Knoll

Mr C.B. Field built a hangar at Kingswood Knoll and flew a wide range of aircraft from an adjoining field, operating north–south, parallel to the line of the A217. In the course of his business, Mr Field handled an extraordinary range of interesting aircraft, some of which he built up or modified; others were simply 'passing through' on their way to new owners. The paragraphs below list most of the aircraft with which he is believed to have been associated.

Five Avro 504K (G-ABSL, G-ABSM, G-ABSN, G-ACAU, G-ACAV) were assembled here by **Field Aircraft Constructions** (C.B. Field) in 1932 and 1933. Further conversions were made in 1932 of Avro 504s to Avro 552 configuration with a Wolseley Viper engine, including G-ACAW, G-ACAX, and G-ACRP. Mr Field also created an Avro 504N equivalent, by fitting G-AEAA with a 115hp Bristol Lucifer engine taken from a Parnall Peto (presumably N182/G-ACOJ). Some of these aircraft were subsequently used for aerial advertising, for example, the luridly painted G-ACAW operated from Abridge by Plane Advertising.

In 1936, Brian Field carried out civil conversions of a number of Hawker Tomtit aircraft, at least five becoming civil registered (as G-AEVO, G-AFFL, G-AFIB, G-AGEF, and G-AFVV). In October 1932 Mr Field purchased SE5A G-EBTK, which had been built at Croydon by the Henderson Flying School from parts supplied by ADC. Mr Field operated the last Martinsyde built, the AV1 G-ABKH, which was built by ADC in 1931, and he also owned the Dudley Watt DWII G-AAWK which was dismantled at Kingswood in December 1934. In May 1935 a further acquisition was a by now very ancient DH9A G-AACP to join the banner towing fleet. Also in 1935, Parnall Peto N182 was rebuilt, emerging as G-ACOJ. Other exotica included two Supermarine S5 (N219, N220), and Gloster IV racer N224! Mr Field also operated Miles Falcon G-ADLI.

From November 1940, Brian Field was engaged in production test-flying for Airspeed Ltd at Christchurch. Sadly, he was killed in an accident involving a Miles Master on 26 August 1943. The hangar at Kingswood was still extant in 1997, used by a tyre company, next to the cornfield alongside the A217 that was used as an airstrip.

Redhill Aerodrome

Airmark Ltd, which was set up by Tom Storey in 1969, built a developed version of the American Cassutt racer, the Cassutt IIIM. At least four of these aircraft were built at Redhill, and they were all raced extensively in the 1970s. The racing names adopted included *Firestreak, Hop along, Blue, Instant Motion, Razor Blade* and *Will o' the Wisp*.

Airmaster Helicopters Ltd built the Airmaster H2-B1 in an attempt to create a practical two-seat light helicopter for private ownership – a market later to be fulfilled by the Robinson R22. The single example built, G-AYNS, was flown in February 1972 (source *Jane's All the World's Aircraft 1973-4*, although the date given in *British Civil Aircraft Since 1919* is 12 September 1972) at Redhill Aerodrome. The type did not reach production status.

Cierva/Servotec/Rotorcraft Ltd produced a series of experimental helicopters including the CR. LTH-1 Grasshopper III, with the unusual arrangement of twin piston engines driving coaxial contra-rotating rotors. Three Grasshopper prototypes were registered, with testing beginning in 1969. The nominal first prototype was registered G-AXFM, while the second prototype (which was actually flown first, on 18 August 1969) was G-AWRP.

The company origins arose from the formation of **Servotec Ltd** by J.S. Shapiro in the 1950s, and **Rotorcraft Ltd**, by J.S. Shapiro and F.G. Mitchell, in 1960. Rotorcraft Ltd designed the Grasshopper I (G-ARVN, built at Feltham and first flown on 11 March 1962), the prototype being constructed by Servotec Ltd. **The Cierva Autogiro Co. Ltd** took over Rotorcraft Ltd in 1965, to form **Cierva Rotorcraft Ltd**, taking over Servotec Ltd in 1969. The Grasshopper III was first flown in August 1969.

F.G. Miles Ltd was set up at Redhill on 4 December 1948, following the demise of Miles Aircraft Ltd at Woodley and the company being taken over by Handley Page Ltd. Initially the Redhill activity was limited to service and repair, and the completion of the three Gemini aircraft purchased from Woodley. F.G. Miles, and his eponymous company, moved back to Shoreham in 1951. One of the Gemini aircraft, G-AMBH, was erected at Redhill as a Gemini 1A, with the other airframes (G-AMDJ, G-AOGA) being constructed as Miles M.75 Aries. The first Miles Aries, G-35-1/G-AMDJ, flew at Redhill on 21 March 1951.

Rollason Aircraft and Engines Ltd: Components for Rollason-built Druine Condor and Turbulent aircraft were manufactured at Croydon, Greater London, with the aircraft being test flown at Redhill.

Five engineers working at Luton (in the ex-Hunting Percival branch of BAC) designed the Luton Group Beta, which was the winner of a 1964 racing aircraft design competition

Above: *The unconventional and unsuccessful Cierva Rotorcraft CR-LTH-1 married twin piston engines and a co-axial contra-rotating rotor.* (Ken Ellis collection)

Left: *The Rollason D31 Turbulent is a popular and economical single-seater which also offers delightful handling qualities.* (Author)

sponsored by Norman Jones. As the prize-winning design, the Luton Beta was then built by Rollason Aircraft and Engines Ltd. While not fully competitive with US Formula 1 designs, the Beta nevertheless offered an exciting 195mph and 2,000ft/min climb rate on an affordable 90hp. The prototype Luton Beta B1 G-ATLY was first flown on 21 April 1967. Three improved Beta B2 aircraft were constructed by Rollason: G-AWHV, G-AWHW and G-AWHX, with G-AWHV flying on 15 February 1969. In 1986, at least two additional Luton Beta aircraft were flying in South Africa. Beta aircraft are also registered in the United States (N545CM), and other examples have been registered in the UK including G-BGFM and G-BUPC.

The **Storey** TSR3 Wonderplane G-AWIV is a single-seat, racing monoplane built by Tom Storey at Redhill and flown in July 1968 prior to his Airmark Cassutt construction activity. While not successful as a racer, its patriotic colour scheme certainly brightened up the Redhill skies. The design rights passed to Airmark in 1969. In 1998, G-AWIV was based at Land's End, having been restored to flying condition for the first time since 1985.

A little known Redhill-based experiment was the unnamed motor glider constructed just after the Second World War, with assistance from **Ken Wallis** (who supplied the engine – a German jet starter motor). The airframe was modified from a Gull-type glider.

Above: *The attractive Rollason Luton Beta was built in small numbers and flown from Redhill. This example G-AWHW* The Red Baron *is a Beta B.2A.* (Author)

Right: *Tom Storey's unmistakably patriotic TSR3 Wonderplane brightened up Redhill's skies in the late 1960s.* (Author)

Sunbury on Thames

The **Cowper-Coles Aircraft Co.**, of 1 French Street, advertised the supply of 'Rustless fittings and metal parts for aircraft', as 'Contractors to the War Office and Admiralty' and 'Contractors to the RAF'. The company was incorporated in January 1917 and announced that it was acquiring a 33-acre site to be used for aircraft production having a 370ft frontage on a backwater of the River Thames. In the summer of 1917 the company was reported to be manufacturing aircraft wings in a temporary building.

Thorpe Water Park

Leisure Sport at Thorpe Water Park were responsible for the commissioning of a series of flying and static replicas of First World War aircraft as follows:

Airworthy replicas: Sopwith Camel (two), Spad XIII, AIRCO DH2, Fokker Dr1, Albatros D.Va, Supermarine S5.
Static replicas: Royal Aircraft Factory SE5A, Sopwith Triplane, AIRCO DH2, Bristol M1C, Sopwith Baby, Hansa Brandenburg W29, Curtiss R3C2, Vickers Viking IV.

Walton on Thames

ABC Motors Ltd, of the ABC Works, Hersham, Walton on Thames, was originally formed at Redbridge, Hampshire, in 1910, as the All British Engine Company Ltd. ABC designed the initially promising, but ultimately disastrous, ABC Dragonfly engine. During the latter stages of the First World War, it was decided to standardise production around this engine, and orders totalling some 11,000 engines were placed. Unfortunately, it was then found that the normal running rpm of the engine coincided with the first natural torsional frequency of the crankshaft, with a catastrophic effect on engine life.

Just how bad the Dragonfly could be is illustrated by the story of Siddeley SR2 C4542, which was so badly damaged by engine vibration during a single flight from Coventry to Martlesham Heath that it had to be scrapped. Around 1,300 of these engines were in fact produced. Fortunately, the Armistice intervened before the consequences of the unfortunate standardisation decision became apparent operationally. The company later produced the twin-cylinder ABC Scorpion, which (although prone to unreliability) proved very popular and was exported to a number of countries.

ABC made one excursion into aircraft design and manufacture, in the form of the single-seat ABC Robin G-AAID of 1929 (see Brooklands for further details). By the end of the Second World War, ABC were building generators, auxiliary power plants and pumping sets. Their origins in engine manufacture were, however, still apparent in their telegraphic address – 'Revs', Walton-on-Thames.

After the formation of Heston Aircraft, Nick Comper and F.R. Walker formed a new company, **Comper Aeroplanes Ltd** (address 2 The Ridgeway, Walton on Thames) which designed and began construction of a twin-boom Mikron II powered pusher design known as the Comper Scamp. The Scamp had not yet been completed when Comper met a most regrettable and tragic death in Hythe in June 1939.

Wisley

The following entry presents the activities of Vickers-Armstrongs Ltd and its successors at Wisley, followed by other test activities conducted from this site.

Vickers-Armstrongs Ltd. Wisley was used as a flight test airfield for Vickers-Armstrongs Ltd. A number of types (noted below) had their first flights here; others flew the short distance from Brooklands to Wisley to enter their flight test programme.

Type	Registration or Serial	Date	Remarks
Windsor	DW512	15 February 1944	2nd prototype
Windsor	NK136	11 July 1944	3rd prototype
Viking	G-AGOK	22 June 1945	
Nene Viking	VX856/G-AJPH	6 April 1948	
Viscount	G-AHRF/VX211	16 July 1948	
Varsity	VX828	17 July 1949	
Valiant	WB210	18 May 1951	

The Vickers Viscount was Britain's most successful commercial aircraft of the immediate post-war period. Apart from the type's reliability and operating economics, its success was also due to its tremendous passenger appeal. A review of the Viscount, based upon an early passenger flight in 1948, was justifiably enthusiastic: 'Without any reservation we can say that,

In-service Valiant aircraft undergoing overhaul at Cambridge. (Marshall Aerospace Ltd)

from a passenger point of view, it is by far the most pleasant airliner we have ever flown in. [...] The large, ellipse-shaped windows are the best thing in airliner windows yet produced.' All who have since had the pleasure of flying in this pioneering turboprop design must have shared these sentiments.

The Valiant was first flown from the grass runway at Wisley, and retreated to Hurn for early testing while a hard runway was built. Three prototypes and a total of 104 production aircraft were constructed, the last of these flying on 27 August 1957. The Valiant served with the RAF from January 1955 until January 1965, when the type was withdrawn due to the early onset of structural fatigue problems.

Vickers-Armstrongs (Aircraft) Ltd (Supermarine Division) flight-testing was moved to Wisley from 1956, following the closure of Chilbolton. The **British Aircraft Corporation** also used Wisley for BAC One-Eleven and VC10 production testing.

The **Vintage Aircraft and Flying Association (VAFA)** built two authentic replicas of early Vickers designs, the F.B.5 Gunbus and the Vimy bomber; both were flown at Wisley. The Gnome-powered replica F.B.5 Gunbus G-ATVP was flown for the first time on 14 June 1966 and is now on display in the RAF Museum at Hendon as 2345 'Bombay II'. The VAFA then built a Vickers Vimy replica G-AWAU, which flew on 3 June 1969 and is also displayed in the RAF Museum as F8614.

David Lockspeiser of 7 Highfield, Christhurst Lane, Shalford (registered office 4 Princes Building, Clifton, Bristol), built the Lockspeiser LDA-01 canard pusher G-AVOR, which flew from Wisley on 24 August 1971. The type was intended as a sub-scale demonstrator for a larger utility aircraft that was never built. G-AVOR was subsequently re-registered G-UTIL and was destroyed by fire at Old Sarum on 17 January 1987 in the arson attack on the Optica Industries factory.

Woking

Martinsyde Ltd, Head Office, Maybury Hill, Woking, Surrey. Martinsyde announced in April 1915 that they were opening premises at Woking 'to augment those at Brooklands'. See Brooklands for further details of Martinsyde products.

George Handasyde set up the **Handasyde Aircraft Co.** with Sidney Camm and F.P. Raynham in 1921, next to the Martinsyde factory. Handasyde designed a glider, which took part in the 1922 Itford Hill trials, the machine being built by Blériot/ANEC (see Fairoaks/Addlestone). This glider was very successful, setting a British endurance record of 1hr 53min during the competition.

A powered ultralight aircraft was then built for the 1923 Motor Glider competition, this (the Handasyde monoplane) flying for the first time at Brooklands on 9 September 1923. The Handasyde monoplane was a single-seat, shoulder-wing monoplane with an open cockpit, powered by a 750cc Douglas engine. Like the 1922 glider, it was built in the Blériot/ANEC

Vickers Gunbus replica G-ATVP/2345 Bombay II was flown at Wisley, and is now displayed in the RAF Museum. (via Author)

Vickers Vimy replica G-AWAU was flown in 1969 and, like its Gunbus stablemate, can now be seen in the RAF Museum. (Author)

David Lockspeiser's LDA01 Land Development Aircraft failed to attract the necessary financial backing. (Author)

works. The Handasyde H.2 was a shoulder-wing cabin monoplane powered by a 350hp Rolls-Royce Eagle engine. The type was distinguished by its cantilever wing and quadricycle undercarriage. The sole, unregistered, example was built by ANEC at Addlestone and flown at Brooklands on 9 December 1922. The type was not a success. The company was disbanded in late 1923 or early 1924.

East Sussex

Brighton & Hove

Brighton Motor Coach Works is listed in *The Aviation Pocket-Book 1919-20* as an aeroplane manufacturer; nothing else is known.

Harrington's Bus Bodies of Hove carried out sub-contract detail design and construction of the rear wing of the tandem-wing Westland Lysander. The prototype Lysander K6127 flew for the first time in its modified tandem-wing form on 27 July 1941.

Short Bros. Initial aerial balloon manufacturing activity by Horace and Eustace Short was undertaken at Hove from April 1901.

In 1912 there was a seaplane hangar (Magnus Volk's seaplane hangar) opposite Paston Place Station, Brighton. One aircraft to use the hangar was the **Radley-England** Waterplane. In Spring 1914, Frank Fowler (founder of the **Eastbourne Aviation Company**) operated EAC-built Farman seaplanes from 'Volk's Waterplane Station'. The facilities consisted of a large canvas hangar erected on the beach.

Eastbourne

The **Brocklehurst** monoplane was reported as being tested at Eastbourne in January 1912. It is not known if this was successful.

Caffyns Garages Ltd of Meads Lane, Eastbourne, is recorded in *The Aviation Pocket-Book 1919-20* as an aeroplane manufacturer. This company, which described itself as 'Engineers,

Aircraft Manufacturers, Eastbourne' built seventy-five sets of SE5A wings, ailerons and rudders under sub-contract. A Maurice Farman biplane was also constructed from salvaged parts during the First World War.

The **Eastbourne Aviation Co.** (EAC) was established on 1 December 1911 by F.B. Fowler and Victor Yates, with telegraphic address 'Aircraft' Eastbourne. In December 1911 the company was advertising 'Tuition on genuine Blériot. Machines built to client's own designs.' The Blériot aircraft were acquired from the New Forest Aviation School (run by McCardle and Drexel) when this enterprise ceased trading in late 1911. A purpose-built trailer was used to transport the aircraft by road to Eastbourne.

Mr Fowler purchased some fifty acres of land 'in the South East corner of the Willingdon levels' (between St Anthony's Hill and the Gas Works) and, by covering the intervening drainage ditches, produced a landing area, Langney aerodrome, some 560 yards long. The landing area was subsequently greatly enlarged for use as an RNAS training airfield, expanding to the north west of the original site, and ultimately extending to 242 acres.

By 1912, the school fleet had been expanded by the purchase of three Bristol 'Boxkite' biplanes, and EAC were advertising 'Tuition on genuine Blériot monoplanes and Bristol biplanes. Inclusive fee for one type £65; for both types £90.' In February 1913, tuition was being advertised on Farman Hydro-aeroplanes, Bristol and Sommer biplanes and three Blériot monoplanes (25, 35 and 50hp).

BRIGHTON,
NEW HYDRO-AEROPLANE STATION.

WE SHALL HAVE AVAILABLE DURING THE COMING SEASON **A LARGE HANGAR** WITH SLIPWAY, ON THE SAME SITE USED WITH GREAT SUCCESS LAST SEASON.

AVIATORS CAN HAVE FREE USE OF SAME SHOULD THEY WISH TO PAY BRIGHTON **"A FLYING VISIT."**

WE ARE ALSO OPEN TO NEGOTIATE FOR EXHIBITION AND PASSENGER-CARRYING FLIGHTS.

ADDRESS: **VOLK'S ELECTRIC RAILWAY.**

Right: *This well-known photograph shows a spirited display of the tandem winged Lysander prototype. The rear wing was constructed by Harrington's Bus Bodies of Hove.* (GKN Westland Helicopters Ltd)

The Eastbourne Aviation Co. was combined with the **Frank Hucks Waterplane Co.** to form the **Eastbourne Aviation Co. Ltd**, this company being registered on 24 February 1913 with an authorised capital of £15,000. The Frank Hucks Waterplane Co. contributed three Farman Hydroplanes to the new company to carry out seaplane joy-riding, with the result that hangars were to be erected on the beach.

The company constructed a number of original designs, one of the most notable being the EAC monoplane, which, powered by a 35hp Anzani radial, flew extremely successfully in 1913. It was designed by Herr Gassler, a pupil of the Eastbourne Aviation School, and was one of the first monoplanes to use aileron control instead of wing warping. The shock of *Flight* is almost palpable: 'Although this is a departure from what has now become almost standard practice as regards monoplane construction, it is a system which works quite well in machines of the biplane type, and there is no reason why it should not be equally successful when applied to monoplanes.'

At the time of the above article (May 1913), one of the buildings in use by the company was a converted galvanised iron church, this having been purchased for £70 and moved to the site. In addition, there were six hangars on the airfield and two more on the seaward side of the main road at the Crumbles, with a slipway to the beach. These latter were known locally as the Seaplane Sheds, or the Seaplane Base, and were equipped with a rail track and turntable to assist in launching the seaplanes. The Seaplane Base gradually expanded to become the main focus of activity, acquiring such facilities as a sawmill and wood-drying store, woodworking and machine shops, and a number of other permanent buildings.

One of the pupils, Mr Vincent Fill, built his own 35hp Anzani-powered Blériot monoplane in the summer of 1913. The Eastbourne Aviation Co. also built a single-seater tractor biplane in February 1914. This aircraft was built for Lt R.E.B. Hunt and featured a square section fuselage with the fuselage carried mid-way between the wings, which were of comparatively high aspect ratio. Power was provided by a 50hp Gnome. An additional biplane (the EAC Military Biplane) was built in 1914 and displayed at the Olympia Aero Show in March. This aircraft seated two crew in tandem and was powered by an 80hp Gnome. Other than the larger than normal gap between the wings, the type was of conventional appearance.

During the First World War, the aerodrome was used for training of RNAS pilots, the EAC being displaced to operate solely from the Seaplane Base, this becoming the company's registered office from February 1916. Here, the company continued to build various types, including the Avro 504 (fifty 504A and 109 504K), Farman S.11 Shorthorn (forty) and BE2C

This BE2E, photographed firing Le Prieur rockets, was manufactured by the Eastbourne Aviation Co. Ltd. The company produced its own designs before the First World War and was also one of many contractors for the Avro 504. (Treadwell/Wood)

(twelve). The company also carried out aircraft repair work. In 1920, EAC were advertising as 'Aeroplane constructors, contractors to the Admiralty'.

Some work on Avro 504 seaplanes continued after the war with six Avro 504L (float-equipped Avro 504K) being built here. The company reverted to the seaplane joy-riding of the pre-war period and, in addition to the float Avros, converted two Short 184 (originally built by J. Samuel White & Co. Ltd) to four-seat configuration as G-EALC and G-EAJT. Like many other companies, there was a brief flirtation with cars and coach bodies, before a receiver was appointed on 16 December 1922. Work ceased in 1924, with the company's assets (other than its buildings) being sold at auction in July. The local council purchased 33,000 sq. ft of buildings in February 1926, but the company was not formally wound up until 8 November 1932.

Rye – Camber Sands

British Aircraft Before The Great War reports that the pioneer aviator Alec Ogilvie had succeeded in flying the **Aerial Manufacturing Co.** monoplane in late 1909 for distances of up to 250 yards at Camber Sands. The machine was of unconventional design, with a number of auxiliary aerofoils associated with an articulating undercarriage.

Alec Ogilvie had a private flying ground at Camber Sands, which he used for flying and developing his Short-Wright (No. 2) biplane, which was delivered at the beginning of September 1909. By November 1910 flights of more than ten minutes' duration were being made.

Ogilvie also took ownership of the No.6 Short-Wright following the death of C.S. Rolls, flying this at Camber in October 1910. Ogilvie modified this machine, turning it into one of the most successful of its type, the changes made including the removal of the front elevator. In December 1910 this aircraft was flown 142 miles in less than four hours. This much-modified aircraft continued flying right up to the outbreak of the First World War. Ogilvie's lease of Camber Sands expired in May 1911, after which he returned to Eastchurch.

The **Howard Wright** biplane of 1909 came to Camber Sands after initial testing at Fambridge.

A contemporary description of the Camber Sands flying area was as follows: 'At low tide, moderately hard sand and soft places. Area about two miles by one mile.'

West Sussex

Bognor Regis

The Middleton on Sea area of Bognor Regis was the base of the White & Thompson Company Ltd who, with their successors the Norman Thompson Flight Company Ltd, manufactured considerable numbers of flying boats during the First World War. The activities of these firms are discussed chronologically below.

White & Thompson Ltd, Aeronautic Works, Middleton on Sea, Bognor. This company was registered in June 1912, although White & Thompson had constructed an unsuccessful experimental design in 1910. Its first product was a pusher biplane of 1913, this being followed by extensive work on flying boats, after the company had become 'sole concessionaires for the Curtiss Flying Boats and Engines'. The company telegraphic address was 'Soaring, Bognor'.

White & Thompson designed a twin-engine flying boat as an entry in the 1914 Circuit of Britain race. Clearly derived from Curtiss designs, this aircraft was known as the White & Thompson Seaplane No. 1 and was taken into RNAS service with serial number 883. For the same event, the company also produced a single engine design as Seaplane No. 2, also taken into RNAS service (with serial number 882). *British Aircraft Before the Great War* indicates that this aircraft was flown for the first time on 1 August 1914.

Early production included the single-engine 'Type 3' Curtiss-type pusher biplane flying boat, the first aircraft of this type being purchased for trials by the Admiralty. At least seven more of these 'improved Curtiss' machines were ordered for the RNAS, followed by ten 'America' flying boats. The profit from these orders was spent in extending the factory, a 25 per cent advance payment being negotiated with the Admiralty in December 1915 for this purpose.

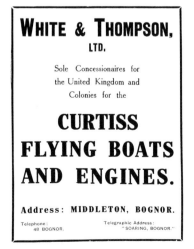

In October 1915 the company was renamed **The Norman Thompson Flight Company Ltd**, advertising as 'Contractors to The Admiralty, manufacturers of seaplanes and aeroplanes' and 'The Firm who gave the Flying Boat to the Navy'. The main production of the Norman Thompson Flight Company Ltd comprised:

- Erection of twenty FBA flying boats that were ordered in July 1916 using hulls built in France. (FBA, Franco-British Aviation, was registered in November 1913 to promote the Lévêque design)
- Twelve NT.3 'Bognor Bloater' single engine biplanes of their own design. Is this the least complimentary name bestowed on a service aircraft?
- More than 130 Norman Thompson NT.2B flying boats, many of which were delivered to store without engines. This type was a development of the White & Thompson Type 3, redesignated NT.2/NT.2A
- More than thirty Norman Thompson NT.4/4A flying boats
- Up to twenty-four Short S.38, the last being delivered in June 1916
- A number of one-off designs, examples including RNAS serials N26, N37 and N82

Difficulties faced by the company caused questions to be asked in Parliament on a number of occasions in 1918 and 1919. The point at issue was whether the company had invested to increase its capacity in both 1915, and again in 1917, at the behest of the Government, only to have received inadequate subsequent orders. The final indignity was that all work except that already in hand was 'cancelled without a day's notice in January 1918'.

The Norman Thompson factory closed in 1919, after acquisition by **Handley Page Ltd**. In February 1920, the assets were auctioned off: 'Freehold – The Norman Thompson Flight Co. Aerodrome, Middleton, Bognor, Sussex. Sale instructed by **The Flying Boat Co. Ltd**. 7.5 acre site overlooking the English Channel with sea and road frontages.' (The Flying Boat

The Norman Thompson Flight Co. Ltd used to advertise as 'The Firm that gave the Flying Boat to the Navy'. This is one of their early products, an FBA flying boat. (Treadwell/Wood)

Ford Aerodrome seen from the air, with the 'sponsors' logo emblazoned on the grass. (Colin Cruddas)

Co. Ltd was presumably a name used by Handley Page Ltd after acquiring the assets). The site is now a Butlins holiday camp.

Hants and Sussex Aviation Ltd had offices at nearby Felpham (and at Portsmouth, Hants, and White Waltham, Berks).

Chichester (see also Goodwood and Tangmere)

The **Virgilio Aircraft Co. Ltd** was registered at Chichester with £5,000 capital in July 1918. Nothing else is known.

The **Wells Aviation Co. Ltd** aerodrome, seaplane station and school of flying was set up at Cobnor, near Chichester, the company being reported in *Flight* to be starting up as a new flying field 'down Chichester way' in October 1916. By February 1917, the School of Flying was active with Caudron biplanes. The origins of this company were with **R.F. Wells & Co.** of Chelsea, which became Wells Aviation Co. Ltd in April 1916. The company was the agent for Benoist flying boats and built both Sopwith and Vickers designs. By October 1917, the company was in liquidation. For details, see the entry for Chelsea in Volume 1 of this series, *British Built Aircraft, Greater London*.

Ford Aerodrome (now Ford Open Prison)

Ford Aerodrome came into being during the First World War as Ford Junction aerodrome and was also sometimes referred to as Yapton. In 1928 or 1929, Mr Dudley Watt was making use of the aerodrome, and he and Mr J.E. Doran-Webb formed the Sussex Aero Club there in 1930. From July 1931, the Ford Motor Co. leased part of the aerodrome as the base for their Trimotor aircraft. This was motivated, at least in part, by the publicity thereby afforded – the airfield even had the Ford logo cut in its grass surface. From 1934, the space previously occupied by Ford was sub-let to National Aviation Day Ltd as the winter base for Sir Alan Cobham's National Aviation Day fleet. This connection probably influenced the move of Cobham's company Flight Refuelling Ltd to Ford at the start of 1936.

DW Aircraft Co., Ford Aerodrome, Yapton, Sussex. The Dudley Watt DW2 G-AAWK was a Warren braced biplane similar in appearance to the Parnall Elf, which was first flown at

Brooklands in May 1930. The DW2 was noted for its slow landing speed and roomy, quiet cockpits. Commenting on a display flown by Dudley Watt, *Flight* said 'His loops were really worth seeing, as he just slowly climbed up one side and slid down the other without any very obvious dive to help him over.' Dudley Watt also operated three Avro 504K from Ford for joy-riding (see also Brooklands).

Flight Refuelling Ltd was registered by Sir Alan Cobham on 29 October 1934, carrying out experiments from Portsmouth using a DH9 (from 1932-33) and an Airspeed Courier G-ABXN (in 1934) as receiver aircraft. The tanker aircraft were Handley Page W.10, G-EBMM and G-EBMR.

Flight Refuelling moved their operations to Ford on 1 January 1936 (although Sir Alan Cobham's National Aviation Tour fleet had made use of the site since 1932). The company address at Ford was Flight Refuelling Ltd, Experimental Factory and Works – Site A, Ford Lane, Ford. In its pioneering work, Flight Refuelling operated an extraordinary variety of aircraft, including two Vickers Virginia, Fairey Hendon, Armstrong Whitworth AW23 G-AFRX, Handley Page Heyford, HP.33 Clive G-ABYX, HP.51 J9833 and HP.54 Harrow. The Harrow tankers, G-AFRG, G-AFRH and G-AFRL were used for experimental fuel transfer to Short C Class flying boat receiver aircraft including *Cabot*, *Cambria* and *Caribou*.

Sixteen transatlantic flights were completed in autumn 1939, with the C-Class flying boats being refuelled by Harrow tankers based in Shannon and Newfoundland. Work on the development of flight refuelling techniques was continued after the war in conjunction with British South American Airways using Avro Lancaster/Lancastrian aircraft. The first non-stop BSAA Lancaster flight from London to Bermuda commenced on 28 May 1947. The route was flown by Lancaster G-AHJV, flown by Air Vice-Marshal D.C.T. Bennett of BSAA, and refuelled by one of Flight Refuelling's Lancaster tanker aircraft G-AHJW, flying from the Azores. Flight Refuelling Ltd operated the following Lancaster fleet – G-AHJT, G-AHJU, G-AHJV, G-AHJW, G-AHVN. Four additional aircraft, G-AKAJ to G-AKAM, were registered to the company, but are reported (A.J. Jackson, *British Civil Aircraft since 1919, Volume 1*) to have only made a single ferry flight to Tarrant Rushton before being disassembled for spares.

A further series of transatlantic trials were carried out with BOAC in 1947 and 1948, their success being reflected in advertising material used in 1948:

> *Proving beyond doubt the practicability and safety of refuelling in flight, 900 gallons – nearly 3 tons of petrol – delivered in 8½ minutes at 10,000ft over mid-Atlantic and the Liberator continues on a non-stop flight from London to Montreal.*
>
> *Following the simple and safe flight refuelling procedure, the tanker located the airliner by radar. Any airliner can be equipped to take on fuel en route, by day or by night, and no extra training or experience is needed by its pilot. Interception and the delivery of fuel is undertaken by the expert tanker crew.*
>
> *The recent trials made with full Government support, first on a summer service between London and Bermuda, followed by the winter service across the Atlantic from London to Montreal, have proved beyond doubt that the operation is practical and safe.*
>
> *The Flight Refuelling service has North Atlantic tanker stations at Shannon, Gander and at Goose Bay.*

Miles Engineering Ltd built three Boxkite replicas at Ford for the film Those Magnificent Men in their Flying Machines. *(J.S. Smith)*

Lancaster XPP tanker conversions G-AKDP, G-AKDR and G-AKDS were based at the tanker stations listed above to support the test Liberator G-AHYD, the trial lasting from 4 February to 28 May 1948.

Flight Refuelling Ltd also operated Lancaster XPP G-AKDO. The Lancaster XPP was a civil transport conversion of the Avro Lancaster, produced in Canada by TCA and Victory Aircraft Ltd. The type had extended nose and tail fairings, and was superficially similar in appearance to a Lancastrian. Lancastrians operated by Flight Refuelling Ltd included G-AGWI, G-AKFF, G-AKFG and G-AKTB. Avro Lincoln RA657 was used for the development of the probe and drogue refuelling system, which the UK eventually adopted for military use.

In June 1948 the operations division of Flight Refuelling Ltd moved from Ford Aerodrome to Tarrant Rushton, Dorset. For further details, see Volume 2 of *British Built Aircraft*.

The **Ford Motor Company** briefly operated two Ford Trimotor aircraft at Ford from mid-1931. The two aircraft (4-AT-E G-ABEF and 5-AT-C G-ABFF) were brought over by sea and assembled at Hooton Park in 1930.

Miles Engineering Ltd (which was set up by F.G. Miles after his withdrawal from Beagle Aircraft) built three Bristol Boxkite replicas for *Those Magnificent Men in their Flying Machines*, and two full-size S.E.5A replicas for *The Blue Max*.

Gatwick Aerodrome, Lowfield Heath

Airwork Ltd operated an approved overhaul facility for Whitley aircraft at Gatwick from 1938.

In 1932-1933 **Air Travel Ltd** converted three Avro 504K (G-ABVH, G-ABVY, G-ACCX) to Avro 504N equivalents, with Armstrong Siddeley Mongoose IIIA radial engines at Penshurst, Kent. Operations were later moved to Gatwick, where the company continued to operate a successful business of conversions, overhaul and refurbishment of the type. Avro 504N civil conversions by Air Travel Ltd included G-ACLV, G-ACOD and G-ACOM.

Redwing Aircraft Ltd ran the Redwing School of Flying and Aeronautical Engineering at Gatwick from summer 1932, the Flying Club being officially opened on 1 July 1932. The company's registered office also moved to Gatwick in July 1932. Redwing owned the site, which it acquired by purchasing Home Counties Aviation Services, from 20 May 1932 until December 1933. Redwing had persistent problems with the drainage of the original aerodrome site, this problem being perhaps reflected in its name of Lowfield Heath.

Goodwood

NDN Aircraft Ltd: The NDN Firecracker piston-engine tandem-seat training aircraft G-NDNI was first flown at Goodwood on 26 May 1977. Only a single example of this aggressive little aircraft was built, the type being developed into the NDN-1T Turbo Firecracker, which competed unsuccessfully in the RAF competition to replace the Jet Provost. The eventually victorious design was a developed version of the Embraer Tucano, built by Shorts in Belfast. NDN and its successor companies were also active at Bembridge, Sandown, Barry, Old Sarum and Hurn.

Littlehampton

José Weiss tested two aircraft on the sands to the west of Littlehampton ('close to Arundel Castle') from April 1910. One was a tailless pusher named *Elsie* flown by Gerald Leake; the second was a powered version of one of Weiss' earlier gliders, this being flown by E.C. Gordon England.

Elsie was flying successfully by mid-April 1910, a flight of 200 yards being recorded on the 16th. *Elsie* featured the crescent-shaped wing planform and washed-out wing tips which so influenced the early Handley Page monoplanes. Good flying results continued into the summer, at which time Weiss decided to move to Brooklands where, in 1911, he flew a further design named *Sylvia*.

The registration of this belligerent little aircraft shows that it is the prototype Norman NDN-1 Firecracker. (Ken Ellis Collection)

Shoreham

Shoreham Aviation Ground dates from 1910, and was the scene of significant pioneer flying, being third only in importance to Brooklands and Hendon. In September 1911, it was advertising as follows: 'Brighton-Shoreham aerodrome – railway station right on aerodrome, tenants share in gate money, large expanse of water available for hydro-aeroplanes.' Uniquely, it has been in more or less continuous use (albeit with differing boundaries, and a break between 1921 and 1925) since 1910, and in 1996 celebrated sixty years as the municipal airport of Brighton and Hove.

An **Aeronautical Syndicate Ltd** Valkyrie B was used on 4 July 1911 to carry the first cargo by air in Britain – a box of OSRAM lamps from Shoreham to Hove, the machine being flown by Horatio Barber.

A.V. Roe & Co. Ltd used Shoreham for seaplane testing, and as the base for the Avro Flying School from October 1912. Contemporary advertising included: 'Avro – Nothing Better' and in March 1913: 'Avro Flying School: Real aeroplanes, no boxkites. Avro Flying School (Brighton) Ltd.' The school used the Avro Type D biplane, and later the Type E prototype and a production Avro 500. The Type E was destroyed here at the end of June 1913. One of the school instructors was John Alcock, later to fly across the Atlantic with Arthur Whitten-Brown in the Vickers Vimy that is preserved in the Science Museum. A.V. Roe & Co. Ltd used Shoreham to test floatplanes, including the Avro 503 first flown on 28 May 1913, which was also known as the 100hp Avro 'Waterplane'. The Avro School left Shoreham in September 1913.

The **Avro-Burga** monoplane was built by A.V. Roe & Co. Ltd for Lt R. Burga of the Peruvian Navy, and was first flown at Shoreham on 11 November 1912 (also reported as 12

This gathering of light aeroplanes celebrates sixty years of Shoreham as a municipal airport. Manufacturers represented include de Havilland, Percival, Miles, Auster, Beagle, Comper, Tipsy, Chrislea and Luton Aircraft. (Author)

The 1911 Avro D tractor biplane photographed at Brooklands. Six were built and the type was used by the Avro Flying School at Shoreham. (Brooklands Museum Trust)

November). The Avro-Burga was a two-seat monoplane, distinguished by having differential rudders mounted above and below the centre fuselage to provide lateral control; no provision was made for wing warping. The aircraft was reported to be very fast with a short take-off run. It is thought that the novel rudders were only tested temporarily.

Beagle Aircraft Ltd (British Executive and General Aviation Limited): This company, a subsidiary of Pressed Steel Ltd, was formed on 7 October 1960. Its chairman was Sir Peter Masefield (previously the Managing Director of the Bristol Aeroplane Co. Ltd). The company took over Auster Aircraft Ltd at Rearsby and produced a series of types of its own design, including, in particular, the Beagle Pup and the Beagle 206. Production facilities were retained at Rearsby, with development and sales activity based at Shoreham. Just over a year after its formation, in November 1961, the company was advertising its actual and projected product range as follows:

The BEAGLES are coming

- *The BEAGLE-Miles-Wallis autogyro – incorporating many new ideas*
- *The BEAGLE Mark Eleven – Primarily a military AOP but has many other uses*
- *The BEAGLE Terrier – training touring aeroplane seating two or three people*
- *The BEAGLE Airedale – a single-engine, four-seat light executive or club aircraft*
- *The BEAGLE M.117 – a single-engine two-seat version of the M.218*
- *The BEAGLE M.218 – a twin-engine four-seat aircraft*
- *The BEAGLE B.206 – a four- to seven-seat luxury aircraft with twin engines.'*

Beagle produced two main designs; the single engine Beagle 121 Pup, and the twin engine Beagle 206. The Beagle Pup was highly successful in sales terms, but unprofitable. The 100hp Pup Srs 1 was somewhat underpowered, but had excellent handling. The prototype G-AVDF first flew at Shoreham on 8 April 1967. The 150hp Srs 2 G-AVLM was first flown on

4 October 1967. The Beagle Pup as a type continues to be much loved by its owners who have an active 'type club'. The Pup is, perhaps, the closest that the post-war industry has come to a production light aircraft that could have been successful on the world stage. (It is, however, unfortunate that its name should have such poor connotations in an American context.) Although orders were received for some 400 aircraft, only 152 had been built when production stopped in 1969.

The second main product of Beagle was the Beagle 206 twin-engine executive, air taxi and military communications aircraft. Some eighty-five Beagle 206 were built, including the twenty Basset used by the RAF. The aircraft was modestly successful, operating with air taxi operators such as the quaintly named 'Steam Chicken Line', which operated out of Gatwick. The type is now regarded as having been over-complex and rather underpowered. The prototype Beagle 206X G-ARRM flew at Shoreham on 15 August 1961. The prototype for the Basset, Beagle 206Z-1 XS742, was flown on 24 January 1964.

Beagle advertised the Beagle 206 in the following terms in October 1965:

BEAGLE 206

Beagle leads with the B.206 Company Executive Aircraft. Most modern, most versatile light twin-piston engine communication aircraft available in production for world markets. Among its many outstanding characteristics are:

Right: *Beagle Pup 100 G-AXPB is an example of Britain's best and most successful post-war production light aircraft.* (Author)

Below: *Great hopes must have been attached to the sight of the Beagle 206 in full production at Shoreham. Like so many other British aviation projects, the promised bright future did not materialise.* (Brooklands Museum Trust)

Chipmunk G-ARWB was modified at Shoreham as a test bed for the 200hp liquid-cooled Aero Bonner Super Sapphire V6 engine, flying for the first time on 2 July 1979. (Author)

- Exceptionally wide instrument panel (54 inches)
- Hydraulically operated air-stairs/baggage door
- Large doors for entrance and freight loading
- Strong floor
- Guaranteed fatigue life of 15,000 flying hours
- Design for maintenance

Beagle was taken over by the British Motor Corporation and nationalised in December 1966, but went into receivership in December 1969. The failure of the company was due to the limited success of the Beagle 206; decisions not to provide the investment required to expand production of the Beagle Pup; and an inability to sell the Pup at a price that covered its high production costs. The Government decided to transfer the assets to Scottish Aviation Ltd at Prestwick. One interpretation of this decision is that it was deemed politically preferable to invest to increase employment in Scotland, rather than to maintain it in the already prosperous south of England.

Scottish Aviation Ltd went on to produce the Bulldog military trainer, which was a 200hp derivative of the Beagle Pup and retained its superb handling qualities. More than 330 Bulldog were subsequently built by Scottish Aviation Ltd, thus demonstrating the true potential of this excellent design. The Beagle-built Bulldog prototype G-AXEH first flew at Shoreham on 19 May 1969.

The names **Beagle-Miles** and **Beagle-Auster** were used briefly to distinguish between the Shoreham and Rearsby components of the Beagle company. The link between Beagle and F.G. Miles Ltd was severed in 1963 due to disagreements over marketing of the composite M.218; see the entry for F.G. Miles Ltd, below. The Beagle B.242 'productionised' derivative of the M.218 was of all-metal construction (abandoning the composite materials of the M.218) and was not actively marketed by Beagle, who were trying to solve the production and financial problems of the Pup and the Beagle 206 at the same time. The prototype B.242 G-ASTX was flown for the first time on 27 August 1964.

Beagle-Wallis. Five WA116 Autogyro were built at Shoreham with Beagle funding. Ken Wallis' first Autogyro, Bensen B7 G-APUD, was also first flown at Shoreham on 23 May 1959. The first Beagle-Wallis WA116 G-ARZA was flown on 10 May 1962.

Bonner. In 1979, de Havilland Canada DHC-1 Chipmunk G-ARWB was modified to act as test bed and demonstrator for the 200hp Aero Bonner Super Sapphire V6 liquid-cooled aero engine. G-ARWB was flown for the first time with its new engine on 2 July 1979 and was subsequently displayed at the SBAC Show at Farnborough.

The **British & Colonial Aeroplane Co.** occupied two sheds at Shoreham in 1911.

Chanter monoplane. The Chanter Flying School moved to Shoreham from Hendon in November 1911, initially with three Blériot plus their own monoplane. The School also acquired the Aeronautical Syndicate Viking 1 and fitted it with floats and a single propeller. The Chanter monoplane made its first flight on New Year's Day 1912 at Shoreham. A fire ended the short residency of the Chanter School on the night of 29 February 1912, destroying three hangars and the Chanter monoplane. A dispute concerning rebuilding works led to closure of the school.

Basil H. England and a Mr Collyer built a tractor biplane, known as the **Collyer-England** biplane, which was tested at Shoreham from August 1911. The aircraft strongly resembled an Avro D biplane with its large wing gap and triangular fuselage section. Dallas-Brett describes the design as not very successful, and it was damaged in early April 1912, having had a change of engine from 30hp Alvaston to 35hp Green. In April 1912, the concern adopted the name 'South Coast Flying School'.

The single experimental **Dowty Rotol** Ducted Propulsor-powered Islander G-FANS was flown at Shoreham on 10 June 1977.

The **Dyott monoplane** was resident at Shoreham in 1913 and later toured very successfully in the United States. The aircraft was making demonstration flights from Shoreham in July 1914. The Dyott monoplane was built at Clapham Junction by Hewlett & Blondeau and was also flown at Hendon.

Mr F.G. Miles set up the **Gnat Aero Company** at Shoreham as a flying school with Cecil Pashley in November 1925. The first student was F.G. Miles himself. Gradually the fleet increased from one Avro 504 to include a BAT Bantam, a Grahame-White-built Boxkite, an additional Avro 504K, two Central Aircraft Centaur biplanes and an Avro Baby G-EAUM. The business was then re-organised into **Southern Aircraft Ltd** (dealing with maintenance and construction) and the Southern Aero Club Ltd (tuition). Later, the Avro Baby was modified into a two-seater, and a surplus SE5A was purchased, together with two further Avro 504. For further associations of F.G. Miles with Shoreham, refer also to the entries for Southern Aircraft Ltd, F.G. Miles Ltd, Miles Marine and Structural Plastics Ltd and Beagle Aircraft Ltd. Other Miles activities were conducted at Reading (Woodley), Redhill, South Marston, Doncaster and Ford.

Hendy Aircraft Co. The Hendy 281 Hobo single-seat monoplane G-AAIG was first flown in October 1929 by Edgar Percival. Initially powered by an ABC Scorpion, the Hobo was re-engined with a Pobjoy R (and later a Pobjoy Cataract) engine. The Hobo had a successful racing career achieving speeds in excess of 130mph on its modest power.

The Hobo was chiefly notable for its use of a novel wing structure, designed by Basil Henderson, which was later taken up by both Parnall and Percival. The Henderson wing made use of two spars with separate diagonal drag bracing attached to the top and bottom of the spars and running across each pair of rib bays, contributing to the torsional stiffness of the wing. The Hobo continued racing until 1938, but was destroyed when its hangar at Lympne was bombed in 1940.

The second product of the company was the Hendy 302 G-AAVT, which was built by Parnall at Yate, and to which the Percival Gull bore more than a passing resemblance. The final design of the Hendy Aircraft Co. was the Hendy 3308 Heck, which was built by Westland at Yeovil, and flew in July 1934. This design was subsequently taken up by Parnall as the Parnall Heck. Hendy Aircraft also built the wing for the Hinkler Ibis. Parnall Aircraft absorbed the Hendy Aircraft Co. in May 1935, purchasing the company from Aircraft Exchange and Mart who had taken over the Hendy assets, including the Hobo, earlier the same year.

The **Lee Richards** Annular Monoplanes were built at Shoreham by James Radley and E.C. Gordon England to the designs of Cedric Lee and G. Tilghmann Richards. The Annular Monoplane No. 1 was flown for the first time on 23 November 1913 by E.C. Gordon England. Unfortunately, the flight was terminated by an engine failure, which occurred on the final approach, resulting in a heavy landing in which the pilot was injured. The aircraft was rebuilt as the Lee Richards Annular Monoplane No. 2, with additional elevator surfaces. This machine was flying successfully in early 1914. *British Aircraft Before The Great War* records that E.C. Gordon England flew some 25 hours on this machine.

At the end of April, experiments with the second machine were concluded as a result of a further accident. A third, almost totally successful, machine was then built with reduced dihedral and further elevator and trailing edge modifications. In all about a year of flying was achieved before the outbreak of the First World War (and a further accident) brought an end to these experiments. A number of sources report that the total time flown by these remarkable conceptions was some 128 hours.

The principles of the annular configuration had been developed in glider experiments at Sellet Banks near Kirkby Lonsdale, and at Ingleborough Dell, Westmorland, in 1912. A powered biplane of annular configuration was also tested unsuccessfully at Middleton Sands, near Heysham. These experiments were associated with the work of Mr J.G.A. Kitchen of Heysham, Lancashire.

F.G. Miles Ltd moved to Shoreham in 1952 from Redhill to continue relatively small-scale aircraft manufacture following the collapse of **Miles Aircraft Ltd** at Woodley. The first new type built was the Miles Sparrowjet G-ADNL, which first flew on 14 December 1953, followed by the Miles M.100 Student G-45-1/G-APLK (first flown on 14 May 1957). The second Miles Aries G-AOGA was flown at Shoreham on 11 July 1955. Other activities centred on early work to exploit composite materials for aircraft construction.

Miles Student G-APLK flies past the now listed Comet hangar, control tower and fire station at Hatfield. (BAE SYSTEMS plc)

The Sparrowjet was a radical conversion of the Gipsy Major-powered M.5 Sparrowhawk to be powered by two 330lb static thrust Turboméca Palas turbo-jet engines mounted at the wing roots. Although a somewhat esoteric one-off, the Sparrowjet proved a successful racer in the hands of Fred Dunkerly, winning the 1957 King's Cup at 228mph.

The Miles Student was advertised in September 1957 as follows: 'F.G. Miles Ltd: The designers of the famous MAGISTER and MASTER trainers for the Royal Air Force have now produced the most economical and versatile basic jet trainer flying today. Miles M.100 STUDENT.' The Miles Student was put back into flying condition during the 1980s after some years in storage, but crashed at Duxford in August 1985. Restoration work was underway in 2000 at the Museum of Berkshire Aviation at Woodley.

In 1955 Miles won a contract to modify Meteor FR.9 VZ608 to test the RB108 lift engine, the aircraft arriving for modification on 15 July 1955. Miles also supplied a thrust reverser for installation on Hunter XF833, under contract to Rolls-Royce.

In June 1955, F.G. Miles entered into collaboration with Société des Avions Hurel-Dubois and announced the formation of **Hurel-Dubois and Miles (Aviation) Ltd**. This led to the construction of the HDM.105, a Miles Aerovan with a high aspect ratio metal wing of 75ft 4in span and 4ft 9in chord. The HDM.105 was a modification of Aerovan G-AJOF and first flew as G-35-3 on 30 March 1957, later acquiring the appropriate registration G-AHDM.

The Miles M.115 project was designed as a Gemini replacement in 1960, and featured attractive lines and extensive use of composite materials. Development of this design was continued (as the Beagle-Miles M.218, or Beagle 218X), following the creation of **Beagle** by Sir Peter Masefield. The Beagle 218X, G-35-6/G-ASCK first flew on 19 August 1962, being rebuilt in 1964 to become the Beagle 242X, G-ASTX. Miles also built the prototype Beagle 206X under contract from Beagle. Another project associated with Beagle was the Beagle Miles M.117 Martlet, a single-engine low-wing monoplane that forms part of the heritage of the B.121 Pup. The M.218 was briefly advertised (September 1961) as the M.218 Merlin.

Two Gipsy Queen-powered SE5A replicas were built at Shoreham in 1965 by **Miles Marine and Structural Plastics Ltd** for use in the film *The Blue Max*. These aircraft were registered G-ATGV and G-ATGW.

Eric and Cecil Pashley built their own biplane at Shoreham in July 1914. The aircraft, which was strongly reminiscent of a Farman Shorthorn, was known as the **Pashley Brothers** biplane. This aircraft was used as a trainer and for joy riding by the Pashley School, which had moved to Shoreham from Brooklands in 1913.

Other aircraft operated by the Pashley Brothers included: Anzani Blériot (1910), Lane monoplane (January 1911), Universal Aviation Co. Sommer biplane (mid-1911), and a Humber monoplane (mid-1912). At the time of transferring to Shoreham in May 1913, a Farman biplane was in use, and the Brothers were reported by *Flight* to be 'flying busily' at Shoreham in July 1913. The company name was changed from 1914 to **Pashley Brothers & Hale**. Cecil Pashley first came to Shoreham in 1911, and continued to instruct at his flying school, now called the Southern Aero Club, until 1962.

The **Piffard** Hydro-biplane was built at Shoreham in 1911. Harold Piffard, its designer, was an artist who had an interest in ballooning before turning to powered flight. The first Piffard design was a pusher biplane with long, curved forward skids rather like a biplane Valkyrie. This first design was constructed in Ealing in 1909, was powered by an eight-cylinder 40hp ENV engine and was tested at Shoreham. A second design achieved short flights at Shoreham in May 1910.

Right: *The Hurel-Dubois Miles HDM.105 G-AHDM shows off the extraordinarily high aspect ratio of its wing planform.* (Mike Hooks)

> **TUITION in FLYING**
>
> Write for particulars of our
>
> **SPECIALLY REDUCED FEES and BONUS FLIGHTS.**
>
> Machines used :— H. FARMAN, AVRO and PASHLEY BIPLANES.
>
> Apply — **PASHLEY BROS. & HALE,**
> THE BRIGHTON—SHOREHAM AERODROME.

The Hydro-biplane was of Boxkite configuration, and was tested with a variety of float configurations without success. Mr Piffard was the first pilot to base his activities at Shoreham, and was thus responsible for the establishment of this pioneering airfield.

The **Popular Flying Association** (PFA) administers the airworthiness certification of British home-built aircraft, and other light aircraft types which fall within the criteria for operation under a Permit to Fly. British designs that have been approved by the PFA for home-built construction include the Clutton-Tabenor FRED, Currie Wot, Isaacs Fury, Phoenix Luton Minor, Shaw Europa, Taylor Monoplane and Taylor Titch. In March 2003, the PFA announced that the organisation would be moving to a new site at Turweston Airfield, Northamptonshire.

The Huntingdon-built **Radley-England** Waterplane was flown very successfully from the River Adur at Shoreham. The aircraft featured a twin-hull design, initially with three Gnome engines, and space for six occupants (three in each float, with the pilot at the front of the starboard float). The Waterplane was rebuilt with a single 150hp Sunbeam driving a Lang propeller for the 1913 *Daily Mail* Round Britain race. The floats (or hulls) were built by The South Coast Yacht Agency. The Radley-England works occupied three sheds at Shoreham and were taken over by Cedric Lee in 1913/14.

Rollason Aircraft & Engines Ltd moved to Shoreham in 1973 from Croydon. By the time of this move, production of the Turbulent and Condor had ceased. The company continued to provide extensive spare parts support for the Tiger Moth and French types such as the Stampe and Jodel series. In 1996 Rollason Aircraft and Engines moved from Shoreham to Burgess Hill.

A single 80hp Henry Farman (serial 1599) was built by **South Coast Aircraft Works**. This company sprang from the remains of the Cedric Lee workforce, who are reported to have built BE2C wings and Avros during the First World War, under Cedric Lee's manager, William Spence. The change in name of Cedric Lee's business was reported in *Flight* during February 1915. The factory was located in the 'Bungalow Town' area.

The **South Coast Aviation Co.** 'official contractors to the Admiralty and War Office'. Twelve BE2C (1424-1435) were ordered and then cancelled – other types, if any, not known.

The similarity in names between the **South Coast Aviation Co.** and the **South Coast Aircraft Works** leads one to speculate that these companies may have been one and the same, with inconsistent reporting leading to a confusion of identity.

Southern Aircraft Ltd was established in 1926 and produced the Southern Martlet, which was designed in 1929 by F.G. Miles and based on the Avro Baby. The first Martlet G-AAII was first flown at Shoreham on 10 July 1929. The type was well known for spirited exhibitions of aerobatics when flown by F.G. Miles. The type was designed from the outset specifically for aerobatics, being described as 'the only aircraft built primarily for private owners who want to stunt'. *Flight* described the type as 'amazingly manoeuvrable'. Seven aircraft, powered by a number of different engines, were built at the Southern Aero Club.

The type was aimed at the 'sporting gentleman', as reflected in the following advertisement:

Martlet: High performance single-seat sports light aeroplane fitted with Genet II, Gipsy II or Hermes type engines. Price from £550. Ample locker accommodation for gun, golf clubs, suitcase fitted standard.

Martlet G-AAVD was reported in *The Aeroplane Spotter* as being still extant at Turnhouse in 1944, albeit in dilapidated condition. The seventh and last Martlet, G-ABJW, was substantially different from its forbears, having a metal fuselage structure, and equal span folding wings without stagger. This type was known as the Metal Martlet. G-AAYX, the fourth Martlet, survives with the Shuttleworth Trust at Old Warden and has been restored to flying condition, flying for the first time on 29 September 2000.

F.G. Miles left Shoreham in 1931, although the Southern Aero Club and Southern Aircraft Ltd continued to operate there until Southern Aircraft Ltd was wound up in 1935. The Southern Aero Club, with an intermediate period as the South Coast Flying Club, operated until 1992, seventy-one years after it was founded.

Above: *Southern Martlet G-AAYX has been restored to flying condition by the Shuttleworth Trust. When first built, the type was noted for its manoeuvrability and aerobatic capabilities.* (James Goggin)

Meteor FR.9 VZ608 was modified for RB108 jet-lift engine trials by F.G. Miles Ltd at Shoreham, before making its first flight in this configuration from RAF Tangmere. (J.S. Smith)

The **Wong** *Tong Mei* was an attractive tractor two-bay biplane powered by a 40hp ABC engine and was tested at Shoreham in spring 1913. 'Tong Mei' is Chinese for dragonfly. The type was followed in 1914 by a much more powerful two-seat derivative powered by a 100hp Anzani engine. Mr Wong was Australian-born of Chinese extraction and learned to fly at the Collyer-England school. A company, **T.K. Wong Ltd**, was formed in December 1913, presumably to promote the design.

RAF Tangmere
F.G. Miles Ltd: Gloster Meteor FR.9 VZ608 was modified to have an RB108 lift engine fitted in the centre fuselage, the conversion being carried out by **F.G. Miles Ltd** at Shoreham in 1955. VZ608 first flew with the RB108 fitted on 18 May 1956 at RAF Tangmere, being delivered to Hucknall on 23 May 1956.

Bibliography

50 Golden Years of Achievement, Hamble 1936–1986 (British Aerospace, 1986)
75 Years of Aviation in Kingston, 1913–1988 (British Aerospace, 1988)
Adventure with Fate, Harald Penrose (Airlife, 1984)
The Aeroplane Directory of British Aviation, Staff of *The Aeroplane* (Temple Press Ltd, 1953)
The Aerospace Chronology, Michael J.H. Taylor (Tri-Service Press, 1989)
Aircraft of the Fighting Powers, Volumes 1–5, ed. D.A. Russell, compiled by H.J. Cooper, Owen Thetford (Harborough Publishing, 1940–1944)
Aircraft of the Fighting Powers, Volume 6, ed. D.A. Russell, compiled by Owen Thetford, C.B. Maycock (Harborough Publishing, 1945)
Aircraft of the Fighting Powers, Volume 7, ed. D.A. Russell, compiled by Owen Thetford, E.J. Riding (Harborough Publishing, 1946)
Aircraft of the RAF, a pictorial record 1918-1978, Paul Ellis (Macdonald & Jane's, 1978)
The Aircraft of the World, William Green, Gerard Pollinger (Macdonald, 1953)
The Aircraft of the World, William Green, Gerard Pollinger (Macdonald, 1955)
The Aircraft of the World, William Green (Macdonald, 1965)
Airlife's General Aviation, R.W. Simpson (Airlife, 1991)
Armstrong Whitworth Aircraft since 1913, Oliver Tapper (Putnam, 1973)
Aviation Archaeology, Bruce Robertson (Patrick Stephens Ltd, second edition 1983)
Aviation in Birmingham, Geoffrey Negus, Tommy Staddon (Midland Counties Publications 1984)
Aviation in Manchester, B.R. Robinson (Royal Aeronautical Society, Manchester Branch, 1977)
Aviation Landmarks, Jean Gardner (Battle of Britain Prints International 1990)
The Aviation Pocket-Book 1919–1920, R. Borlase-Matthews (Crosby, Lockwood & Son, 7th edn, 1919)
Avro (Archive Photographs series), Harry Holmes (Chalford Publishing, 1996)
Avro Aircraft since 1908, A.J. Jackson (Putnam, 1965)
AVRO: The History of an Aircraft Company, Harry Holmes (Airlife, 1994)
Balloons to Buccaneers – Yorkshire's role in aviation since 1785, Brian Catchpole (Maxiprint, 1994)
The Blackburn Story 1909-1959, Blackburn Aircraft Ltd, 1960
Boulton Paul Aircraft (Archive Photographs series), Boulton Paul Association (Chalford Publishing, 1996)
Brassey's World Aircraft & Systems Directory, Michael Taylor (Brassey's (UK) Ltd, 1996)
Bristol Aircraft since 1910, C.H. Barnes (Putnam, 1964)
Bristol: An Aircraft Album, James D. Oughton (Ian Allan, 1973)
'Britain's Air Strength', *The Air Defence of Great Britain,* Lt Cdr R. Fletcher, MP (Penguin, October 1938)
Britain's Motor Industry – The first hundred years, Nick Georgano, Nick Baldwin, Anders Clausager, Jonathan Wood (G.T. Foulis & Co., 1995)
British Aeroplanes, 1914–1918, J.M. Bruce (Putnam, 1962)
British Aerospace – The Facts, BAe Corporate Communications (British Aerospace, 1992 & 1996)
British Aircraft at War 1939–45, Gordon Swanborough (HPC Publishing, 1997)
British Aircraft Before the Great War, Michael H. Goodall, Albert E. Tagg (Schiffer Publishing Ltd, 2001)
British Aircraft Manufacturers since 1908, Günter Endres (Ian Allan Publishing, 1995)
British Aircraft of World War II, David Mondey (Chancellor Press, 1994)
British Aircraft, 1809–1914, Peter Lewis (Putnam, 1962)
British Aviation – Ominous Skies, Harald Penrose (HMSO, 1980)

Bibliography

British Aviation – The Adventuring Years, Harald Penrose (Putnam, 1973)
British Aviation – The Pioneer Years, Harald Penrose (Cassell Ltd, revised edition 1980)
British Aviation – Widening Horizons, Harald Penrose (HMSO, 1979)
The British Bomber since 1914, F.K. Mason (Putnam, 1994)
British Civil Aircraft since 1919, A.J. Jackson (Putnam, 2nd edn, Vol. 1 1973, Vol. 2 1973, Vol. 3 1974)
British Commercial Aircraft – sixty years in pictures, Paul Ellis (Jane's Publishing, 1980)
The British Fighter since 1912, F.K. Mason (Putnam, 1992)
British Flight Testing: Martlesham Heath 1920–1939, Tim Mason (Putnam, 1993)
British Floatplanes, G.R. Duval (D. Bradford Barton, 1976)
British Homebuilt Aircraft since 1920, Ken Ellis (Merseyside Aviation Society, 2nd edn, 1979)
British Light Aeroplanes – Their Evolution, Development and Perfection 1920–1940, Arthur W.J.G. Ord-Hume (GMS Enterprises, 2000)
British Military Aircraft Serials 1878–1987, Bruce Robertson (Midland Counties Publications, 1987)
British Prototype Aircraft, Ray Sturtivant (The Promotional Reprint Co. Ltd, 1995)
British Racing and Record Breaking Aircraft, Peter Lewis (Putnam, 1970)
Brush Aircraft production at Loughborough, A.P. Jarram (Midland Counties Publications, 1978)
Cobham – The Flying Years (Archive Photographs Series), Colin Cruddas (Chalford Publishing, 1997)
In Cobham's Company – Sixty Years of Flight Refuelling Ltd, Colin Cruddas (Cobham plc, 1994)
The Cold War Years – Flight Testing at Boscombe Down 1945–1975, Tim Mason (Hikoki Publications Ltd, 2001)
Dangerous Skies The, A.E. Clouston (Pan Books, 1956)
Discover Aviation Trails, Paul Shaw (Midland Publishing, 1996)
Dizzy Heights – The Story of Lancashire's First Flying Men, Chris Aspin (Helmshore Local History Society, 1988)
English Electric Aircraft and their Predecessors, S. Ransom, R. Fairclough (Putnam, 1987)
Fairey Aircraft since 1915, H.A. Taylor (Putnam, 1974)
Fairey Aviation (Archive Photographs Series), J.W.R. Taylor (Chalford Publishing, 1997)
Fighters of the Fifties, Bill Gunston (Patrick Stephens Ltd, 1981)
Filton and the Flying Machine (Archive Photographs Series), Malcolm Hall (Chalford Publishing, 1995)
The First Croydon Airport 1915–1928, Douglas Cluett (ed.), Bob Learmonth, Joanna Nash (Sutton Libraries and Arts Services, 1977)
First Through the Clouds, F. Warren Merriam (B.T. Batsford Ltd, 1954)
The Flight of the Mew Gull, Alex Henshaw (John Murray, 1980)
Flying Corps Headquarters 1914–1918, Maurice Baring (Buchan & Enright, Publishers, Ltd (reprint), 1985)
The Flying Scots – A century of aviation in Scotland, Jack Webster (The Glasgow Royal Concert Hall, 1994)
Forever Farnborough – Flying the Limits 1904–1996, P.J. Cooper (Hikoki Publications, 1996)
The Forgotten Pilots, Lettice Curtis (Nelson Saunders, 3rd edn, 1985)
Forty Years of the Spitfire – Proceedings of the Mitchell Memorial Symposium, R.A. East, I.C. Cheeseman (Royal Aeronautical Society, Southampton Branch, 1976)
From Spitfire to Eurofighter, Roy Boot (Airlife, 1990)
Gloucestershire Aviation – A History, Ken Wixey (Alan Sutton, 1995)
Handley Page (Images of Aviation Series), Alan Dowsett (Tempus Publishing, 1999)
Hawker – A Biography of Harry Hawker, L.K. Blackmore (Airlife, 1993)
Hawker Aircraft since 1920, F.K. Mason (Putnam, 1961)
Helicopters and Autogyros of the World, Paul Lambermont, Anthony Pirie (Cassell, 1958)
Hendon Aerodrome – A History, David Oliver (Airlife, 1994)
The History of Black Country Aviation, Alec Brew (Alan Sutton, 1993)
History of British Aviation 1908–1914, R. Dallas Brett (Air Research Publications & Kristall Productions, 80th anniversary edn, 1988)

A History of the Eastbourne Aviation Company 1911–1924, Lou McMahon & Michael Partridge (Eastbourne Local History Society, 2000)
I Kept No Diary, Air Cdr F.R. Banks (Airlife, 1978)
Industry and Air Power. The Expansion of British Aircraft Production, 1935–1941, Sebastian Ritchie (Frank Cass, 1997)
The Jet Aircraft of the World, William Green, Roy Cross (Macdonald, 1955)
Knights of the Air, Peter King (Constable & Co. Ltd, 1989)
Lend-Lease Aircraft of World War II, Arthur Pearcy (Motorbooks International, 1996)
Leysdown – the Cradle of Flight, Brian Slade (Santa-Maria Publications, 1990)
Lion Rampant and Winged, Alan Robertson (Alan Robertson, 1986)
Mach One, Mike Lithgow (Allan Wingate, 1954)
The Magic of a Name, Harold Nockholds (G.T. Foulis & Co. Ltd, 1949)
The Marshall Story, Sir Arthur Marshall (Patrick Stephens Ltd, 1994)
Men with Wings, W/Cdr H.P. 'Sandy' Powell (Allan Wingate, 1957)
More Tails of the Fifties, ed. Peter G. Campbell (Cirrus Associates (SW), 1998)
Not much of an Engineer, Sir Stanley Hooker (Airlife, 1984)
Parnall's Aircraft (Images of England Series), Ken Wixey (Tempus Publishing, 1998)
Peaceful Fields.... Volume 1, The South, J.F. Hamlin (GMS Enterprises, 1996)
Plane Speaking, Bill Gunston (Patrick Stephens Ltd, 1991)
Per Ardua – The Rise of British Air Power 1911–1939, Hilary St George Saunders (Oxford University Press, 1944)
Proud Heritage – A Pictorial History of British Aerospace Aircraft, Phil Coulson (Royal Air Force Benevolent Fund, 1995)
Pure Luck – The Authorized Biography of Sir Thomas Sopwith 1888–1989, Alan Bramson (Patrick Stephens Ltd, 1990)
The Quick and The Dead, W.A. Waterton (Frederick Muller Ltd, 1956)
The Redwing Story, John Lane (Mrs Phyllis Lane, 1992)
The Royal Flying Corps (Images of Aviation Series), Terry C. Treadwell & Alan C. Wood (Tempus Publishing Ltd, 2000)
The Royal Naval Air Service (Images of Aviation Series), Terry C. Treadwell & Alan C. Wood (Tempus Publishing Ltd, 1999)
Schneider Trophy, The, David Mondey (Robert Hale, 1975)
Sent Flying, A.J. 'Bill' Pegg (Macdonald, 1959)
Shoreham Airport, Sussex, T.M.A. Webb, Dennis L. Bird (Cirrus Associates (SW), 1996)
Shorts Aircraft since 1900, C.H. Barnes (Putnam, 1989)
Sigh for a Merlin, Alex Henshaw, Crécy Publishing, 1999 reprint
Slide Rule, Nevil Shute (Readers Union, 1956)
Sopwith – The Man and His Aircraft, Bruce Robertson (Air Review Ltd, 1970)
The Speed Seekers, Thomas G. Foxworth (Macdonald and Jane's, 1975)
The Spider Web, Sqn Ldr T.D. Hallam (Arms & Armour Press (reprint), 1979)
Spirit of Hamble – Folland Aircraft, Derek N. James (Tempus Publishing, 2000)
Spitfire – A Test Pilot's Story, J.K. Quill (John Murray, 1983)
The Spitfire Story, Alfred Price (Arms & Armour Press, second edition, 1995)
Staffordshire and Black Country Airfields (Archive Photographs Series), Alec Brew (Chalford Publishing, 1997)
Stirling Wings – The Short Stirling goes to War, Jonathan Falconer (Budding Books, 1995)
The Story of Acton Aerodrome and the Alliance Factory (London Borough of Ealing Library Service, second edition, 1978 with addenda and corrigenda)
The Story of the British Light Aeroplane, Terence Boughton (John Murray, 1963)
Supermarine (Archive Photographs Series), Norman Barfield (Chalford Publishing, 1996)
Supermarine Spitfire – 40 Years On, G.N.M. Gingell (Royal Aeronautical Society, Southampton Branch, 1976)
Tails of the Fifties, ed. Peter G. Campbell (Cirrus Associates (SW), 1997)
Test Pilot, Nevil Duke (Allan Wingate, 1953)
Test Pilots – The Story of British Test Flying 1903–1984, Don Middleton (Willow Books, 1985)

Testing Time, Constance Babington Smith (Cassell & Co. Ltd, 1961)
That Nothing Failed Them, Air Cdre A.H. Wheeler (G.T. Foulis & Co. Ltd, 1963)
Three Centuries to Concorde, Charles Burnet (Mechanical Engineering Publications Ltd, 1979)
A Time to Fly, Sir Alan Cobham (Shepheard-Walwyn, 1978)
Ultralights – The Early British Classics, Richard Riding (Patrick Stephens Ltd, 1987)
Vapour Trails, Mike Lithgow (Allan Wingate, 1956)
Vickers Aircraft since 1908, C.F. Andrews, E.B. Morgan (Putnam, 2nd edn, 1988)
War in the Air, Edward Smithies (Penguin, 1992)
Westland 50, J.W.R. Taylor, Maurice F. Allward (Ian Allan, 1965)
Westland Aircraft since 1919, D.N. James (Putnam, 1991)
Wings over Woodley – The Story of Miles Aircraft and the Adwest Group, Julian C. Temple (Aston Publications, 1987)
World Encyclopaedia of Aircraft Manufacturers, Bill Gunston (Patrick Stephens Ltd, 1993)

Magazines and other publications:

Flight: Numerous editions of 'The First Aero Weekly in the World – A Journal Devoted to the Interests, Practice and Progress of Aerial Locomotion and Transport. Official Organ of The Royal Aero Club of the United Kingdom'
The Aeroplane: Numerous editions, Temple Press Ltd, eds C.G. Grey, Thurstan James
Aeroplane Monthly: Numerous editions, IPC Magazines Ltd
The Aeroplane Spotter July 1941–December 1945, Temple Press Ltd
Jane's All the World's Aircraft: various editions from 1909 to date, published by Samson Low, Jane's Information Group, and (reprints) David & Charles Ltd, Collins & Jane's
Popular Flying The Magazine of the Popular Flying Association
Royal Air Force Flying Review: 1954–55, 1957–58, 1961–62, Mercury House

Index

Abbott-Baynes Aircraft Ltd, 66, 183
ABC Motors Ltd, 138, 187
   Robin, 138, 188
Addlestone, 16, 136-139, 153, 157, 190, 191
Aerial Manufacturing Co. monoplane, 194
Aero Construction Co., 139, 141
Aeronautical Corporation of Great Britain Ltd
   (Aeronca), 138
Aeronautical Syndicate Ltd, The, 201, 205
   Valkyrie, 201, 208
AgustaWestland, see Westland
Air Service Training Ltd, 28
Air Travel Ltd, 125, 199
Airbus Integrated Company (also Airbus Industrie,
   BAe Airbus Ltd, BAE SYSTEMS Airbus Ltd), 37,
   42, 142
Airbus Integrated Company (also BAe Airbus Ltd,
   BAE SYSTEMS Airbus Ltd)
   A300-A380, 42, 43
   A400M, 43
AIRCO (also The Aircraft Manufacturing Co. Ltd),
   14, 19, 21, 23, 48, 66, 73, 128
   DH2, 187
   DH4, 14, 18
   DH6, 14, 66
   DH9 & DH9A, 14, 128, 184, 198
Aircraft Disposal Co. Ltd, The (also AIRDISCO), 20,
   111, 152, 156
Airflight Ltd, 79
Airmark Ltd, 185, 186
   Cassutt IIIM, 185, 186
Airmaster Helicopters Ltd H2-B1, 175, 185
Airspeed Ltd (also Airspeed (1934) Ltd), 24, 28, 48, 185
   AS.5 Courier, 198
   AS.6 Envoy, 24
   AS.10/AS.40 Oxford, 24, 27, 29, 30, 56, 81, 98,
      103
   AS.51 Horsa, 56
   AS.57 Ambassador, 32, 97
   AS.65 Consul, 80
Airtech Ltd, 10, 80
Airtraining (Fairoaks) Ltd, 182
Airwork Ltd, 75, 172, 182, 199
AJD Engineering, 84, 85
AJEP Developments Wittman Tailwind, 103
Aldenham, 26, 91, 92, 104
Aldergrove, 100
Aldermaston, 52, 66, 68
ANEC (Air Navigation & Engineering Co. Ltd), 124,
   125, 136, 137, 139, 190, 191
   ANEC I monoplane, 124, 137, 139
   ANEC II, 137
   ANEC III, 137, 139
   ANEC IV Missel Thrush, 125, 137
ARIII Construction (Hafner Gyroplane) Ltd, 74
   Hafner ARIII, 74
Armstrong Whitworth Aircraft Ltd, Sir W.G., 21, 28,
   47, 148, 169, 177
   A.W.23, 198
   A.W.38 Whitley, 81, 199
   Siskin, 171
Ashingdon, 81

Astley, H.J.D., 139, 162
Audley End, 82
Auster Aircraft Ltd, 202
Austin Motor Co. Ltd (also Austin Motor Co. (1914)
   Ltd), 19, 25, 28, 29, 132, 151, 152
Autokraft Ltd, 139
Aviation Enterprises Ltd (and AMF Aviation
   Enterprises Ltd), 53
   Chevvron, 52, 53
   Magnum, 53, 54
Aviation Traders Engineering Ltd, 11, 86-89, 173
   Accountant, 86, 87
   Carvair, 73, 86, 87
   Vanguard Merchantman, 87
Avro (A.V. Roe)
   Roe I-IV triplanes, 13, 140
Avro (A.V. Roe & Co.)
   Type D, 140, 201, 202
   Type E, 141, 147, 201
   Type F, 140, 141
   500, 140, 141, 201
Avro (A.V. Roe & Co. Ltd), 19, 21, 23, 28, 35, 40, 47,
   124, 125, 182, 201
   504 (all variants), 14, 56, 80, 84-86, 111, 112, 125,
      136, 140, 141, 184, 193, 194, 198, 199, 205
   548, 147, 152
   552, 184
   558, 124
   560, 124
   562 Avis, 125
   581/594/616 Avian (all models), 125
   652A Anson and Avro XIX, 29, 30, 141
   683 Lancaster, 26, 29, 30, 32, 67, 80, 100, 135,
      171, 176, 198, 199
   685 York, 32, 176
   688/689 Tudor, 32, 79, 86, 88, 101
   691 Lancastrian, 32, 100, 198, 199
   694 Lincoln, 80, 101, 199
   696 Shackleton, 68
   698 Vulcan, 34
   707, 182
Avro School (Brighton) Ltd, 140
Avro-Burga monoplane, 201, 202
Ayot St Lawrence, 89

BAE SYSTEMS plc, 6, 7, 9, 41, 42-44, 46, 47, 102,
   142, 180, 181
   F-35 Joint Strike Fighter (with Lockheed Martin),
      42, 46, 180
Barton-le-Clay, 74
Batchelor monoplane, 134
Battersea, 116, 152
Beagle Aircraft Ltd, 6, 11, 37, 39, 47, 199, 202-205
   B.242 & B.242X, 204
   Beagle 206 and Basset, 37, 38, 39, 202-204,
      207
   Bulldog, 38, 204
   M.117, 202, 207
   M.218, 202, 204, 207
   Pup, 38, 39, 202-204
Beardmore, Wm. & Co. Ltd, 19, 124, 125, 137, 144
   Wee Bee, 124, 125

Index

Beaulieu, 157
Belfast, 9, 26, 28, 35, 107, 132-134, 139, 200
Bembridge, 38, 200
Benton B.I – B.VII, 66
Berkshire, 7, 52-73, 65, 66, 87, 110, 207
Bexleyheath, 112, 166, 167
Billing, Mr Eardley, 88, 141
    'Oozeley Bird' biplane, 141, 142
Blackburn Aeroplane & Motor Co. Ltd, The (also Blackburn Aircraft Ltd and Blackburn & General Aircraft Ltd), 19, 22, 28, 125, 161
    Beverley, 34
    Bluebird, 125
    Mercury monoplanes, 141
Blackburn, Mr Robert, 141
Blackbushe, 70, 86, 139
Blair Atholl, 121
Blair Atholl Aeroplane Syndicate Ltd, 121
Blériot & SPAD Manufacturing Co., 136
Blériot & SPAD Manufacturing Co., 16, 136, 138, 139
Bodmin, 86
Bognor Regis, 195-197
Bolotoff, Prince Serge de, 135, 142
    Biplane, 135
Bonner-powered Chipmunk, 204, 205
Boscombe Down, 65, 76, 79, 177
Boulton & Paul Ltd, 19, 22, 161
Boulton Paul Aircraft Ltd, 81, 150
    Defiant, 29, 81, 151
Brabazon Committee, 31, 99
Brighton & Hove, 191
Bristol Aeroplane Co. Ltd, 13, 22, 28, 48, 78, 124, 149, 202
    Type 91 Brownie, 124, 125
    Type 105 Bulldog, 148
    Type 120, 23
    Type 130 Bombay, 28
    Type 142M/149 Blenheim, 26, 27, 29, 30, 91, 182
    Type 152 Beaufort, 29
    Type 156 Beaufighter, 27, 29, 30, 182
    Type 167 Brabazon, 32
    Type 170 Freighter, 32, 88
    Type 171 Sycamore, 34
    Type 175 Britannia, 32
    Type 192 Belvedere, 34
British & Colonial Aeroplane Co. Ltd, The, 21, 142
    Boxkite, 119, 143, 199
    Bristol F.2B Fighter, 18, 161
British Aerospace plc, 6, 7, 11, 37, 39-47, 49, 51, 82, 96, 101, 102, 110, 142, 176, 180, 181
    ATP (and Jetstream 61), 43, 44, 102
    BAe 146, HS146, Avro RJ, RJX, 37, 44, 96, 101, 102
    Jetstream 41, 43, 44
    Sea Harrier, 41, 179, 181
    T-45 Goshawk (with Boeing), 42, 180
British Aircraft Company Ltd, 125, 125
    BAC I-IX, 125
    Drone (also Kronfeld Drone & Super Drone), 125
    Planette, 125
British Aircraft Corporation, 6, 11, 19, 35-37, 39-41, 46-48, 51, 73, 101, 138, 142, 167, 170, 173, 185, 189
    BAC 167 Strikemaster, 39
    Concorde, 36, 37, 73, 142
    One-Eleven, 36, 37, 73, 102, 142, 170, 189
    TSR.2, 35, 39, 73, 142
British Deperdussin Co. Ltd, 83, 144
    Seagull, 83
British South American Airways Corporation, 79, 80, 198

Britten-Norman Ltd (and its successors), 6
    Islander, 38, 39, 45, 205
Broburn Wanderlust, 66
Brocklehurst monoplane, 191
Brooklands, 6, 9-13, 16, 22, 26, 72, 78, 83, 85, 87, 122, 135-176, 188, 190, 191, 198, 200-202, 208
Brooklands Aviation Ltd, 143
Brough, 41, 75, 77, 89, 141, 180, 181
Broughton (Chester), 26, 99, 101
Broughton-Blayney Brawney, 114
Broxbourne, 90
Brush Electrical Engineering Co. Ltd, The (also Brush Coachworks Ltd), 19, 92, 127
Buckinghamshire, 7, 73-81

Caffyns Garages Ltd, 191
Camber Sands, 13, 85, 194, 195
Camberley, 175, 176
Campbell Aircraft Ltd (also Campbell Gyroplanes Ltd), 11, 54
    Cougar, 54
    Cricket & Super Cricket, 53, 54
Carden-Baynes Scud III, 66, 183
Castle Bromwich, 27
Central Aircraft Centaur, 139, 205
Chalgrove, 76, 81
Champel biplane, 143
Chanter monoplane, 205
Chichester, 197
Chichester Miles Consultants Ltd, 89
Chilbolton, 182, 189
Chilton Aircraft Ltd DW1 Monoplane, 53, 54
Christchurch, 41, 97, 99, 100, 185
Christchurch Division of The de Havilland Aircraft Co. Ltd, 97
Churchill, W.S. (later Sir Winston Churchill), 15, 17
Cierva Rotorcraft Ltd (also Servotec Ltd), 185
    CR. LTH-1 Grasshopper III, 185, 186
Cinque Ports Aviation Ltd, 125
Clacton, 13, 83
Clarke Cheetah, 75, 77
Clayton & Shuttleworth Ltd, 167
CLW Aviation Co. Ltd (also CLW Aviation (1936) Ltd), 112
    Curlew, 112, 113
CMC Leopard, 89
Coates, J.R., 103, 105
    Swalesong, 103, 105
Cobham, 170, 176
Cody, S.F., 12
Colchester, 83, 84, 153
Collyer-England biplane, 205
Collyer-Lang monoplane, 143
Comper Aeroplanes Ltd, 188
    Scamp, 188
Coventry, 19, 143, 153, 188
Coventry Ordnance Works Ltd, 19, 48, 143
Cowes, 147, 157
Cowper-Coles Aircraft Co. Ltd, 10, 16, 187
Cranleigh, 176
Cranwell Light Aero Club, 125
    CLA.2, CLA.3, CLA.4, 125
Cross, Mr Jack, 112
Croydon, 20, 24, 80, 83, 84, 91, 156, 184, 185, 206
Croydon Aviation & Engineering Co., 10, 73
Cunliffe-Owen Aircraft Ltd, 28, 32
    Concordia, 32
Currie Wot, 124, 125, 176, 206
Curtiss, 13, 195
CW Aircraft Cygnet, 67

Daimler Co. Ltd, The, 19, 25, 144
Darracq Motor Engineering Co. Ltd, The, 19, 161, 166
de Havilland (Canada) DHC1 Chipmunk, 34, 99, 111, 205
de Havilland Aircraft Co. Ltd, The, 22, 24, 28, 47, 67, 92, 101, 111, 124
   DH53, 75, 77
   DH60 Moth (all models), 24, 92, 125
   DH82 Tiger Moth, 26, 27, 29, 30, 56, 80, 81, 98, 102, 206
   DH84 Dragon, 24, 97
   DH87 Hornet Moth, 7, 9, 92, 96
   DH88 Comet, 92, 97, 112
   DH89 Dragon Rapide (and Dominie), 24, 29, 80, 92, 93, 97-99
   DH90 Dragonfly, 92, 97
   DH91 Albatross, 92, 93, 97
   DH94 Moth Minor, 92
   DH95 Flamingo, 93, 97
   DH98 Mosquito (and Sea Mosquito), 26, 29, 30, 56, 67, 82, 92, 93, 98, 103, 104, 110, 111, 135, 143, 176
   DH100 Vampire (all marks), 28, 33, 93, 94, 95, 98-100
   DH103 Hornet (and Sea Hornet), 33, 92-94, 98
   DH104 Dove, 33, 58, 92, 94, 99
   DH106 Comet, 32, 33, 36, 92, 94-96, 99, 102
   DH110 Sea Vixen, 33, 95
   DH112 Venom (all marks including Sea Venom), 33, 94, 95, 98-100
   DH114 Heron, 95, 99, 100
de Havilland, Geoffrey, 13, 55
Deal, 111
Deekay Aircraft Corporation, 90
   Knight, 90
Denham, 74-77, 80, 81, 125
Denny, Wm. & Bros., 19, 47
DFW Aircraft Co., 144
DH Technical School, 54, 102
   TK1-TK5, 102, 103
Dilton Marsh, 89
Dudbridge Iron Works Ltd, The, 19
Dumbarton, 133
Dunne, J.W., 121
   Dunne D.5-D.10, 121
Dunne-Huntington triplane, 121
Dunsfold, 6, 8, 11, 33, 34, 41, 42, 79, 176-182
DW Aircraft Co., 144, 197
   Dudley Watt DW1, 144
   Dudley Watt DW2, 144, 184, 197

Earls Colne, 84
East Anglian Aviation Co. Ltd, 7, 83
East Sussex, 7, 191-195
Eastbourne, 7, 12, 13, 191-194
Eastbourne Aviation Co. Ltd, 7, 12, 13, 191-194
Eastchurch, 11, 12, 24, 115-122, 127, 138, 175, 194
Eastleigh, 89, 125
Edgar Percival Aircraft Ltd, 88, 89
   E.P.9 Prospector, 88, 89
Edgley Aircraft Co. Ltd
   Optica, 189
Elliotts of Newbury Ltd, 11, 56, 67
   Newbury Eon, 56, 67
Elstree, 73, 88, 91, 92, 104
English Electric Co. Ltd, The (and English Electric Aviation Ltd), 26, 28, 35, 48, 94, 99, 106, 108, 109
   Canberra (all marks), 34, 39, 66, 108, 109
   P1A & Lightning, 39, 40, 73
   Wren, 124

Essex, 7, 81-89, 91, 153, 174
Essex Aero Ltd, 112, 114
   Sprite, 112
Eurofighter GmbH
   Eurofighter (and Typhoon), 41, 180

Fairey Aviation Co. Ltd, The (also Fairey Aviation Ltd), 6, 11, 22, 27, 28, 35, 52, 67-69, 90, 108, 109, 115, 127, 157
   Albacore, 27
   Barracuda, 27, 29, 158
   Battle, 22, 25, 26, 27, 29, 150
   F.127, 115
   F.128/Fairey III and IIIA, 115
   Fawn, 22
   Firefly, 27, 29, 67, 158, 181
   Flycatcher, 22
   Gannet, 52, 67, 68
   Gordon, 22
   Gyrodyne and Jet Gyrodyne, 34, 68, 69
   IIIF, 22
   N.4 Atalanta and Titania, 115
   Rotodyne, 34, 68, 69
   Seal, 22
   Swordfish, 22, 29, 158
   Ultralight, 35, 68, 69
Fairey, C.R. Mr (later Sir Richard Fairey), 13, 120, 121
Fairfield Aviation Ltd, 7, 91, 104
Fairoaks, 70, 182, 190
Fairtravel Ltd, 69, 70
   Linnet, 70
Fambridge, 13, 85, 153, 174, 194
Farm Aviation Ltd, 111
   Chipmunk 23, 111
Farnborough, 12, 76, 79, 84, 102, 121, 138, 162, 170, 176, 205
Farnham, 66, 176, 183
Felixstowe (Seaplane Experimental Station)
   F.3, 128
   F.5, 128, 129
Field, C.B., 184, 185
Filey, 141
Filton, 27, 41, 142, 143, 168
Fitch Biplane, 83
Flanders, L. Howard Ltd, 146
   Flanders B.2, F.2-F.4, 144
Flight Refuelling Ltd (also FR Aviation, Cobham plc), 75, 197, 198, 199
FLS Aerospace (Lovaux Ltd)
   Sprint, 86
Folland Aircraft Ltd, 9, 28, 31, 47, 182
   Gnat (fighter and trainer), 182
Ford (Yapton), 197-199
Foster Wikner Aircraft Co. Ltd, 89
   Wicko, 89
Frank Hucks Waterplane Co. Ltd, 193
Fritz monoplane, 12

Garland-Bianchi (also Garland Aircraft Ltd), 69, 70, 182
   Linnet, 70, 182
Gaskell-Blackburn biplane, 147
Gatwick, 83, 125, 199, 200, 203
General Aircraft Ltd, 24, 47, 67, 147, 151, 182
   Hamilcar and Hamilcar X, 56
Gerrard's Cross, 74, 122
Gillingham, 112
Glenny & Henderson Ltd, 7, 147, 152
   Gadfly, 144, 147
Gloster Aircraft Co. Ltd, 28, 47, 148, 149, 151, 152
   Gloster IV, 185

Javelin, 100
Meteor (all marks), 33, 81, 100, 182, 210, 211
Gloucestershire Aircraft Co. Ltd, The, 22
   Bamel (and Gloster I), 185
   Gannet, 124
Gnat Aero Co., 205
Gnosspelius Gull, 124, 125, 135
Goodwood, 83, 197, 200
Gordon Dove, 81
Gordon England, Mr E.C., 85, 147, 174, 200, 206
Gosport, 115
Gouge, Sir Arthur, 128, 134
Gowland Jenny Wren, 105, 106
Grahame-White Aviation Co. Ltd, The, 19
Gravesend, 6, 11, 24, 112-114, 132
Greater London, 6, 7, 11, 12, 67, 74, 83, 115, 185, 197
Grey, C.G., Mr, 37, 118, 138
Guildford, 176, 183

Hall School of Flying Ltd, 129
Halton Aero Club, 75, 76
   HAC.1 Mayfly, 75, 76
   HAC.2 Minus, 75, 77
Hamble, 28, 41, 52, 115, 167, 182
Hammond, Mr E.V., 147
Hampshire, 56, 84, 115
Hampshire Aero Club, 125
Hamsey Green, 184
Handasyde Aircraft Co., 190
   Handasyde H.2 monoplane, 137, 190, 191
Handley Page (Reading) Ltd, 11, 33, 60, 63-66, 108
   HPR.2, 66
   HPR.3 Herald and HPR.7 Dart Herald, 38, 65, 66, 73, 108, 110
   HPR.5, 66
   Marathon, 33, 62, 64-66
Handley Page Ltd, 6, 11, 19, 22, 26, 28, 35, 38, 47, 64, 65, 88, 104-110, 124, 146, 147, 156, 185, 196, 197
   Clive, 198
   Halton, 32, 80, 87
   HP.12 O/400, 15, 106
   HP.15 V/1500, 106
   HP.38/50 Heyford, 106, 107, 198
   HP.42/45, 23, 106-108
   HP.52 Hampden, 28, 29, 106
   HP.53 Hereford, 28, 106
   HP.54 Harrow, 107, 198
   HP.57 Halifax, 26-30, 67, 80, 81, 86-88, 91, 92, 101, 104-109, 176
   HP.67 Hastings, 34, 107, 108
   HP.68 Hermes, 33, 107, 110
   HP.88, 88
   HP.75 Manx, 107
   HP.80 Victor, 34, 106, 108-110
   HP.137 Jetstream, 38, 39, 43, 105, 108-110
   W.10, 198
Hanriot (England) Ltd, 147, 156
Hants & Sussex Aviation Ltd, 70
Hanworth, 24, 67, 74, 125
Harmondsworth, 52, 55
Harris Lebus Ltd, 56
Hatfield, 6, 8, 11, 24, 37, 41, 44, 76, 92-102, 111
Hawarden, 99, 101
Hawker Aircraft Ltd (also H.G. Hawker Engineering Co. Ltd), 6, 11, 20, 28, 47, 77, 78, 125, 138, 147, 148, 175, 176, 182
   Audax, 149-152
   Cygnet, 125, 137
   Demon, 150, 151
   Duiker, 148
   Fury, 22, 72, 148, 149, 151, 152
   Fury F.2/43, 78
   Hardy, 150, 151
   Hart and Hart Trainer, 20, 22, 91, 148-152, 171
   Hartbees, 150
   Hector, 80, 151
   Henley, 26, 101, 151
   Hind, 22, 80, 150-152
   Hornet, 148, 152
   Horsley, 148, 151
   Hotspur, 151
   Hunter, 33, 34, 40, 72, 79, 177, 178, 181, 210
   Hurricane, 22, 26, 29, 30, 72, 77, 78, 81, 82, 85, 98, 139, 150-152, 175, 182
   Nimrod, 149
   Osprey, 23, 125, 129, 149, 151
   P.1040, 79
   P.1052, 79
   P.1072, 79
   P.1081, 79
   P.1127 and Kestrel, 33, 34, 178, 181
   Sea Fury, 33, 72, 78, 79, 178
   Sea Hawk, 33, 177, 181
   Tempest (all marks), 29, 72, 77-79, 139, 176
   Tomtit, 148, 149, 184
   Tornado, 78
   Typhoon, 26, 27, 29, 72, 77, 78, 176
   Woodcock, 148
Hawker Restorations, 84
Hawker Siddeley Aviation Ltd, 6, 35- 38, 40, 44, 46, 47, 101, 110, 176, 178-180, 182
   Buccaneer, 40
   DH121 Trident, 37, 40, 73, 96, 101
   Harrier, 33, 40-42, 72, 178, 179, 181
   HS1182 Hawk, 40-42, 142, 178- 181
   HS125 (and DH125, BAe125), 38, 40, 43, 96, 101, 181
   HS748, 40, 43
Hayes, 52, 68, 72, 115
Helmy Aerogypt, 70
Henderson School of Flying Ltd, 10, 147, 152
   HSF.1, 152
Hendon, 12, 13, 83, 106, 141, 147, 157, 175, 189, 198, 201, 205
Hendy Aircraft Co., 206
Hobo, 206
Hertfordshire, 7, 89-111
Herts & Essex Aviation Ltd, 90
Heston, 28, 52, 67, 68, 70, 74, 75, 80, 97, 183
Hewlett & Blondeau Ltd, 10, 19, 147, 152, 153, 165, 205
High Post, 83
High Wycombe (also Booker), 10, 16, 71, 73, 74
Hinkler, H.J. 'Bert', 124, 206
   Ibis, 206
Historic Flying Ltd, 82, 83
Hitchin, 103, 105, 111
Holle Varioplane, 153
Hordern-Richmond Aircraft Ltd, 7, 74, 80, 81
   Autoplane, 74, 80
Howard Wright, 13, 85, 174, 175, 194
Hucclecote, 78, 152
Humber Ltd, 153
Humphreys monoplane, 153
Hungerford, 11, 53, 54
Hurel Dubois & Miles Aviation Ltd HDM.105, 210, 208
Hurn, 41, 86, 142, 170, 172, 189, 200

Isaacs, John, 24, 125, 206
Isle of Grain, 16, 114, 115
Isle of Sheppey, 6, 11, 12, 115-122, 125, 127

Jetstream Aircraft Ltd (and Terravia Trading Services Ltd), 105
Jezzi brothers, 24, 121, 122
Jouques Aviation Works, 19
Joyce Green, 13, 16, 122, 124, 165, 166

Kent, 7, 11, 111-135, 142, 165, 166, 199
Kent Aircraft Services Ltd, 7, 111, 112
Kingsbury Aviation Ltd, 167
Kingsbury Works Ltd, 111
Kingston upon Thames, 16, 22, 26, 41, 148, 152, 158, 181
Kingswood Knoll, 184

Lakes Flying Co., 129, 141
Lang Propeller Ltd (also Lang, Garnett & Co.), 138
Langley, 6, 11, 26, 77-80, 152, 176, 177
Larkhill, 12, 13, 124, 142, 143, 147
Latimer-Needham, Mr C.H., 74, 75, 76, 77, 176, 184
Leavesden, 6, 11, 26-28, 91, 92, 100, 103-105, 108
Lee Richards Annular Monoplane, 206
Leeds, 141
Leisure Sport, 187
Leysdown, 12, 13, 115-118, 122, 125
Littlehampton, 85, 174, 200
Lockspeiser LDA-01, 189, 191
London Aero and Motor Services Ltd, 80, 88, 91
London Aircraft Production Group, 26-28, 30, 91, 104, 105, 108, 109
Louis Blériot Aeronautics (and L. Blériot Aeronautics), 136
Luton, 24, 75, 89, 90, 113, 114, 152, 153, 185
Luton Aircraft Ltd, 55, 74, 75, 176
    LA.4 & LA.4A Minor, 74, 75, 77, 105, 106, 176, 182, 183, 206
    LA.5 Major, 74, 75
Lympne, 24, 56, 124, 125, 129, 135, 168, 206

Macfie, Mr R.F., 85, 153, 154, 162
    Empress, 85, 153
Maidenhead, 54, 66, 70, 72
Maidstone, 113, 125, 125
Mann, Egerton & Co. Ltd, 19, 127, 128
Marendaz Aircraft Ltd (and associated companies), 54, 55
    Marendaz III, 55
    Special Monoplane, 55
    Trainer, 55
Martin & Handasyde Ltd, 154, 155
    Nº 3 monoplane, 154
    Nº 4B 'Dragonfly', 154
Martin Monoplane, 75
Martin-Baker Aircraft Ltd, 9, 28, 74-76, 81
    MB1, 75, 76
    MB2, 75
    MB3, 75, 81
    MB5, 28, 75, 76
Martinsyde Ltd (also Martinsyde Aircraft Co.), 6, 16, 18, 19, 21, 47, 136-138, 154-156, 184, 190
    F.1, 155
    F.3, 18, 155
    F.4, 155
    G.100/G.102, 155
    S.1, 155
    Semiquaver, 138, 155
    Type A, 155

Medway (river), 112, 120, 125-129, 132, 135
Membury, 53, 54
Metropolitan Wagon Co. Ltd, 167
Mickleborough L107 Sparrow, 80
Middleton on Sea, 13, 16, 195-197
Miles Engineering Ltd, 199
Miles, F.G. Ltd, 64, 185, 204-207, 211
    M.100 Student, 206, 207
    Sparrowjet, 206, 207
Miles, F.G., Mr, 37, 57, 64, 65, 185, 199, 205, 207, 210
Milton Keynes, 80, 81
Mitchell Brothers hydro-aeroplane, 112
Mitchell-Procter Aircraft Ltd, 176, 183
    Kittiwake I, 176, 183, 184
ML Engineering Co. Ltd (also ML Aviation Co. Ltd), 67, 70, 71
    Utility, 70
Moore-Brabazon, J.T.C. (later Lord Brabazon of Tara), 12, 115, 118, 122
Morgan & Co., 167
Morris Motors Ltd, 26, 28, 62
Mulliners Coachworks Ltd, 158
Muntz, Alan & Co. Ltd, 80
Mussel Manor (alternatively Muswell Manor), 116

Napier, D. & Son Ltd, 19, 106, 107
Nash Aircraft Ltd, 183
NDN Aircraft (UK) Ltd (also NDN Aircraft Ltd), 200
    Firecracker, 200
    NDN-1T Turbo Firecracker, 200
Neale's Aeroplane Works
    Neale 6 & 7, 156
Newbury, 11, 54, 55, 56
Northolt, 52, 68, 70, 75, 137, 138, 153

Oakley, 76, 81
Old Sarum, 189, 200
Ord-Hume, A.W.J., Mr, 8, 55, 74, 102, 135, 139, 176, 184
Orsett, 86
Osea Island, 83
Oyler, H. & D.J. & Co., 146

Panavia, 40
    Tornado, 40, 41
Parker, John Lankester, 129, 131, 135, 165
Parnall & Sons (also George Parnall & Co. Ltd), 22, 115, 124
Parnall & Sons Ltd (also George Parnall & Co. Ltd), 19, 127, 128
    Elf, 197
    Hendy 302, 206
    Peto, 184, 185
    Pixie, 124
    Puffin, 115
Parsons Biplane, 156
Pashley Brothers (later Pashley Brothers & Hale), 157, 208
Pemberton Billing, Mr, 18, 85, 165
Pemberton-Billing Ltd, 48, 119
Penshurst, 125, 199
Percival Aircraft Ltd (and Hunting Percival Aircraft Ltd), 6, 11, 20, 28, 48, 112, 135
    Gull, 113, 124, 125, 186, 206
    Jet Provost, 39, 200
    Merganser, 32
    Mew Gull, 85, 112, 113
    Pembroke, 34
    Prentice, 34, 86-89

Proctor, 19, 29, 65, 80, 90, 135
Provost, 34, 66, 112
Vega Gull, 113, 114
Percival, Mr N.S
Percival biplane, 141, 142
Perman Parasol, 114
Perry-Beadle & Co., 157
Personal Plane Services Ltd, 71, 73
Replica Aircraft, 71
Phillips & Powis Aircraft Ltd (also Miles Aircraft Ltd), 6, 11, 20, 24, 28, 31, 47, 56-62, 64-66, 185, 206
M.1 Satyr (Parnall-built), 57
M.2 Hawk, 24, 57
Hawk Major, 57
Hawk Speed Six, 57, 58
Hawk Trainer I & II, 57
M.3 Falcon, 18, 57-59, 185
M.4 Merlin, 57
M.5 Sparrowhawk, 57, 207
M.8 Peregrine, 58
M.9 PV Trainer, 58
M.9/M.19 Master, 26, 27, 29, 58, 60, 62, 91, 185
M.11 Straight & Whitney Straight, 58, 59
M.14 Hawk Trainer III & Magister, 29, 58, 59, 62, 81
M.16 Mentor, 58
M.17 Monarch, 58
M.18, 58, 59
M.20, 60
M.25 Martinet, 56, 60, 62
M.28, 60
Miles M.30 X-Minor, 62
M.33 Monitor, 60, 61
M.35 Libellula, 61
M.38 Messenger, 60-62, 64, 66
M.39, 61
M.57 Aerovan, 62-64, 66, 207
M.65 Gemini, 60, 62, 64, 66, 185, 207
M.68 Boxcar, 64
M.71 Merchantman, 64, 112
M.75 Aries, 64, 185
Phoenix Aircraft Ltd, 74, 82, 125, 176
Phoenix Duet, 182, 183
Phoenix Dynamo Manufacturing Co. Ltd, 19, 48, 127, 128
Piffard Hydro-biplane, 208
Pobjoy Airmotors & Aircraft Ltd, 132, 135
Pirate, 135
Popular Flying Association, 80, 206
Port Victoria, 16, 114, 115
PV1-PV8, 114, 115
Portsmouth, 24, 32, 70, 100, 197, 198
Portsmouth Aviation Ltd, 135
Aerocar, 32, 135
Practavia Ltd, 73
Sprite, 73
Premier Aircraft Constructions Ltd, 81
Preston, 26, 28, 41, 94, 99, 108, 115
Prestwick, 35, 39, 41, 43, 44, 105, 110, 204
Procter (later Nash) Petrel, 176, 183, 184
Procter, Roy (also Procter Aircraft Associates Ltd), 176

Radlett, 6, 11, 23, 26, 35, 39, 65, 66, 106-110
Radley-England
Waterplane, 147, 157, 191, 193, 201, 206
Radley-Moorhouse, 157
RAE Aero Club, 124, 125
RAF Halton, 76, 77
RAF Kemble, 28, 72
RAF Tangmere, 211

Reading, 52, 56-66, 205
Rearsby, 35, 37, 202, 204
Redhill, 64, 176, 185-188, 205, 206
Redwing Aircraft Ltd, 83, 91, 104, 200
Robinson Redwing, 83, 84
Robey & Co. Ltd, 19, 127, 160
Robinson Aircraft, 83
Rochester, 6, 11, 16, 23, 26, 29, 120, 125-135
Rollason Aircraft & Engines Ltd, 206
Condor, 185
Luton Beta, 186, 187
Turbulent, 185, 186, 206
Rolls, C.S., 115-118, 194
Rootes Securities Ltd, 25, 28, 108, 109
Rotol Ltd (and Dowty Rotol Ltd), 81, 205
Rover Company Ltd, The, 25
Royal Aircraft Factory, The, 14, 167
BE2 (all models), 14, 18, 152, 153-155, 167, 193, 194, 206
BE8, 167
BE12, 14
FE2 (all models), 14
FE8, 167
RE8, 14
SE5, SE5A, 14, 18, 84, 136, 144, 152, 155, 167, 184, 187, 192, 199, 205, 208
Rush Green, 111
Ruston, Proctor & Co. Ltd, 19, 161

Sage, Fredk. & Co. Ltd, 19, 127, 147
Salisbury, 134
Salisbury Hall, 93, 110, 111
Samlesbury, 26, 28, 41, 42, 181
Samlesbury Engineering Ltd, 89
Sandown, 200
Saunders, S.E. Ltd, 19, 22, 127
Saunders-Roe Ltd, 35, 128, 134, 157
P.531, 34, 38
Princess, 32
Skeeter, 34
Scottish Aviation Ltd, 35, 47, 51, 105, 110, 204
Sevenoaks, 135, 142
Shellbeach, 115, 116, 118, 122
Sherburn-in-Elmet, 70, 73, 153, 161
Shoreham, 11-13, 16, 24, 37, 57, 93, 140, 141, 147, 157, 185, 201-211
Short Brothers Ltd
S.27-S.38, 118, 119, 132, 196
S.36, 120
S.39 Triple Twin, 119
S.41 and 'improved S.41', 120, 127
S.47 Triple Tractor, 120
S.80 & S.81 Nile Seaplane, 119
Short-Wright biplane, 12, 13, 116, 118, 125
Tandem Twin, 119
Short Brothers (Rochester & Bedford) Ltd, 6, 11, 16, 22, 28, 114, 124-125, 129, 134, 135
Short 74, 127
Short 166, 127
Short 184, 14, 120, 125-128, 160, 194
Short 225 Bomber, 127, 128
Short 310/320, 128
Short 827, 127
Short 830, 120, 127
Silver Streak, 128-129
S.4 Satellite, 125, 129
S.5 Singapore, 128-129, 132
S.7 Mussel/Mussel II, 129
S.8 Calcutta, 128-129
S.8/8 Rangoon, 129, 129

S.10 Gurnard, 125, 129
S.11 Valetta, 34, 128, 129
S.16 Scion, 114, 131, 132, 135
S.17 Kent, 129
S.17L Scylla, 132
Sarafand, 128, 129, 131
Knuckleduster, 129
S.20 Mercury, 129-132
S.21 Maia, 129-132
S.22 Scion Senior, 132
S.23 C-Class (and S.30, S.33), 23, 24, 128, 129, 132, 198
S.25 Sunderland, 28, 29, 32, 128, 129-134
S.26 Golden Hind, 128, 129, 132
S.25 Sandringham, 32, 131, 133, 134
Hythe, 32, 133, 134
S.29 Stirling, 26, 28, 29, 32, 80, 128, 132, 133, 135
S.35 Shetland, 128, 131, 134
S.45 Seaford, 129, 133, 134
S.45 Solent, 32, 133, 134
SA-1 Sturgeon, 134
Short & Harland Ltd, 26, 28, 107, 134
Short Bros & Harland Ltd (and Shorts plc, Bombardier Aerospace), 134
SC-7 Skyvan, 37, 38, 44
SD330, 44
SD360, 44
PD-6 Sperrin, 100
Tucano, 44, 200
Siddeley-Deasy Motor Car Co. Ltd, The, 19
Simmonds Aircraft Ltd
Spartan, 56
Sir W.G. Armstrong, Whitworth & Co. Ltd, 17, 19
Skinner Monoplane, 158
Slingsby Aviation Ltd, 6, 45, 71
T.57 Camel replica, 71
T.67, 45
Slough, 66, 67
Society of British Aircraft Constructors, 6, 19, 21, 205
Somers Kendall SK1, 66
Sopwith Aviation Co. Ltd, The, 6, 11, 16, 19, 138, 148, 158, 162
1½ Strutter, 14, 159, 160, 167
Baby (and Fairey Hamble Baby), 114, 159, 160, 187
Bat Boat, 159
Buffalo, 162
Bulldog, 162
Camel, 14, 71, 85, 144, 159, 161, 187
Cuckoo, 161
Dolphin, 18, 159, 161
Dragon, 162
Hippo, 161
Hybrid, 159
Pup, 14, 85, 159, 160, 207
Salamander, 136, 161, 162
Schneider, 159, 160
Scooter, 144
Snipe, 10, 14, 15, 159, 161, 162
Sopwith-Wright, 158
Spinning Jenny, 160
Tabloid, 159
Three-Seater, 158, 159
Type 807, 159
Type 860, 160
Sopwith, T.O.M. (later Sir Thomas Sopwith), 13, 122, 143, 147, 152, 154, 158, 174, 175
South Coast Aircraft Works, 16, 206, 210

South Coast Aviation Co., 206, 210
South Marston, 26, 29, 60, 132, 205
Southend, 11, 82, 86-88
Southern Aircraft Ltd, 57, 205, 210
Martlet, 210
Spencer-Stirling biplane, 154, 162
St Albans, 92, 104, 111
Standard Motor Co. Ltd, The, 19, 25, 28
Stansted, 11, 80, 86, 88, 91
Stapleford Tawney, 88, 89, 112
Star monoplane, 162
Stockport, 52, 68, 108
Storey TSR3 Wonderplane, 186, 187
Sunbeam Motor Car Co. Ltd, The, 18, 19, 127, 128
Sunbury on Thames, 16, 187
Supermarine Aviation Works Ltd, The (also The Supermarine Aviation Works (Vickers) Ltd), 22, 48, 119, 125, 127, 169
Seafire, see Vickers-Armstrongs
Seagull, see Vickers-Armstrongs
Sea Otter, see Vickers-Armstrongs
Sparrow, 125
Spitfire, see Vickers-Armstrongs
Swift, see Vickers-Armstrongs
Walrus, 29, 157
Surrey, 7, 83, 85, 136-191
Sywell, 105, 143

Tarrant Rushton, 199
Tarrant, W.G., 162
Tawney Aircraft Ltd
Tawney Owl, 89
Taylor, C.F. (Metalworkers) Ltd, 73
Taylor, John, 24, 71, 72, 87
Taylor Monoplane, 71, 72, 87, 206
Taylor Titch, 87, 88, 206
Taylor, Richard, 184
Monoplane, 184
Thame, 10, 74, 76, 80, 81
The Varioplane Co. Ltd, 153
Trago Mills Ltd (Aircraft Division)
SAH1, 86

Universal Aviation 'Birdling', 139, 164

Vickers Ltd, 11, 13, 16, 19, 20, 22, 122-125, 165, 168, 169
Type 1-8 monoplanes, 166
Experimental Fighting Biplane, 165, 166
F.B.5, 124, 166
F.B.9, 166
F.B.14, 166
F.B.19, 166
F.B.26A, 122
Vimy (and Vimy Commercial), 15, 20, 122, 124, 166, 167, 173, 201
Vernon, 167, 168
Type 54 Viking (amphibian)(all models), 167, 187
Type 57 Virginia (all models), 167, 168, 173, 198
Type 61 Vulcan (all models), 168
Type 71 Vixen (all models), 168
Type 81 Victoria (all models), 84, 167, 168
Type 89 Viget, 124, 168
Type 92 Valparaiso (all models), 168
Type 113 Vespa (all models), 168
Type 130 Vivid, 169
Type 132 Vildebeest (all models), 20, 168, 173
Type 166 Vellore (all models), 122
Type 212 Vellox, 169
Type 264 Valentia, 167, 168

Type 266 Vincent, 20, 168, 173
Type 279 Venom, 168
Vickers-Armstongs Ltd (also Vickers Ltd (Aviation Dept), Vickers (Aviation) Ltd, Vickers-Armstrongs (Aircraft) Ltd), 6, 11, 28, 31, 32, 48, 52, 66, 72, 138, 142, 148, 168, 169, 175, 188, 189
Seafire, 29, 81, 82, 85
Supermarine Attacker, 33
Supermarine Sea Otter, 157
Supermarine Seagull, 59
Supermarine Spitfire (all marks), 26, 27, 29, 30, 33, 52, 56, 62, 66, 67, 81-83, 85, 100, 152, 171, 176
Supermarine Swift, 33
Type 246 Wellesley (all models), 20, 25, 26, 170, 173
Type 271 Wellington (all models), 20, 26, 29, 30, 91, 167, 170, 171, 173, 176
Type 284 Warwick (all models), 72, 170, 171
Type 392 (E.10/44), 112
Type 432, 170, 176
Type 447 Windsor, 170, 188
Type 491 VC1 Viking (all models), 32, 33, 167, 171-173, 188
Type 618 Nene Viking, 188
Type 637 Valetta (all models), 34, 171, 172
Type 630/700/800 Viscount, 32, 33, 36, 73, 87, 167, 170, 172, 173, 176, 188
Type 648 Varsity, 34, 143, 170-172, 188
Type 680 Valiant, 34, 172, 173, 176, 188, 189
Type 950 Vanguard, 37, 87, 172, 173
Type 1100 VC10 and Type 1151 Super VC10, 37, 73, 173, 174, 189
Vintage Aircraft & Flying Association, 189
F.B.5 Replica, 189, 190
Vimy Replica, 189, 190
Virgilio Aircraft Co. Ltd, 197

Wallis, K.H., Wing Cdr., 186
Beagle-Wallis WA116, 205
Walton & Edwards Aeroplane Co. Ltd, 146, 173
Elephantoplane/Colossoplane, 173
Walton on Thames, 138, 187, 188
Warton, 41, 42, 73, 179-181
Watney, Messrs. Gordon & Co. Ltd, 173
Weir, G. & J. group (also Weir, G. & J. Ltd), 19
Weiss, José, 13, 85, 147, 174, 200
Wells Aviation Co. Ltd (also R.F. Wells & Co.), 19, 197
West Sussex, 7, 144, 157, 195
Westlake, Mr A. and Westlake monoplane, 13, 83
Westland Aircraft Works (Branch of Petters Ltd) (also Westland Aircraft Ltd), 19, 22, 28, 69, 71, 124, 127, 149, 151, 167, 206

Lysander, 29, 91, 191, 192
Widgeon, 124, 125
Woodpigeon, 124
Wyvern, 33
Westland Helicopters Ltd (also GKN Westland Helicopters Ltd, AgustaWestland), 6, 19, 38, 44, 45, 47
Dragonfly, 34
EH101 and Merlin, 44, 45
Lynx, 38, 45
Scout, 72
Sea King, 38
WAH-64 Apache, 45
Wasp, 38, 72
Wessex, 38
WG30, 44
Whirlwind, 34, 38
Weston-super-Mare (and Old Mixon), 54
Weybridge, 6, 11, 26, 41, 138, 142, 143, 155-157, 166, 167, 169-175
Whitchurch, 27
White & Thompson Ltd (also The Norman Thompson Flight Co. Ltd), 13, 16, 19, 195, 196
NT.2/NT.2A/NT.2B, 196
NT.3 'Bognor Bloater', 196
NT.4/NT.4A, 196
Seaplane No. 1, 195
Seaplane No. 2, 195
White Waltham, 11, 52, 67-73, 87, 182, 197
White, J. Samuel & Co. Ltd, 19, 127, 194
Whitehead Aircraft Co. Ltd, 19, 139
Whitway, 56
Winchester, 24
Windermere, Lake, 133, 141, 157
Windsor, 70, 72
Wing, 81
Wisley, 11, 170-172, 176, 188-190
Witney, 54, 92, 98
Woking, 16, 137, 154, 156, 190
Wokingham, 73
Wolseley Motors Ltd, 19, 167
Wong Tong Mei, 211
Woodford, 41-44, 102, 110
Woodley, 6, 11, 24, 56-66, 108, 110, 183, 185, 205-207
Woolston, 27
Worsell Monoplane, 135
Wycombe Aircraft Constructors Ltd, 7, 10, 16, 48, 73, 74

Yate, 57, 113, 206
Yeovil, 72, 206

Other local interest titles published by Tempus:

LEADING FROM THE FRONT Bristow Helicopters – the first 50 years
ANDREW HEALEY

Andrew Healey documents the history of Bristow Helicopters, and Alan Bristow's early career, from joining Westland as its first helicopter test pilot to setting up his original company, Air Whaling Ltd., to search for whales in the Antarctic. His business expanded into oil, before becoming established as a leading light in the burgeoning North Sea industry. Today it remains a world-class helicopter operation, still supports the oil industry around the globe, and provides search and rescue services and student military pilot training,
0 7524 2697 4

BAC ONE-ELEVEN – The Whole Story
STEPHEN SKINNER

In August 1963 the first One-Eleven took to the air with an order book for sixty aircraft, unprecedented for a British civil aircraft, the first project for the newly formed British Aircraft Corporation which came into being in 1960. It remained in production throughout the entire seventeen-year history of the organisation, the last commercial flights taking place in March 2002. This book, the product of much original research, illustrated with 180 photographs and images, considers what transpired in those four decades and the special place the aircraft holds in British aviation history.
0 7524 2774 1

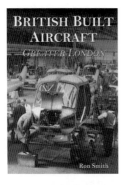

BRITISH BUILT AIRCRAFT
Greater London

RON SMITH

British Built Aircraft – Greater London is the first in a series covering all of the aircraft manufacturers in the United Kingdom. The names of some of the companies are well-known but some others, who constructed aeroplanes purely on a contract basis, are surprising. Inside are the names and details of hundreds of firms once involved in aircraft manufacture, from the first decade of the twentieth century to the present day.
0 7524 2770 9

BRITISH BUILT AIRCRAFT
South West and Central Southern England

RON SMITH

Following on from *British Built Aircraft – Greater London*, this volume documents the complete evolution and history of aircraft construction and activity in South West and Central Southern England from 1908 until the present day. This series sheds light on the sheer scale of effort involved in the construction of aircraft during the First World War, while paying tribute to the heritage of the British aircraft industry.
0 7524 2785 7

To discover more Tempus titles please visit us at:
www.tempus-publishing.com